MW00624544

Most mobile telephone
subscribers
Page 98

Fastest average broadband
download speed
Page 99

Least
dependent
on trade
Page 32

Canada

United States

Japan

Haiti

Mexico

Cuba

Guatemala Honduras
El Salvador Nicaragua
Costa Rica Pan. Venezuela

Guyana
Suriname
Fr. Guiana

Colombia

PACIFIC

Ecuador

Brazil

Papua New
Guinea

OCEAN

Peru

Fiji

Bolivia

Chile

Paraguay

Australia

Uruguay

New Zealand

Argentina

Philippines

van

ippines

Greatest number
of plant species
under threat
Page 89

Biggest
producer
of coffee
Page 49

Biggest registered
merchant fleet
Page 80

The Economist

POCKET
WORLD IN
FIGURES

2022 Edition

Published by
Profile Books Ltd
29 Cloth Fair
London EC1A 7JQ

Published under exclusive licence from
The Economist by Profile Books, 2021

Copyright © The Economist Newspaper Ltd, 1991, 1992,
1993, 1994, 1995, 1996, 1997, 1998, 1999, 2000, 2001, 2002,
2003, 2004, 2005, 2006, 2007, 2008, 2009, 2010, 2011, 2012,
2013, 2014, 2015, 2016, 2017, 2018, 2019, 2020, 2021

Material researched by
Andrea Burgess, Lisa Davies, Mark Doyle, Ian Emery,
Conrad Heine, Carol Howard, Adam Meara, David McKelvey,
Georgina McKelvey, Christopher Wilson, Pip Wroe

All rights reserved. Without limiting the rights under copyright
reserved above, no part of this publication may be reproduced,
stored in or introduced into a retrieval system, or transmitted, in
any form or by any means (electronic, mechanical, photocopying,
recording or otherwise), without the prior written permission of
both the copyright owner and the above publisher of this book.

The greatest care has been taken in compiling this book. However,
no responsibility can be accepted by the publishers or compilers
for the accuracy of the information presented.

Typeset in Econ Sans Condensed by MacGuru Ltd

Printed and bound in Italy by L.E.G.O. Spa

A CIP catalogue record for this book is available
from the British Library

ISBN 978 1 78816 764 2

Contents

CONTENTS

CONTENTS

Introduction

This 2022 edition of *The Economist Pocket World in Figures* presents and analyses data about the world in two sections:

The **world rankings** consider and rank the performance of 188 countries against a range of indicators in five sections: geography and demographics, business and economics, politics and society, health and welfare, and culture and entertainment. The countries included are those which had (in 2019) a population of at least 1m or a GDP of at least $3bn; they are listed on pages 250–53. New rankings this year include topics as diverse as the best cities for culture, origins and destinations of migrants, tax rates for individuals, cryptocurrencies, speed cameras, active paramilitary forces, the burdens of overweight populations resulting in life years lost and extra deaths, media manipulation and trust in the news, and a selection of covid-19 indicators including tests, cases, deaths, vaccines and working-days lost during the pandemic. Some of the rankings data are shown as charts and graphs.

The **country profiles** look in detail at 64 major countries, listed on page 109, plus profiles of the euro area and the world.

Test your *Pocket World in Figures* knowledge with our **World Rankings Quiz** on pages 242–7. Answers can be found in the corresponding world rankings section.

The extent and quality of the statistics available vary from country to country. Every care has been taken to specify the broad definitions on which the data are based and to indicate cases where data quality or technical difficulties are such that interpretation of the figures is likely to be seriously affected. Nevertheless, figures from individual countries may differ from standard international statistical definitions. The term "country" can also refer to territories or economic entities.

Definitions of the statistics shown are given on the relevant page or in the glossary on pages 248–9. Figures may not add exactly to totals, or percentages to 100, because of rounding or, in the case of GDP, statistical adjustment. Sums of money have generally been converted to US dollars at the official exchange rate ruling at the time to which the figures refer.

Some country definitions

North Macedonia was formerly known as Macedonia until officially changed in February 2019. North Macedonia is used in this book. Data for Cyprus normally refer to Greek Cyprus only. Data for China do not include Hong Kong or Macau. For countries such as Morocco they exclude disputed areas. Congo-Kinshasa refers to the Democratic Republic of Congo, formerly known as Zaire. Congo-Brazzaville refers to the other Congo. Eswatini was known as Swaziland until April 2018. Eswatini is used in this book. Euro area data normally refer to the 19 members that had adopted the euro as at December 31 2019: Austria, Belgium, Cyprus, Estonia, Finland, France, Germany, Greece, Ireland, Italy, Latvia, Lithuania, Luxembourg, Malta, Netherlands, Portugal, Slovakia, Slovenia and Spain. Data referring to the European Union include the United Kingdom unless the data are from 2020 or later. The United Kingdom officially left the EU on January 31st 2020. For more information about the EU, euro area and OECD see the glossary on pages 248–9.

Statistical basis

The all-important factor in a book of this kind is to be able to make reliable comparisons between countries. Although this is never quite possible for the reasons stated above, the best route, which this book takes, is to compare data for the same year or period and to use actual, not estimated, figures wherever possible. In some cases, only OECD members are considered. Where a country's data are excessively out of date, they are excluded. The research for this edition was carried out in 2021 using the latest available sources that present data on an internationally comparable basis.

Data in the country profiles, unless otherwise indicated, refer to the year ending December 31 2019. Life expectancy, crude birth, death and fertility rates are based on 2020–25 estimated averages; energy data are for 2018 and religion data for 2010; marriage and divorce, employment, health and education, consumer goods and services data refer to the latest year for which figures are available.

Other definitions

Data shown in country profiles may not always be consistent with those shown in the world rankings because the definitions or years covered can differ.

Statistics for principal exports and principal imports are normally based on customs statistics. These are generally compiled on different definitions to the visible exports and imports figures shown in the balance of payments section.

Energy-consumption data are not always reliable, particularly for the major oil-producing countries; consumption per person data may therefore be higher than in reality. Energy exports can exceed production and imports can exceed consumption if transit operations distort trade data or oil is imported for refining and re-exported.

Abbreviations and conventions

(see also glossary on pages 248–9)

bn	billion (one thousand million)	km	kilometre
		m	million
EU	European Union	PPP	purchasing power parity
GDP	gross domestic product	TOE	tonnes of oil equivalent
GNI	gross national income	trn	trillion (one thousand billion)
ha	hectare		
kg	kilogram	...	not available

World rankings

Countries: natural facts

Countries: the largest[a]
'000 sq km

1	Russia	17,098	33	Namibia	824
2	Canada	9,985	34	Pakistan	796
3	United States	9,832	35	Mozambique	786
4	China	9,563	36	Turkey	785
5	Brazil	8,516	37	Chile	757
6	Australia	7,741	38	Zambia	753
7	India	3,287	39	Myanmar	677
8	Argentina	2,780	40	South Sudan	659
9	Kazakhstan	2,725	41	Afghanistan	653
10	Algeria	2,382	42	Somalia	638
11	Congo-Kinshasa	2,345	43	Central African Rep.	623
12	Saudi Arabia	2,150	44	Ukraine	604
13	Mexico	1,964	45	Madagascar	587
14	Indonesia	1,914	46	Botswana	582
15	Sudan	1,879	47	Kenya	580
16	Libya	1,760	48	France	549
17	Iran	1,745	49	Yemen	528
18	Mongolia	1,564	50	Thailand	513
19	Peru	1,285	51	Spain	506
20	Chad	1,284	52	Turkmenistan	488
21	Niger	1,267	53	Cameroon	475
22	Angola	1,247	54	Papua New Guinea	463
23	Mali	1,240	55	Morocco	447
24	South Africa	1,219		Sweden	447
25	Colombia	1,142		Uzbekistan	447
26	Ethiopia	1,104	58	Iraq	435
27	Bolivia	1,099	59	Paraguay	407
28	Mauritania	1,031	60	Zimbabwe	391
29	Egypt	1,001	61	Norway	385
30	Tanzania	947	62	Japan	378
31	Nigeria	924	63	Germany	358
32	Venezuela	912	64	Congo-Brazzaville	342

Coastlines: the longest
Length, km

1	Canada	202,080	15	Brazil	7,491
2	Indonesia	54,716	16	Denmark	7,314
3	Russia	37,653	17	Turkey	7,200
4	Philippines	36,289	18	India	7,000
5	Japan	29,751	19	Chile	6,435
6	Australia	28,855	20	Croatia	5,835
7	Norway	28,735	21	Papua New Guinea	5,152
8	United States	19,924	22	Argentina	4,989
9	New Zealand	15,134	23	Iceland	4,970
10	China	14,500	24	Spain	4,964
11	Greece	13,676	25	France	4,853
12	United Kingdom	12,429	26	Madagascar	4,828
13	Mexico	9,330	27	Malaysia	4,675
14	Italy	7,600	28	Estonia	3,794

a Includes freshwater.

Mountains: the highest[a]

		Location	Height (m)
1	Everest	China-Nepal	8,849
2	K2 (Godwin Austen)	China-Pakistan	8,611
3	Kangchenjunga	India-Nepal	8,586
4	Lhotse	China-Nepal	8,516
5	Makalu	China-Nepal	8,463
6	Cho Oyu	China-Nepal	8,201
7	Dhaulagiri	Nepal	8,167
8	Manaslu	Nepal	8,163
9	Nanga Parbat	Pakistan	8,126
10	Annapurna I	Nepal	8,091

Rivers: the longest

		Location	Length (km)
1	Nile	Africa	6,695
2	Amazon	South America	6,516
3	Yangtze (Chang Jiang)	Asia	6,380
4	Mississippi-Missouri system	North America	5,969
5	Ob'-Irtysh	Asia	5,568
6	Yenisey-Angara-Selanga	Asia	5,550
7	Yellow (Huang He)	Asia	5,464
8	Congo	Africa	4,667

Deserts: the largest non-polar

		Location	Area ('000 sq km)
1	Sahara	Northern Africa	8,600
2	Arabian	South-western Asia	2,300
3	Gobi	Mongolia/China	1,300
4	Patagonian	Argentina	673
5	Syrian	Middle East	520
6	Great Basin	South-western United States	490
7	Great Victoria	Western & Southern Australia	419
8	Great Sandy	Western Australia	395

Lakes: the largest

		Location	Area ('000 sq km)
1	Caspian Sea	Central Asia	371
2	Superior	Canada/United States	82
3	Victoria	East Africa	69
4	Huron	Canada/United States	60
5	Michigan	United States	58
6	Tanganyika	East Africa	33
7	Baikal	Russia	31
	Great Bear	Canada	31
9	Malawi	East Africa	30

a Includes separate peaks which are part of the same massif.
Notes: Estimates of the lengths of rivers vary widely depending on, eg, the path to take through a delta. The definition of a desert is normally a mean annual precipitation value equal to 250mm or less.

Population: size and growth

Largest populations

m, 2019

1	China	1,433.8		37	Afghanistan	38.0
2	India	1,366.4		38	Poland	37.9
3	United States	329.1		39	Canada	37.4
4	Indonesia	270.6		40	Morocco	36.5
5	Pakistan	216.6		41	Saudi Arabia	34.3
6	Brazil	211.1		42	Uzbekistan	33.0
7	Nigeria	201.0		43	Peru	32.5
8	Bangladesh	163.0		44	Malaysia	32.0
9	Russia	145.9		45	Angola	31.8
10	Mexico	127.6		46	Ghana	30.4
11	Japan	126.9			Mozambique	30.4
12	Ethiopia	112.1		48	Yemen	29.2
13	Philippines	108.1		49	Nepal	28.6
14	Egypt	100.4		50	Venezuela	28.5
15	Vietnam	96.5		51	Madagascar	27.0
16	Congo-Kinshasa	86.8		52	Cameroon	25.9
17	Germany	83.5		53	Ivory Coast	25.7
18	Turkey	83.4			North Korea	25.7
19	Iran	82.9		55	Australia	25.2
20	Thailand	69.6		56	Taiwan	23.8
21	United Kingdom	67.5		57	Niger	23.3
22	France	65.1		58	Sri Lanka	21.3
23	Italy	60.6		59	Burkina Faso	20.3
24	South Africa	58.6		60	Mali	19.7
25	Tanzania	58.0		61	Romania	19.4
26	Myanmar	54.0		62	Chile	19.0
27	Kenya	52.6		63	Kazakhstan	18.6
28	South Korea	51.2			Malawi	18.6
29	Colombia	50.3		65	Zambia	17.9
30	Spain	46.7		66	Guatemala	17.6
31	Argentina	44.8		67	Ecuador	17.4
32	Uganda	44.3		68	Netherlands	17.1
33	Ukraine	44.0			Syria	17.1
34	Algeria	43.1		70	Cambodia	16.5
35	Sudan	42.8		71	Senegal	16.3
36	Iraq	39.3		72	Chad	15.9

Largest populations

m, 2035

1	India	1,553.7		11	Russia	141.1
2	China	1,461.1		12	Congo-Kinshasa	137.3
3	United States	358.7		13	Egypt	130.3
4	Indonesia	309.8		14	Philippines	130.0
5	Nigeria	295.0		15	Japan	117.2
6	Pakistan	282.9		16	Vietnam	106.3
7	Brazil	227.2		17	Iran	95.8
8	Bangladesh	184.4		18	Turkey	91.9
9	Ethiopia	160.2		19	Tanzania	90.4
10	Mexico	145.8		20	Germany	82.7

Note: Populations include migrant workers.

Fastest-growing populations
Average annual rate of change, 2020–25, %

1	Syria	5.5		Liberia	2.4
2	Niger	3.7		Rwanda	2.4
3	Angola	3.2		Sudan	2.4
4	Equatorial Guinea	3.1	31	Guinea-Bissau	2.3
5	Congo-Kinshasa	3.0		Iraq	2.3
6	Burundi	2.9		Togo	2.3
	Chad	2.9		West Bank & Gaza	2.3
	Mali	2.9	35	Afghanistan	2.2
	Somalia	2.9		Gabon	2.2
	Tanzania	2.9		Kenya	2.2
	Zambia	2.9	38	South Sudan	2.1
12	Burkina Faso	2.8		Yemen	2.1
	Gambia, The	2.8	40	Central African Rep.	2.0
	Mozambique	2.8		Ghana	2.0
15	Guinea	2.7		Sierra Leone	2.0
	Malawi	2.7		Tajikistan	2.0
	Uganda	2.7		Venezuela	2.0
18	Benin	2.6	45	Papua New Guinea	1.9
	Madagascar	2.6		Timor-Leste	1.9
	Mauritania	2.6	47	Bahrain	1.8
	Senegal	2.6		Botswana	1.8
22	Cameroon	2.5		Egypt	1.8
	Ivory Coast	2.5		Guatemala	1.8
	Nigeria	2.5		Namibia	1.8
25	Congo-Brazzaville	2.4		Oman	1.8
	Ethiopia	2.4		Pakistan	1.8
	French Guiana	2.4			

Slowest-growing populations
Average annual rate of change, 2020–25, %

1	Lebanon	-1.3		Martinique	-0.2
2	Latvia	-1.0		Poland	-0.2
	Lithuania	-1.0	24	Belarus	-0.1
4	Bulgaria	-0.8		Cuba	-0.1
5	Maldives	-0.7		Germany	-0.1
	Ukraine	-0.7		North Macedonia	-0.1
7	Croatia	-0.6		Russia	-0.1
8	Greece	-0.5		Slovenia	-0.1
	Romania	-0.5		Spain	-0.1
	Serbia	-0.5	31	Guadeloupe	0.0
11	Bosnia & Herz.	-0.4		Montenegro	0.0
	Japan	-0.4		Slovakia	0.0
13	Albania	-0.3		South Korea	0.0
	Bermuda	-0.3	35	Andorra	0.1
	Estonia	-0.3		Armenia	0.1
	Georgia	-0.3		Barbados	0.1
	Hungary	-0.3		Chile	0.1
	Moldova	-0.3		Czech Republic	0.1
	Portugal	-0.3		Finland	0.1
	Virgin Islands (US)	-0.3		Mauritius	0.1
21	Italy	-0.2		Taiwan	0.1

Population: matters of breeding and sex

Crude birth-rates
Births per 1,000 population, annual av., 2020–25

Highest			Lowest		
1	Niger	44.2	1	Monaco	6.6
2	Somalia	40.9		Puerto Rico	6.6
3	Chad	39.9	3	South Korea	6.8
4	Mali	39.5	4	Andorra	6.9
5	Angola	38.9		Greece	6.9
6	Congo-Kinshasa	38.8	6	Italy	7.0
7	Burundi	36.3		Japan	7.0
	Gambia, The	36.3	8	Bosnia & Herz.	7.5
9	Nigeria	36.0	9	Portugal	7.7
10	Burkina Faso	35.9	10	Spain	7.9
	Mozambique	35.9	11	Croatia	8.3
12	Tanzania	35.1		Singapore	8.3
	Uganda	35.1	13	Taiwan	8.4
14	Zambia	34.9	14	Finland	8.6
15	Benin	34.6		Ukraine	8.6
	Guinea	34.6	16	Bulgaria	8.7
17	Central African Rep.	34.5	17	Qatar	8.8
18	Ivory Coast	34.3	18	Slovenia	8.9
19	Cameroon	33.4	19	Serbia	9.1
	South Sudan	33.4	20	Poland	9.2
21	Malawi	32.9	21	Hungary	9.3
22	Guinea-Bissau	32.7		Romania	9.3
23	Senegal	32.2			
24	Mauritania	31.9			

Teenage birth rates
Number of births per 1,000 women aged 15–19, annual av., 2020–25

1	Niger	171.4	23	Lesotho	92.0
2	Mali	157.8	24	Dominican Rep.	88.1
3	Chad	145.2	25	Somalia	87.9
4	Equatorial Guinea	144.8	26	Togo	87.1
5	Angola	137.7	27	Venezuela	83.5
6	Mozambique	136.8	28	Gabon	82.9
7	Liberia	134.0	29	Bangladesh	79.7
8	Malawi	129.8	30	Panama	77.9
9	Guinea	125.6	31	Ecuador	76.8
10	Central African Rep.	118.5	32	Nicaragua	76.6
11	Congo-Kinshasa	116.1	33	Benin	75.8
12	Tanzania	111.1	34	Iraq	71.8
	Zambia	111.1	35	Zimbabwe	71.7
14	Ivory Coast	110.3	36	Eswatini	70.0
15	Congo-Brazzaville	105.8	37	Kenya	69.9
16	Uganda	105.0	38	Paraguay	68.9
17	Madagascar	100.3	39	Honduras	67.6
18	Sierra Leone	99.8		South Africa	67.6
19	Nigeria	97.9	41	Guyana	66.8
20	Guinea-Bissau	96.8	42	Gambia, The	65.8
21	Cameroon	94.3	43	El Salvador	65.2
22	Burkina Faso	93.0	44	Guatemala	65.1

Fertility rates
Number of children per woman, annual av., 2020–25

Highest			Lowest		
1	Niger	6.5	**1**	South Korea	1.1
2	Somalia	5.7	**2**	Bosnia & Herz.	1.2
3	Congo-Kinshasa	5.5		Puerto Rico	1.2
	Mali	5.5		Singapore	1.2
5	Chad	5.3		Taiwan	1.2
6	Angola	5.2	**6**	Cyprus	1.3
7	Nigeria	5.1		Greece	1.3
8	Burundi	5.0		Italy	1.3
9	Gambia, The	4.9		Macau	1.3
10	Burkina Faso	4.8		Moldova	1.3
11	Tanzania	4.6	**11**	Andorra	1.4
12	Benin	4.5		Croatia	1.4
	Mozambique	4.5		Finland	1.4
14	Central African Rep.	4.4		Hong Kong	1.4
	Guinea	4.4		Japan	1.4
	Ivory Coast	4.4		Luxembourg	1.4
	South Sudan	4.4		Mauritius	1.4
	Uganda	4.4		Portugal	1.4
	Zambia	4.4		Serbia	1.4
20	Cameroon	4.3		Spain	1.4
	Mauritania	4.3		Ukraine	1.4
	Senegal	4.3		United Arab Emirates	1.4
23	Congo-Brazzaville	4.2			
	Equatorial Guinea	4.2			
	Guinea-Bissau	4.2			
	Sudan	4.2			

Women[a] who use modern methods of contraception
2019, %

Highest			Lowest		
1	China	82.7	**1**	Chad	6.3
2	Norway	79.3	**2**	South Sudan	6.4
3	Nicaragua	78.4	**3**	Guinea	7.9
4	Thailand	77.8	**4**	Somalia	9.2
5	Germany	77.6	**5**	Congo-Kinshasa	10.4
6	Finland	77.4	**6**	Eritrea	11.8
7	Brazil	76.9	**7**	Benin	13.0
	Uruguay	76.9		Nigeria	13.0
9	Canada	76.8	**9**	Equatorial Guinea	13.2
10	Colombia	76.4	**10**	Sudan	13.4
11	Czech Republic	75.7	**11**	Gambia, The	13.5
12	France	75.2	**12**	Angola	14.2
13	New Zealand	74.5	**13**	Montenegro	14.3
14	United Kingdom	73.8	**14**	Mauritania	14.7
15	Puerto Rico	73.7	**15**	Maldives	15.8
16	Cuba	73.5	**16**	Cameroon	16.3
17	Denmark	73.4	**17**	Niger	16.7

a Married women aged 15–49; excludes traditional methods of contraception, such as the rhythm method.

Population: age

Median age[a]

Highest, 2019		Lowest, 2019	
1 Monaco	53.1	1 Niger	15.1
2 Japan	48.0	2 Mali	16.2
3 Italy	46.9	3 Chad	16.5
4 Martinique	46.6	Uganda	16.5
5 Andorra	45.8	5 Angola	16.6
6 Germany	45.7	Somalia	16.6
Portugal	45.7	7 Congo-Kinshasa	17.0
8 Greece	45.2	8 Burundi	17.3
9 Lithuania	44.6	9 Zambia	17.4
10 Hong Kong	44.5	10 Burkina Faso	17.5
11 Bulgaria	44.4	Central African Rep.	17.5
Spain	44.4	Mozambique	17.5
13 Slovenia	44.2	13 Gambia, The	17.7
14 Croatia	44.1	14 Guinea	17.8
15 Isle of Man	44.0	15 Malawi	17.9
16 Latvia	43.6	Tanzania	17.9
17 Austria	43.4	17 Nigeria	18.1
18 Guadeloupe	43.3	18 Afghanistan	18.2
19 Puerto Rico	43.2	19 Senegal	18.4
20 Netherlands	43.1	20 Cameroon	18.6
South Korea	43.1	Zimbabwe	18.6

Most old/young people

% of population, 2025

Aged 65 or over

Monaco
Japan
Italy
Martinique
Portugal
Finland
Greece
Malta
Virgin Is. (US)
Germany
Bermuda
Slovenia
Croatia
Puerto Rico
Lithuania
Latvia
Bulgaria
Isle of Man
France
Guadeloupe
Netherlands
Hong Kong
Spain

Aged 0–19

Niger
Mali
Somalia
Angola
Chad
Congo-Kinshasa
Uganda
Burundi
Burkina Faso
Mozambique
Gambia, The
Central African Rep.
Zambia
Nigeria
Tanzania
Guinea
Malawi
Senegal
Cameroon
Benin
Ivory Coast
Guinea-Bissau
Zimbabwe

a Age at which there is an equal number of people above and below.

City living

Biggest cities[a]
Population, m, 2019

1	Tokyo, Japan	37.4	26	Shenzhen, China	12.1
2	Delhi, India	29.4	27	Bangalore, India	11.9
3	Shanghai, China	26.3	28	Paris, France	11.0
4	São Paulo, Brazil	21.8	29	Bogotá, Colombia	10.8
5	Mexico City, Mexico	21.7	30	Chennai, India	10.7
6	Cairo, Egypt	20.5	31	Jakarta, Indonesia	10.6
7	Dhaka, Bangladesh	20.3		Lima, Peru	10.6
8	Mumbai, India	20.2	33	Bangkok, Thailand	10.4
9	Beijing, China	20.0	34	Seoul, South Korea	10.0
10	Osaka, Japan	19.2	35	Hyderabad, India	9.7
11	New York, United States	18.8	36	Nagoya, Japan	9.5
12	Karachi, Pakistan	15.7	37	Taipei, Taiwan	9.3
13	Chongqing, China	15.4	38	London, United Kingdom	9.2
14	Buenos Aires, Argentina	15.1	39	Chengdu, China	9.0
15	Istanbul, Turkey	15.0		Tehran, Iran	9.0
16	Kolkata, India	14.8	41	Chicago, United States	8.9
17	Lagos, Nigeria	13.9	42	Nanjing, China	8.5
18	Kinshasa, Congo-Kinshasa	13.7	43	Ho Chi Minh City, Vietnam	8.4
	Manila, Philippines	13.7	44	Wuhan, China	8.3
20	Rio de Janeiro, Brazil	13.4	45	Luanda, Angola	8.0
	Tianjin, China	13.4	46	Ahmedabad, India	7.9
22	Guangzhou, China	13.0	47	Kuala Lumpur, Malaysia	7.8
23	Moscow, Russia	12.5	48	Xi'an, China	7.7
24	Los Angeles, United States	12.4	49	Hong Kong	7.5
25	Lahore, Pakistan	12.2			

City growth[b]
Total % change, 2015–25

Fastest			Slowest		
1	Malappuram, India	84.5	1	Bucharest, Romania	-4.9
2	Abuja, Nigeria	72.4	2	Khulna, Bangladesh	-3.9
3	Can Tho, Vietnam	69.5	3	Detroit, United States	-2.9
4	Suqian, China	68.9	4	Daegu, South Korea	-2.8
5	Dar es Salaam, Tanzania	67.4	5	Volgograd, Russia	-2.5
6	Kozhikode, India	66.0	6	Osaka, Japan	-2.0
7	Kampala, Uganda	65.5	7	Hiroshima, Japan	-1.9
8	Port Harcourt, Nigeria	61.9	8	Kharkiv, Ukraine	-1.8
9	Antananarivo, Madagascar	61.5	9	Fukuoka, Japan	-1.3
10	Suzhou, China	61.0	10	Samara, Russia	-1.2
11	Putian, China	60.4		San Juan, Puerto Rico	-1.2
12	Ouagadougou, Burkina Faso	60.0	12	Naples, Italy	-1.0
13	Mogadishu, Somalia	59.6	13	Nizhny Novgorod, Russia	-0.7
14	Kollam, India	59.4	14	Tokyo, Japan	-0.6
15	Onitsha, Nigeria	59.3	15	Pittsburgh, United States	-0.5
16	Lusaka, Zambia	58.7	16	Odessa, Ukraine	-0.3
17	Thrissur, India	57.9	17	Athens, Greece	-0.2
18	Wuhu, China	57.8		Changwon, South Korea	-0.2

a Urban agglomerations. Data can change from year to year based on reassessments of agglomeration boundaries.
b Urban agglomerations with a population of at least 1m in 2015.

Best culture and environment[a]

100=ideal, 2019

1	London, United Kingdom	100.0
	Vancouver, Canada	100.0
3	Melbourne, Australia	98.6
4	Auckland, New Zealand	97.9
5	Amsterdam, Netherlands	97.2
	Berlin, Germany	97.2
	Frankfurt, Germany	97.2
	Munich, Germany	97.2
	Paris, France	97.2
	Sydney, Australia	97.2
	Toronto, Canada	97.2
12	Manchester, United Kingdom	96.5
13	Brisbane, Australia	96.3
	Vienna, Austria	96.3
	Zurich, Switzerland	96.3
16	Seattle, US	95.8
17	Copenhagen, Denmark	95.4
18	Lisbon, Portugal	95.1
19	Düsseldorf, Germany	94.9
	Geneva, Switzerland	94.9
21	Barcelona, Spain	94.4
	Los Angeles, US	94.4
	Madrid, Spain	94.4
	San Francisco, US	94.4
	Tokyo, Japan	94.4
	Washington, DC, US	94.4
	Wellington, New Zealand	94.4
28	Adelaide, Australia	94.2
29	Hamburg, Germany	93.5
	Osaka, Japan	93.5

Tallest buildings[b]

Height, metres, 2020

Burj Khalifa, Dubai
Shanghai Tower, Shanghai
Makkah Royal Clock Tower, Mecca
Ping An Finance Centre, Shenzhen
Lotte World Tower, Seoul
One World Trade Centre, New York
CTF Finance Centre, Guangzhou
CTF Finance Centre, Tianjin
CITIC Tower, Beijing
Taipei 101, Taipei
World Financial Centre, Shanghai
Int. Commerce Centre, Hong Kong
Central Park Tower, New York
Lakhta Centre, St Petersburg
Vincom Landmark, Ho Chi Minh City
IFS Tower T1, Changsha
Petronas Twin Towers, Kuala Lumpur
Suzhou IFS, Suzhou
Zifeng Tower, Nanjing
The Exchange 106, Kuala Lumpur
Willis Tower, Chicago
KK100, Shenzhen
Int. Finance Centre, Guangzhou
Centre Tower, Wuhan

a Based on factors such as censorship, climate, corruption, culture, food, sport.
b Completed.

Foreign-born and refugees

Largest foreign-born populations[a]

2019[b], m

1	United States	50.1	24	Japan	2.7
2	Germany	14.7	25	Ivory Coast	2.5
3	Saudi Arabia	12.9		Singapore	2.5
4	Russia	11.6	27	Switzerland	2.4
5	United Kingdom	9.2	28	Netherlands	2.3
6	United Arab Emirates	8.6		Oman	2.3
7	France	8.4	30	Argentina	2.2
8	Canada	7.9	31	Qatar	2.1
9	Australia	7.5	32	Bangladesh	2.0
10	Spain	6.7		Belgium	2.0
11	Italy	6.3		Israel	2.0
12	Turkey	5.7	35	Sweden	1.9
13	Ukraine	5.0	36	Lebanon	1.8
14	India	4.9	37	Austria	1.7
15	Kazakhstan	3.7		South Korea	1.7
16	Thailand	3.6	39	Colombia	1.6
17	Jordan	3.4	40	Uganda	1.5
	Malaysia	3.4	41	Chile	1.4
19	Pakistan	3.3	42	Greece	1.3
20	Kuwait	3.1		New Zealand	1.3
21	Hong Kong	2.9		Nigeria	1.3
	South Africa	2.9		Venezuela	1.3
23	Iran	2.8			

Foreign-born as % of total population

2019[b]

Highest			Lowest		
1	United Arab Emirates	87.8	1	Cuba	0.0
2	Qatar	75.0	2	China	0.1
3	Kuwait	73.2		Indonesia	0.1
4	Monaco	68.0		Madagascar	0.1
5	Liechtenstein	67.0		Myanmar	0.1
6	Macau	62.2		Vietnam	0.1
7	Andorra	58.0	7	Haiti	0.2
8	Bahrain	54.5		North Korea	0.2
9	Virgin Islands (US)	54.3		Philippines	0.2
10	Isle of Man	50.6		Sri Lanka	0.2
11	Channel Islands	48.6	11	Morocco	0.3
12	Guam	47.5	12	Eritrea	0.4
13	Luxembourg	46.9		Honduras	0.4
14	Oman	45.9		India	0.4
15	Cayman Islands	44.1		Papua New Guinea	0.4
16	Singapore	43.4		Somalia	0.4
17	French Guiana	40.1	17	Afghanistan	0.5
18	Hong Kong	39.5		Brazil	0.5
19	Saudi Arabia	37.7		Cambodia	0.5
20	Jordan	33.9		Egypt	0.5
21	Curaçao	32.6		Guatemala	0.5
22	Bermuda	31.4		Lesotho	0.5
23	Australia	29.7		Tunisia	0.5

a Includes migrant workers and illegal immigrants.   b 2020 revisions.

Biggest immigrant[a] groups by country of origin

m, 2019

1	India	17.5	15	Kazakhstan	4.1
2	Mexico	11.3	16	West Bank & Gaza	4.0
3	Russia	10.6	17	Romania	3.9
4	China	10.4	18	Germany	3.8
5	Syria	8.1	19	Egypt	3.5
6	Bangladesh	7.3		Myanmar	3.5
7	Pakistan	6.2	21	Turkey	3.3
8	Ukraine	6.1		Vietnam	3.3
9	Philippines	6.0	23	Morocco	3.2
10	Afghanistan	5.8	24	Italy	3.1
11	Poland	4.7	25	Colombia	3.0
	United Kingdom	4.7	26	United States	2.9
13	Indonesia	4.5	27	Nepal	2.5
	Venezuela	4.5			

Biggest immigrant[a] groups

m, 2019

	Host country	Origin of foreign-born group	
1	United States	Mexico	11.0
2	Turkey	Syria	3.6
3	United Arab Emirates	India	3.4
4	Russia	Ukraine	3.3
	Ukraine	Russia	3.3
6	Iran	Afghanistan	2.7
	United States	India	2.7
8	Russia	Kazakhstan	2.6
9	India	Bangladesh	2.5
	Kazakhstan	Russia	2.5
11	Hong Kong	China	2.4
	Saudi Arabia	India	2.4
13	Jordan	West Bank & Gaza	2.2
14	Germany	Poland	2.0
	United States	Philippines	2.0

Stock of a population displaced by conflict

'000, as of end 2019

1	Syria	6,495	14	Azerbaijan	730
2	Colombia	5,576	15	Ukraine	651
3	Congo-Kinshasa	5,512	16	Burkina Faso	592
4	Yemen	3,635	17	Central African Rep.	560
5	Afghanistan	2,993	18	India	470
6	Nigeria	2,648	19	Libya	457
7	Somalia	2,583	20	Myanmar	451
8	Sudan	2,134	21	Bangladesh	427
9	Iraq	1,555	22	Georgia	345
10	Ethiopia	1,414	23	Ivory Coast	303
11	South Sudan	1,352	24	Mexico	301
12	Turkey	1,099	25	Chad	247
13	Cameroon	969	26	Cyprus	243

a Includes migrants, illegal immigrants and refugees.

Refugees,[a] country of origin

'000, 2019

1	Syria	6,617.0	11	Iraq	344.5
2	Afghanistan	2,728.9	12	Vietnam	316.4
3	South Sudan	2,234.8	13	Nigeria	295.6
4	Myanmar	1,078.3	14	Rwanda	246.7
5	Somalia	905.1	15	China	212.9
6	Congo-Kinshasa	807.4	16	Colombia	189.5
7	Sudan	734.9	17	Mali	164.5
8	Central African Rep.	610.2	18	Pakistan	137.2
9	Eritrea	505.1	19	Iran	129.7
10	Burundi	381.5	20	Sri Lanka	110.4

Countries with largest refugee[a] populations

'000, 2019

1	Turkey	3,579.5	11	Congo-Kinshasa	523.7
2	Pakistan	1,419.6	12	Chad	442.7
3	Uganda	1,359.5	13	Kenya	438.9
4	Germany	1,146.7	14	France	407.9
5	Sudan	1,055.5	15	Cameroon	406.3
6	Iran	979.4	16	United States	341.7
7	Lebanon	916.2	17	China	303.4
8	Bangladesh	854.8	18	South Sudan	298.3
9	Ethiopia	733.1	19	Iraq	274.0
10	Jordan	693.7	20	Yemen	268.5

Applications for asylum by country of origin

'000, 2019

1	Venezuela	439.9	11	Colombia	50.5
2	Afghanistan	113.3	12	Cuba	45.6
3	Syria	89.5	13	Haiti	40.2
4	Nigeria	82.6	14	Mexico	40.0
5	Honduras	79.9	15	Pakistan	39.1
6	Iraq	61.0	16	China	37.3
7	Guatemala	59.8	17	Iran	36.9
8	El Salvador	57.2	18	Somalia	36.6
9	Congo-Kinshasa	55.5	19	Eritrea	35.2
10	Nicaragua	52.4	20	Turkey	34.1

Countries where asylum applications were lodged

'000, 2019

1	United States	305.8	11	United Kingdom	49.7
2	Peru	259.7	12	Niger	43.1
3	France	187.5	13	Costa Rica	39.8
4	Germany	159.1	14	Australia	39.5
5	Spain	116.9	15	Italy	33.5
6	Brazil	80.9	16	Uganda	33.3
7	Greece	75.3	17	Sweden	30.6
8	Mexico	69.4	18	Malaysia	26.8
9	Canada	56.3	19	Egypt	24.7
10	Turkey	54.1	20	Netherlands	21.5

a According to UNHCR. Includes people in refugee-like situations.

The world economy

Biggest economies
GDP, $bn, 2019

1	United States	21,433	24	Thailand	544
2	China	14,343	25	Belgium	533
3	Japan	5,082	26	Sweden	531
4	Germany	3,861	27	Nigeria	448
5	India	2,869	28	Argentina	445
6	United Kingdom	2,829		Austria	445
7	France[a]	2,716	30	United Arab Emirates	421
8	Italy	2,004	31	Norway	403
9	Brazil	1,840	32	Israel	395
10	Canada	1,736	33	Ireland	389
11	Russia	1,700	34	Philippines	377
12	South Korea	1,647	35	Singapore	372
13	Australia	1,397	36	Hong Kong	366
14	Spain	1,393	37	Malaysia	365
15	Mexico	1,269	38	South Africa	351
16	Indonesia	1,119	39	Denmark	350
17	Netherlands	907	40	Colombia	324
18	Saudi Arabia	793	41	Bangladesh	303
19	Turkey	761		Egypt	303
20	Switzerland	703	43	Chile	282
21	Taiwan	612	44	Pakistan	278
22	Poland	596	45	Finland	269
23	Iran	581	46	Vietnam	262

Biggest economies by purchasing power
GDP PPP, $bn, 2019

1	China	23,523	24	Iran	1,071
2	United States	21,433	25	Netherlands	1,062
3	India	9,560	26	Pakistan	1,061
4	Japan	5,504	27	Argentina	1,035
5	Germany	4,783	28	Philippines	1,006
6	Russia	4,433	29	Malaysia	946
7	France[a]	3,420	30	Vietnam	810
8	Indonesia	3,338	31	Bangladesh	809
9	United Kingdom	3,337	32	Colombia	806
10	Brazil	3,229	33	South Africa	763
11	Italy	2,757	34	United Arab Emirates	685
12	Mexico	2,672	35	Belgium	647
13	Turkey	2,347	36	Romania	645
14	South Korea	2,276	37	Switzerland	621
15	Spain	2,048	38	Sweden	582
16	Canada	1,942	39	Singapore	580
17	Saudi Arabia	1,681	40	Ukraine	562
18	Australia	1,354	41	Austria	536
19	Thailand	1,342	42	Algeria	517
20	Poland	1,335	43	Chile	512
21	Taiwan	1,261	44	Kazakhstan	509
22	Egypt	1,233	45	Czech Republic	473
23	Nigeria	1,078	46	Hong Kong	469

a Includes overseas territories.   b IMF coverage.

Regional GDP

$bn, 2019		*% annual growth 2014–19*	
World	87,345	World	3.4
Advanced economies	51,975	Advanced economies	2.1
Euro area (19)	13,365	Euro area (19)	1.9
G7	39,741	G7	1.9
Emerging & dev. Asia	20,554	Emerging & dev. Asia	6.4
Emerging & dev. Europe	3,932	Emerging & dev. Europe	2.6
Latin America and the Carib.	5,192	Latin America and the Carib.	0.5
Middle East, N. Africa & Central Asia	3,977	Middle East, N. Africa & Central Asia	2.7
Sub-Saharan Africa	1,715	Sub-Saharan Africa	2.8

Regional purchasing power

GDP, % of total, 2019		*$ per person, 2019*	
World	100.0	World	17,811
Advanced economies	40.3	Advanced economies	54,182
Euro area (19)	11.2	Euro area (19)	49,336
G7	29.7	G7	55,639
Emerging & developing Asia	34.1	Emerging & dev. Asia	11,615
Emerging & dev. Europe	7.1	Emerging & dev. Europe	27,075
Latin America & the Carib.	7.2	Latin America and the Carib.	16,204
Middle East, N. Africa & Central Asia	8.1	Middle East, N. Africa & Central Asia	11,816
Sub-Saharan Africa	3.1	Sub-Saharan Africa	4,064

Regional population

% of total (7.7bn), 2019		*No. of countries[b], 2019*	
World	100.0	World	194
Advanced economies	14.2	Advanced economies	39
Euro area (19)	4.5	Euro area (19)	19
G7	10.2	G7	7
Emerging & developing Asia	48.2	Emerging & developing Asia	30
Emerging & dev. Europe	5.0	Emerging & developing Europe	16
Latin America & the Carib.	8.3	Latin America & the Caribbean	33
Middle East, N. Africa & Central Asia	10.7	Middle East, N. Africa & Central Asia	31
Sub-Saharan Africa	13.6	Sub-Saharan Africa	45

Regional international trade

Exports of goods & services *% of total, 2019*		*Current-account balances* *$bn, 2019*	
World	100.0	World	394
Advanced economies	63.0	Advanced economies	394
Euro area (19)	26.3	Euro area (19)	307
G7	33.4	G7	-100
Emerging & developing Asia	18.2	Emerging & dev. Asia	131
Emerging & dev. Europe	6.2	Emerging & dev. Europe	52
Latin America & the Caribbean	5.1	Latin America and the Carib.	-89
Middle East, N. Africa & Central Asia	5.9	Middle East, N. Africa & Central Asia	21
Sub-Saharan Africa	1.7	Sub-Saharan Africa	-63

Living standards

Highest GDP per person
$, 2019

1	Monacoª	185,829	26	Israel	43,592
2	Liechtensteinª	180,432	27	United Arab Emirates	43,103
3	Bermuda	117,089	28	United Kingdom	42,330
4	Luxembourg	114,705	29	New Zealand	42,084
5	Isle of Manª	89,108	30	Andorra	40,886
6	Cayman Islandsª	85,975	31	France	40,494
7	Macau	84,096	32	Japan	40,247
8	Switzerland	81,994	33	Virgin Islands (US)ᵇ	35,938
9	Ireland	78,661	34	Guamª	35,713
10	Norway	75,420	35	Bahamas	34,864
11	Iceland	66,945	36	New Caledonia	34,567
12	United States	65,298	37	Italy	33,228
13	Singapore	65,233	38	Puerto Rico	32,874
14	Qatar	62,088	39	Kuwait	32,000
15	Channel Islands	60,174	40	South Korea	31,846
16	Denmark	60,170	41	Brunei	31,087
17	Australia	55,060	42	Malta	29,821
18	Netherlands	52,331	43	Spain	29,600
19	Sweden	51,615	44	Cyprus	27,858
20	Austria	50,138	45	Slovenia	25,946
21	Finland	48,783	46	Taiwan	25,936
22	Hong Kong	48,713	47	Estonia	23,723
23	Germany	46,445	48	Bahrain	23,504
24	Belgium	46,421	49	Czech Republic	23,495
25	Canada	46,195	50	Portugal	23,252

Lowest GDP per person
$, 2019

1	Burundi	261	22	Rwanda	820
2	South Sudan	310	23	Ethiopia	856
3	Somalia	338	24	Tajikistan	871
4	Malawi	412	25	Mali	879
5	Sudan	442	26	Guinea	963
6	Central African Rep.	468	27	Nepal	1,071
7	Mozambique	504	28	Lesotho	1,118
8	Afghanistan	507	29	Tanzania	1,122
9	Madagascar	523	30	Syria	1,139
10	Sierra Leone	528	31	North Korea	1,208
11	Niger	554	32	Benin	1,219
12	Eritrea	567	33	Haiti	1,272
13	Congo-Brazzaville	581	34	Pakistan	1,285
14	Liberia	622	35	Zambia	1,305
15	Togo	679	36	Kyrgyzstan	1,309
16	Guinea-Bissau	697	37	Myanmar	1,408
17	Chad	710	38	Senegal	1,447
18	Yemen	774	39	Zimbabwe	1,464
19	Gambia, The	778	40	Cameroon	1,507
20	Burkina Faso	787	41	Timor-Leste	1,561
21	Uganda	794	42	Cambodia	1,643

a 2018   b 2017

Highest purchasing power
GDP per person in PPP (US = 100), 2019

1	Macau	198.2	35	Japan	66.8
2	Luxembourg	190.8	36	Spain	66.6
3	Singapore	155.7	37	Israel	65.7
4	Qatar	144.0	38	Slovenia	65.0
5	Ireland	137.3	39	Cyprus	63.2
6	Bermuda	130.8	40	Lithuania	61.3
7	Cayman Islands[a]	112.2	41	Estonia	61.2
8	Switzerland	110.8	42	Bahamas	59.3
9	United Arab Emirates	107.3	43	Portugal	58.1
10	Norway	107.2	44	Puerto Rico	55.2
11	Taiwan	101.8	45	Poland	53.9
12	United States	100.0	46	Hungary	53.5
13	Brunei	99.3	47	Slovakia	51.3
14	Hong Kong	95.7	48	Romania	51.1
15	Denmark	95.1	49	Latvia	50.6
16	Netherlands	93.9	50	Panama	50.3
17	Austria	92.5	51	Greece	49.8
18	Iceland	92.1	52	Croatia	47.7
19	Germany	88.1	53	Malaysia	45.4
20	Sweden	86.7	54	Russia	44.7
21	Belgium	86.3	55	Oman	43.7
22	Australia	81.8	56	Turkey	43.1
23	Finland	81.4	57	Kazakhstan	42.1
24	Kuwait	79.7	58	Trinidad & Tobago	41.9
25	Canada	79.1	59	Chile	41.4
26	France	78.1	60	Curaçao	39.1
27	United Kingdom	76.5	61	Bulgaria	38.8
28	Saudi Arabia	75.1	62	Montenegro	36.8
29	Malta	72.9	63	Mauritius	36.6
30	Bahrain	72.0	64	Argentina	35.3
31	Italy	70.0	65	Uruguay	34.5
32	New Zealand	69.5	66	Costa Rica	33.3
33	Czech Republic	67.8	67	Mexico	32.1
34	South Korea	67.4	68	Maldives	31.2

Lowest purchasing power
GDP per person in PPP (US = 100), 2019

1	Burundi	1.20	15	Eritrea	3.47
2	South Sudan	1.46	16	Burkina Faso	3.48
3	Central African Rep.	1.51	17	Uganda	3.50
4	Malawi	1.69	18	Ethiopia	3.55
5	Congo-Kinshasa	1.76		Gambia, The	3.55
6	Niger	1.96	20	Rwanda	3.56
7	Mozambique	2.05	21	Mali	3.71
8	Liberia	2.28	22	Guinea	4.10
9	Chad	2.53	23	Tanzania	4.24
10	Togo	2.55	24	Lesotho	4.32
11	Madagascar	2.63	25	Zimbabwe	4.54
12	Sierra Leone	2.75	26	Haiti	4.65
13	Guinea-Bissau	3.18	27	Benin	5.26
14	Afghanistan	3.30	28	Tajikistan	5.40

The quality of life

Human development index[a]

Highest, 2019		Lowest, 2019	
1 Norway	95.7	1 Niger	39.4
2 Ireland	95.5	2 Central African Rep.	39.7
Switzerland	95.5	3 Chad	39.8
4 Hong Kong	94.9	4 Burundi	43.3
Iceland	94.9	South Sudan	43.3
6 Germany	94.7	6 Mali	43.4
7 Sweden	94.5	7 Burkina Faso	45.2
8 Australia	94.4	Sierra Leone	45.2
Netherlands	94.4	9 Mozambique	45.6
10 Denmark	94.0	10 Eritrea	45.9
11 Finland	93.8	11 Yemen	47.0
Singapore	93.8	12 Guinea	47.7
13 United Kingdom	93.2	13 Congo-Kinshasa	48.0
14 Belgium	93.1	Guinea-Bissau	48.0
New Zealand	93.1	Liberia	48.0
16 Canada	92.9	16 Malawi	48.3
17 United States	92.6	17 Ethiopia	48.5
18 Austria	92.2	18 Gambia, The	49.6
19 Israel	91.9	19 Haiti	51.0
Japan	91.9	Sudan	51.0
Liechtenstein	91.9	21 Afghanistan	51.1
22 Slovenia	91.7	22 Senegal	51.2
23 Luxembourg	91.6	23 Togo	51.5
South Korea	91.6	24 Lesotho	52.7

Gini coefficient[b]

Highest, 2010–18		Lowest, 2010–18	
1 South Africa	63.0	1 Slovenia	24.2
2 Namibia	59.1	2 Czech Republic	24.9
3 Zambia	57.1	3 Belarus	25.2
4 Central African Rep.	56.2	Slovakia	25.2
5 Eswatini	54.6	5 Moldova	25.7
6 Mozambique	54.0	6 Ukraine	26.1
7 Brazil	53.9	7 Iceland	26.8
8 Botswana	53.3	8 Norway	27.0
9 Honduras	52.1	9 Belgium	27.4
10 Angola	51.3	Finland	27.4
11 Guinea-Bissau	50.7	11 Kazakhstan	27.5
12 Colombia	50.4	12 Algeria	27.6
13 Panama	49.2	13 Kyrgyzstan	27.7
14 Congo-Brazzaville	48.9	14 Netherlands	28.5
15 Guatemala	48.3	15 Denmark	28.7
16 Costa Rica	48.0	Timor-Leste	28.7
17 Benin	47.8	17 Sweden	28.8

a GDP or GDP per person is often taken as a measure of how developed a country is, but its usefulness is limited as it refers only to economic welfare. The UN Development Programme combines statistics on average and expected years of schooling and life expectancy with income levels (now GNI per person, valued in PPP US$). The HDI is shown here scaled from 0 to 100; countries scoring over 80 are considered to have very high human development, 70–79 high, 55–69 medium and those under 55 low.
b The lower its value, the more equally household income is distributed.

Individual tax rates, top marginal rate
%, 2020

1	Finland	57.0	23	Italy	43.0
2	Japan	56.0	24	India	42.7
3	Denmark	55.9	25	Papua New Guinea	42.0
4	Austria	55.0		South Korea	42.0
5	Aruba	52.0	27	Chile	40.0
6	Belgium	50.0		Congo-Kinshasa	40.0
	Israel	50.0		Mauritania	40.0
	Slovenia	50.0		Senegal	40.0
9	Netherlands	49.5		Switzerland	40.0
10	Ireland	48.0		Taiwan	40.0
	Portugal	48.0		Turkey	40.0
12	Curaçao	46.5		Uganda	40.0
13	Iceland	46.2		Zimbabwe	40.0
14	Luxembourg	45.8	36	Colombia	39.0
15	Australia	45.0	37	Norway	38.2
	China	45.0	38	Morocco	38.0
	France	45.0		Suriname	38.0
	Germany	45.0	40	Zambia	37.5
	South Africa	45.0	41	Namibia	37.0
	Spain	45.0		United States	37.0
	United Kingdom	45.0	43	Croatia	36.0
22	Greece	44.0		Uruguay	36.0

Corporate tax rates, net effective rate
%, 2020

1	United Arab Emirates[a]	55.0		Ethiopia	30.0
2	Suriname	36.0		Gabon	30.0
3	Congo-Kinshasa	35.0		Germany	30.0
	Malta	35.0		India	30.0
	Pakistan	35.0		Kenya	30.0
	Sudan	35.0		Malawi	30.0
	Zambia	35.0		Mexico	30.0
8	Brazil	34.0		Nicaragua	30.0
	Venezuela	34.0		Nigeria	30.0
10	Cameroon	33.0		Papua New Guinea	30.0
	Monaco	33.0		Philippines	30.0
12	Colombia	32.0		Rwanda	30.0
	Mozambique	32.0		Senegal	30.0
	Namibia	32.0		Sierra Leone	30.0
15	Gambia, The	31.0		Tanzania	30.0
	Morocco	31.0		Trinidad & Tobago	30.0
17	Japan	30.6		Uganda	30.0
18	Angola	30.0	43	Peru	29.5
	Argentina	30.0	44	Belgium	29.0
	Australia	30.0	45	Burkina Faso	28.0
	Benin	30.0		France	28.0
	Burundi	30.0		New Zealand	28.0
	Congo-Brazzaville	30.0		South Africa	28.0
	Costa Rica	30.0		Sri Lanka	28.0
	El Salvador	30.0		Syria	28.0

a Foreign oil firms.

Economic growth

Highest economic growth
Average annual % increase in real GDP, 2009–19

1	Ethiopia	9.8		Turkey	5.8
2	Turkmenistan[a]	9.0	27	Togo	5.7
3	China	7.7	28	Dominican Rep.	5.6
4	Mongolia	7.6		Zimbabwe	5.6
5	Laos	7.2	30	Malta	5.5
6	Rwanda	7.1		Mozambique	5.5
7	Cambodia	7.0		Qatar	5.5
	Tajikistan	7.0	33	Indonesia	5.4
9	Bangladesh	6.8		Iraq	5.4
	Myanmar	6.8		Papua New Guinea	5.4
11	Ghana	6.7		Uganda	5.4
	India	6.7	37	Malaysia	5.3
13	Uzbekistan	6.6	38	Sri Lanka	5.2
14	Maldives	6.4	39	Senegal	5.1
	Philippines	6.4	40	Georgia	4.9
16	Tanzania	6.3		Nepal	4.9
	Vietnam	6.3		Zambia	4.9
18	Congo-Kinshasa	6.2	43	Benin	4.8
	Ivory Coast	6.2		Singapore	4.8
	Panama	6.2	45	Botswana	4.7
21	Ireland	6.1	46	Afghanistan	4.6
	Niger	6.1		Bolivia	4.6
23	Burkina Faso	6.0		Macau	4.6
	Guinea	6.0		Timor-Leste	4.6
25	Kenya	5.8	50	Sierra Leone	4.5

Lowest economic growth
Average annual % change in real GDP, 2009–19

1	South Sudan	-7.5	23	Croatia	1.0
2	Yemen	-4.3		Spain	1.0
3	Virgin Islands (US)[b]	-3.8	25	Lebanon	1.1
4	Equatorial Guinea	-3.5	26	Finland	1.2
5	Libya	-2.5		Suriname	1.2
6	Greece	-2.1	28	Argentina	1.3
7	Bermuda	-1.2		Bahamas	1.3
	Central African Rep.	-1.2		Brazil	1.3
9	Puerto Rico	-1.1		Cyprus	1.3
10	Curaçao	-0.9		Japan	1.3
11	Congo-Brazzaville	-0.3	33	Euro area	1.4
12	Trinidad & Tobago	-0.2		France	1.4
13	North Korea	-0.1		Netherlands	1.4
14	Barbados	0.0		Sudan	1.4
15	Andorra	0.1	37	Austria	1.5
16	Italy	0.3		Haiti	1.5
	Ukraine	0.3		Kuwait	1.5
18	Brunei	0.5		Norway	1.5
19	Iran	0.7	41	Azerbaijan	1.6
	Jamaica	0.7		Belgium	1.6
21	Portugal	0.8	43	South Africa	1.7
22	Guam[a]	0.9	44	Belarus	1.8

a 2009–18   b 2009–17

Highest economic growth
Average annual % increase in real GDP, 1999–2009

1	Equatorial Guinea	20.2	11	Cambodia	8.4
2	Azerbaijan	15.4	12	Armenia	8.3
3	Qatar[c]	12.6		Rwanda	8.3
4	Myanmar	12.4		Tajikistan	8.3
5	China	10.3	15	Ethiopia	8.0
6	Macau	9.4	16	Nigeria	7.6
7	Afghanistan[d]	9.2	17	Mozambique	7.5
	Chad	9.2	18	Turkmenistan	7.3
9	Angola	8.6	19	Belarus	7.2
10	Kazakhstan	8.5			

Lowest economic growth
Average annual % change in real GDP, 1999–2009

1	Zimbabwe	-5.5	10	Jamaica	0.9
2	Eritrea	-1.0		Portugal	0.9
3	Gabon	0.5	12	Bahamas	1.0
	Italy	0.5		Denmark	1.0
	Japan	0.5		Puerto Rico	1.0
6	Curaçao[c]	0.7	15	Fiji	1.1
	Germany	0.7		Virgin Islands (US)[d]	1.1
	Ivory Coast	0.7	17	Euro area	1.3
9	Liberia[c]	0.8			

Highest services growth
Average annual % increase in real terms, 2009–19

1	Ethiopia	11.1	13	Cambodia	6.8
2	Myanmar[e]	9.2		Tanzania[b]	6.8
3	China	8.4	15	Ghana	6.6
4	Togo	8.1		Guinea-Bissau	6.6
5	India	7.8	17	Indonesia	6.5
	Rwanda	7.8	18	Azerbaijan	6.3
7	Zimbabwe[a]	7.5		Kenya	6.3
8	Uzbekistan	7.3		Maldives	6.3
9	Philippines	7.2		Zambia	6.3
10	Mongolia[f]	7.0	22	Malaysia	6.2
11	Laos[g]	6.9		Mozambique	6.2
	Macau[a]	6.9			

Lowest services growth
Average annual % change in real terms, 2009–19

1	Libya	-5.0		Italy	0.4
2	Yemen	-3.5	10	Sudan	0.5
3	Greece	-2.0	11	North Korea	0.8
4	Puerto Rico	-1.7	12	Japan[h]	0.9
5	Bermuda[f]	-1.1		Portugal	0.9
6	Suriname	-0.7	14	Bahamas	1.0
7	Jamaica	0.3	15	Finland	1.1
8	Barbados	0.4		Ukraine	1.1

c 2000–09 d 2002–09 e 2010–18 f 2010–19 g 2012–19 h 2011–19
Note: Rankings of highest and lowest industrial growth 2009–19 can be found on page 44.

Trading places

Biggest exporters
% of total world exports (goods, services and income), 2019

1	Euro area (19)	16.57		22	Australia	1.36
2	United States	12.73		23	Luxembourg	1.32
3	China	10.09		24	Poland	1.20
4	Germany	7.20		25	Thailand	1.16
5	Japan	4.23		26	Hong Kong	1.11
6	United Kingdom	4.02		27	Sweden	1.09
7	France	3.83		28	Saudi Arabia	1.06
8	Netherlands	3.80		29	Brazil	0.99
9	Italy	2.49		30	Austria	0.98
10	South Korea	2.44			Vietnam	0.98
11	Canada	2.32		32	Malaysia	0.88
12	Switzerland	2.23			Turkey	0.88
13	Ireland	2.17		34	Denmark	0.82
14	India	1.98		35	Indonesia	0.72
15	Spain	1.93		36	Czech Republic	0.69
16	Russia	1.86		37	Norway	0.66
17	Belgium	1.77		38	Hungary	0.52
	Singapore	1.77		39	Finland	0.46
19	Mexico	1.76		40	Israel	0.45
20	Taiwan	1.46		41	Kuwait	0.40
21	United Arab Emirates	1.43				

Trade dependency
Trade[a] as % of GDP, 2019

Most				Least		
1	Vietnam	96.8		1	Cuba	5.8
2	Slovakia	81.1		2	Bermuda	7.8
3	Cambodia	68.7		3	Hong Kong	9.1
4	United Arab Emirates	66.1		4	Iran	9.6
5	Hungary	64.8		5	United States	9.7
	Slovenia	64.8		6	Ethiopia	9.9
7	Czech Republic	60.2		7	Tanzania	11.1
8	Lesotho	59.9		8	Brazil	11.2
9	South Sudan	59.3		9	Kenya	11.7
10	Belgium	58.6		10	Yemen[b]	11.8
	Puerto Rico	58.6		11	Argentina	12.6
12	Netherlands	56.8		12	Pakistan	12.8
13	North Macedonia	56.3		13	Macau	13.1
14	Lithuania	55.6		14	Bahamas	13.3
15	Belarus	54.6		15	Niger	13.4
16	Suriname	50.4		16	Cayman Islands	13.6
17	Bulgaria	49.9		17	Japan	13.7
	Malaysia	49.9		18	Burundi[c]	14.1
19	Taiwan	49.3		19	Egypt	14.2
20	Estonia	49.0			Nigeria	14.2
21	Ireland	48.4		21	India	14.3

Notes: The figures are drawn wherever possible from balance of payment statistics so have differing definitions from statistics taken from customs or similar sources. For Hong Kong and Singapore, only domestic exports and retained imports are used. Euro area data exclude intra-euro area trade.

a Average of imports plus exports of goods.   b 2016   c 2018

Biggest traders of goods[a]
% of world, 2020

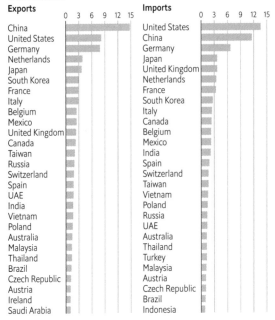

Exports		Imports	
	0 3 6 9 12 15		0 3 6 9 12 15
China		United States	
United States		China	
Germany		Germany	
Netherlands		Japan	
Japan		United Kingdom	
South Korea		Netherlands	
France		France	
Italy		South Korea	
Belgium		Italy	
Mexico		Canada	
United Kingdom		Belgium	
Canada		Mexico	
Taiwan		India	
Russia		Spain	
Switzerland		Switzerland	
Spain		Taiwan	
UAE		Vietnam	
India		Poland	
Vietnam		Russia	
Poland		UAE	
Australia		Australia	
Malaysia		Thailand	
Thailand		Turkey	
Brazil		Malaysia	
Czech Republic		Austria	
Austria		Czech Republic	
Ireland		Brazil	
Saudi Arabia		Indonesia	

Biggest earners from services and income
% of world exports of services and income, 2019

1	Euro area (19)	18.94	19	South Korea		1.33
2	United States	18.38	20	Sweden		1.26
3	United Kingdom	6.23	21	Australia		1.10
4	Germany	5.59	22	Russia		1.06
5	Netherlands	4.96	23	Denmark		1.05
6	Japan	4.75	24	Austria		1.01
7	China	4.73	25	United Arab Emirates		0.88
8	France	4.62	26	Thailand		0.84
9	Ireland	3.38	27	Taiwan		0.83
10	Luxembourg	3.27	28	Norway		0.80
11	Singapore	2.98	29	Poland		0.77
12	Hong Kong	2.88	30	Israel		0.64
13	Switzerland	2.70		Turkey		0.64
14	India	2.18	32	Brazil		0.54
15	Spain	2.07		Finland		0.54
16	Canada	1.99	34	Malaysia		0.52
17	Italy	1.89	35	Philippines		0.50
18	Belgium	1.79	36	Macau		0.48

a Individual countries only.

Balance of payments: current account

Largest surpluses
$m, 2019

1	Euro area (19)	312,827		26	Libya[a]	11,276
2	Germany	289,605		27	Norway	10,439
3	Japan	176,811		28	Venezuela[a]	8,613
4	China	102,910		29	Australia	8,033
5	Netherlands	90,206		30	Puerto Rico	7,974
6	Taiwan	65,161		31	Turkey	6,759
7	Russia	64,806		32	Angola	5,137
8	Italy	64,011		33	Papua New Guinea	4,999
9	South Korea	59,676		34	Azerbaijan	4,365
10	Singapore	53,399		35	Qatar	4,260
11	Switzerland	49,151		36	Iran	3,754
12	Saudi Arabia	38,230		37	Luxembourg	3,095
13	Thailand	38,206		38	Slovenia	3,049
14	Kuwait	33,811		39	Poland	2,931
15	Denmark	30,937		40	Cuba[b]	1,899
16	United Arab Emirates	29,653		41	Belgium	1,842
17	Spain	29,605		42	Lithuania	1,817
18	Sweden	27,162		43	Guatemala	1,792
19	Hong Kong	21,807		44	Iceland	1,579
20	Macau	18,556		45	Croatia	1,455
21	Iraq	15,763		46	Bulgaria	1,234
22	Israel	13,135		47	Trinidad & Tobago	1,056
23	Vietnam	13,101		48	Zimbabwe	920
24	Austria	12,664		49	Czech Republic	898
25	Malaysia	12,296		50	Brunei	894

Largest deficits
$m, 2019

1	United States	-480,228		22	Sudan	-5,215
2	United Kingdom	-87,545		23	Ethiopia	-4,934
3	Brazil	-65,030		24	Morocco	-4,407
4	Ireland	-44,934		25	Mexico	-4,238
5	Canada	-35,688		26	Oman	-4,140
6	Indonesia	-30,279		27	Ukraine	-4,124
7	India	-29,763		28	Cambodia	-4,065
8	France	-18,419		29	Argentina	-3,997
9	Algeria	-17,148		30	Afghanistan	-3,792
10	Nigeria	-14,627		31	Serbia	-3,535
11	Colombia	-14,285		32	Peru	-3,531
12	Romania	-12,191		33	Uzbekistan	-3,366
13	Lebanon	-11,540		34	Panama	-3,332
14	South Africa	-10,667		35	Tunisia	-3,284
15	Chile	-10,454		36	Greece	-3,112
16	Egypt	-10,222		37	Philippines	-3,047
17	Pakistan	-8,558		38	Mozambique	-3,022
18	Kazakhstan	-7,296		39	Bangladesh	-2,949
19	New Zealand	-6,843		40	Slovakia	-2,842
20	Turkmenistan[c]	-5,581		41	Uganda	-2,333
21	Kenya	-5,559		42	Mongolia	-2,162

Note: Euro area data exclude intra-euro area trade.
a 2018   b 2017   c 2015

Largest surpluses as % of GDP
2019

1	Macau	34.5		Malta	5.8
2	Kuwait	25.1	27	Slovenia	5.6
3	Libya[a]	21.4	28	Sweden	5.1
4	Papua New Guinea	20.1	29	Vietnam	5.0
5	Eritrea[a]	15.4	30	Saudi Arabia	4.8
6	Singapore	14.4	31	Eswatini	4.4
7	Bermuda	11.1		Luxembourg	4.4
8	Taiwan	10.6		Trinidad & Tobago	4.4
9	Netherlands	9.9	34	Zimbabwe	4.3
10	Azerbaijan	9.1	35	Bahamas	3.9
11	Denmark	8.8	36	Russia	3.8
12	Venezuela[a]	8.7	37	South Korea	3.6
13	Puerto Rico	7.6	38	Japan	3.5
14	Germany	7.5	39	Malaysia	3.4
15	Switzerland	7.0	40	Israel	3.3
	Thailand	7.0		Lithuania	3.3
	United Arab Emirates	7.0	42	Italy	3.2
18	Iraq	6.7	43	Austria	2.8
19	Brunei	6.6	44	Norway	2.6
	Timor-Leste	6.6	45	Croatia	2.4
21	Iceland	6.5		Qatar	2.4
22	South Sudan	6.2	47	Euro area (19)	2.3
23	Hong Kong	6.0		Guatemala	2.3
	Nicaragua	6.0	49	Spain	2.1
25	Angola	5.8			

Largest deficits as % of GDP
2019

1	Guyana	-32.8	22	Mauritania	-10.9
2	Maldives	-26.8	23	West Bank & Gaza	-10.8
3	Malawi	-24.0	24	Algeria	-10.0
4	Lebanon	-22.2	25	Cayman Islands	-9.7
	Sierra Leone	-22.2	26	Guinea-Bissau	-9.5
6	Liberia	-21.3	27	Moldova	-9.4
7	Mozambique	-19.8	28	Chad[c]	-9.1
8	Afghanistan	-19.7		Senegal	-9.1
9	Curaçao	-17.4	30	Tunisia	-8.5
10	Sudan	-17.1	31	Albania	-8.0
11	Turkmenistan[b]	-15.6	32	Botswana	-7.6
12	Mongolia	-15.4	33	Armenia	-7.2
13	Montenegro	-15.1	34	Serbia	-6.9
14	Cambodia	-15.0	35	Uganda	-6.6
15	Fiji	-12.6	36	Cyprus	-6.3
	Kyrgyzstan	-12.6	37	Equatorial Guinea[d]	-5.8
17	Niger	-12.2		Gambia, The[a]	-5.8
18	Rwanda	-12.1		Georgia	-5.8
	Suriname	-12.1		Kenya	-5.8
20	Burundi	-11.7		Uzbekistan	-5.8
21	Ireland	-11.6			

a 2018   b 2015   c 2013   d 2017

Official reserves[a]
$m, end-2020

1	China	3,357,022	16	France	223,962
2	Japan	1,390,723	17	Italy	210,411
3	Switzerland	1,083,287	18	Mexico	199,056
4	Euro Area (19)	1,076,715	19	United Kingdom	180,019
5	United States	627,454	20	Israel	173,292
6	Russia	596,511	21	Czech Republic	166,116
7	India	590,151	22	Poland	154,193
8	Taiwan	555,620	23	Indonesia	135,907
9	Hong Kong	491,775	24	Philippines	109,969
10	Saudi Arabia	472,815	25	Malaysia	107,639
11	South Korea	443,451	26	United Arab Emirates	106,695
12	Singapore	369,820	27	Turkey	93,431
13	Brazil	355,607	28	Canada	90,428
14	Germany	268,030	29	Spain	81,256
15	Thailand	258,087	30	Libya[b]	80,241

Official gold reserves
Market prices, $m, end-2020

1	Euro Area (19)	653,748	14	Kazakhstan	23,538
2	United States	493,605	15	Portugal	23,217
3	Germany	204,061	16	Uzbekistan	20,178
4	Italy	148,798	17	Saudi Arabia	19,606
5	France	147,848	18	United Kingdom	18,831
6	Russia	139,494	19	Lebanon	17,407
7	China	118,239	20	Spain	17,088
8	Switzerland	63,116	21	Austria	16,992
9	Japan	46,440	22	Poland	13,877
10	Turkey	43,473	23	Belgium	13,800
11	India	41,064	24	Philippines	11,457
12	Netherlands	37,169	25	Algeria	10,533
13	Taiwan	25,709	26	Thailand	9,344

Workers' remittances
Inflows, $m, 2019

1	India	83,332	16	Italy	10,459
2	China	68,398	17	Russia	10,432
3	Mexico	39,022	18	Spain	9,975
4	Philippines	35,167	19	Uzbekistan	8,546
5	France	26,838	20	Nepal	8,250
6	Egypt	26,781	21	Thailand	8,162
7	Nigeria	23,809	22	Romania	8,142
8	Pakistan	22,245	23	Dominican Rep.	7,421
9	Bangladesh	18,364	24	Lebanon	7,410
10	Germany	18,271	25	South Korea	7,166
11	Vietnam	17,000	26	Morocco	6,963
12	Ukraine	15,788	27	Colombia	6,762
13	Belgium	12,157	28	Sri Lanka	6,749
14	Indonesia	11,666	29	United States	6,724
15	Guatemala	10,656	30	Poland	6,501

a Foreign exchange, SDRs, IMF position and gold at market prices.   b November 2020

Exchange rates

The Economist's Big Mac index

Local currency under (-)/over (+) valuation against the $ᵃ, %
January 2021

	Big Mac price, $ᵇ
Switzerland	7.29
Sweden	6.37
Norway	6.09
United Statesᶜ	5.66
Israel	5.35
Canada	5.29
Euro areaᵈ	5.16
Australia	4.98
Denmark	4.90
New Zealand	4.87
Uruguay	4.80
United Kingdom	4.44
Singapore	4.43
Thailand	4.25
Czech Republic	4.12
South Korea	4.10
Chile	4.09
UAE	4.02
Bahrain	3.98
Brazil	3.98
Costa Rica	3.83
Kuwait	3.79
Argentina	3.75
Colombia	3.74
Japan	3.74
Saudi Arabia	3.73
Sri Lanka	3.70
Croatia	3.69
Honduras	3.61
Qatar	3.57
Nicaragua	3.56
Poland	3.51
Chinaᵉ	3.46
Pakistan	3.43
Peru	3.29
Jordan	3.24
Guatemala	3.20

a Based on purchasing-power parity: local price of a Big Mac burger divided by United States price. b At market exchange rates. c Average of four cities. d Weighted average of prices in euro area. e Average of five cities.

Inflation

Consumer-price inflation

Highest, 2020 or latest, %		Lowest, 2020 or latest, %	
1 Venezuela	2,355.1	1 Qatar	-2.7
2 Zimbabwe	557.2	2 Fiji	-2.6
3 Sudan	163.3	3 Bahrain	-2.3
4 Lebanon	88.2	4 United Arab Emirates	-2.1
5 Argentina	42.0	5 Maldives	-1.6
6 South Sudan	38.0	6 Panama	-1.6
7 Iran	36.5	7 Greece	-1.3
8 Suriname	34.9	Puerto Rico	-1.3
9 Yemen	26.2	9 Cyprus	-1.1
10 Haiti	22.9	Ivory Coast	-1.1
11 Angola	22.3	Malaysia	-1.1
Libya	22.3	12 Oman	-0.9
13 Ethiopia	20.4	13 Thailand	-0.8
14 Liberia	17.0	14 Switzerland	-0.7
15 Zambia	16.4	West Bank & Gaza	-0.7
16 Sierra Leone	15.7	16 Bosnia & Herz.	-0.6
17 Nigeria	13.2	Cayman Islands	-0.6
18 Uzbekistan	12.9	Estonia	-0.6
19 Turkey	12.3	Israel	-0.6
20 Congo-Kinshasa	11.3	20 Ireland	-0.5

Highest average annual consumer-price inflation, 2010–20, %		Lowest average annual consumer-price inflation, 2010–20, %	
1 Venezuela	637.2	1 Switzerland	-0.1
2 South Sudan[a]	70.1	2 Somalia	0.0
3 Sudan	42.9	3 Brunei	0.1
4 Zimbabwe	39.2	4 Eritrea	0.2
5 Argentina	25.3	Greece	0.2
6 Iran	23.0	6 Bosnia & Herz.	0.5
7 Belarus	18.3	Cyprus	0.5
Yemen	18.3	Ireland	0.5
9 Angola	16.6	Japan	0.5
10 Malawi	16.1	10 Israel	0.7
11 Suriname	14.8	Puerto Rico	0.7
12 Ethiopia	14.7	12 Denmark	0.9
13 Curaçao[b]	12.9	Mali	0.9
14 Ivory Coast[b]	12.7	Morocco	0.9
Liberia	12.7	Niger	0.9
16 Egypt	12.1	Taiwan	0.9
Uzbekistan	12.1	17 Bulgaria	1.0
18 Nigeria	11.7	Croatia	1.0
19 Ghana	11.5	Slovenia	1.0
Libya	11.5	Spain	1.0
21 Guinea	11.3	21 Burkina Faso	1.1
22 Haiti	11.2	El Salvador	1.1
Ukraine	11.2	Italy	1.1
24 Sierra Leone	10.5	Portugal	1.1
25 Zambia	8.9	Sweden	1.1
		West Bank & Gaza	1.1

a 2011–20 b 2010–19

Commodity prices

End 2020, % change on a year earlier			*2015–20, % change*	
1	Timber	118.6	1	Iron ore	285.3
2	Iron ore	76.9	2	Timber	245.0
3	Silver	46.6	3	Nickel	98.7
4	Soya meal	42.4	4	Silver	88.0
5	Soya beans	37.4	5	Palm oil	81.1
6	Copper	27.4	6	Gold	76.5
7	Gold	24.1	7	Zinc	76.4
8	Soya oil	23.2	8	Copper	67.4
9	Nickel	21.5	9	Soya meal	58.4
10	Rice	21.2	10	Rice	49.3
11	Palm oil	20.8	11	Soya beans	48.9
12	Corn	20.2	12	Soya oil	39.2
13	Zinc	19.9	13	Rubber	30.5
14	Aluminium	11.1	14	Aluminium	30.3
15	Wheat	10.7	15	Wheat	30.0
16	Pulp	9.2	16	Corn	28.6
17	Cotton	6.4	17	Cotton	17.4
18	Sugar	5.8	18	Beef (Aus)	17.1
19	Rubber	2.9	19	Pork	13.6
20	Lead	0.7	20	Oil[a]	10.8
21	Coffee	0.6	21	Lead	9.9
22	Cocoa	-2.8	22	Coffee	1.8
23	Pork	-5.9	23	Sugar	-0.3
24	Beef US	-6.3	24	Beef (US)	-6.2
25	Tea	-14.5	25	Wool (Aus)	-7.4
26	Beef Aus	-17.7	26	Pulp	-11.1

Real[b] residential house prices

Q3 2020[c], % change on a year earlier			*Q3 2015–Q3 2020[c], % change*	
1	Turkey	13.9	1	Hungary	50.9
2	Luxembourg	10.3	2	Portugal	47.8
3	Canada	8.7	3	Iceland	41.1
4	Austria	7.9	4	Luxembourg	38.9
	Germany	7.9	5	Czech Republic	37.7
6	Poland	7.7	6	Latvia	34.7
7	Croatia	7.1		Slovakia	34.7
	Netherlands	7.1	8	Netherlands	32.9
9	Portugal	7.0	9	Canada	32.6
10	Slovakia	6.8	10	Germany	32.0
11	Russia	5.9	11	Ireland	31.0
12	Lithuania	5.4	12	Slovenia	30.4
13	Greece	5.1	13	Bulgaria	28.1
	Thailand	5.1	14	Croatia	26.9
15	Denmark	5.0	15	New Zealand	25.4
	Switzerland	5.0	16	Austria	25.3
17	Czech Republic	4.9	17	Poland	24.8
	Estonia	4.9	18	Lithuania	23.9
	United States	4.9	19	Chile	23.0
20	New Zealand	4.8	20	Spain	22.6

a Brent.　b Deflated by CPI.　c Or latest.

Debt

Highest foreign debt[a]
$bn, 2019

#	Country		#	Country	
1	China	2,114.2	26	Ukraine	123.8
2	Hong Kong	710.0	27	Vietnam	117.3
3	Singapore	674.1	28	Romania	117.2
4	Brazil	569.4	29	Egypt	115.1
5	India	560.0	30	Israel	105.0
6	Russia	490.7	31	Pakistan	100.8
7	Mexico	469.7	32	Panama	99.1
8	Turkey	440.8	33	Iraq	86.0
9	South Korea	430.9	34	Philippines	83.7
10	Indonesia	402.1	35	Lebanon	74.0
11	Poland	354.0	36	Bahrain	73.1
12	Argentina	279.3	37	Oman	70.9
13	Saudi Arabia	254.1	38	Peru	64.2
14	United Arab Emirates	245.8	39	Angola	61.6
15	Malaysia	231.0	40	Kuwait	59.7
16	Qatar	198.9	41	Bangladesh	57.1
17	Chile	198.1	42	Sudan	56.6
18	Czech Republic	194.1	43	Sri Lanka	56.1
19	South Africa	187.7	44	Morocco	55.0
20	Taiwan	184.7	45	Nigeria	54.8
21	Thailand	180.2	46	Ecuador	51.7
22	Venezuela	168.1	47	Croatia	43.5
23	Kazakhstan	156.3	48	Uruguay	42.6
24	Hungary	147.3	49	Belarus	40.7
25	Colombia	138.7	50	Bulgaria	40.5

Highest foreign debt burden[a]
Total foreign debt as % of GDP, 2019

#	Country		#	Country	
1	Venezuela	281.6	21	Laos	88.7
2	Mongolia	224.0	22	Kazakhstan	88.6
3	Hong Kong	194.1	23	Papua New Guinea	88.3
4	Bahrain	189.6	24	Armenia	86.9
5	Singapore	180.0	25	Tajikistan	81.7
6	Panama	148.4	26	Bosnia & Herz.	80.8
7	Montenegro	147.9	27	Ukraine	80.5
8	Sudan	140.5	28	Iceland	77.8
9	Lebanon	138.0	29	Czech Republic	77.4
10	Mozambique	133.0	30	Jordan	75.7
11	Zambia	118.2	31	Croatia	71.6
12	Qatar	113.1		North Macedonia	71.6
13	Jamaica	101.3	33	Mauritania	70.6
14	Georgia	99.1	34	Chile	70.2
15	Kyrgyzstan	98.6	35	Serbia	69.7
16	Tunisia	97.3	36	Angola	69.4
17	Nicaragua	93.4	37	Uruguay	69.3
18	Oman	92.8	38	Namibia	68.6
19	Hungary	90.3	39	El Salvador	66.9
20	Mauritius	89.6	40	Sri Lanka	66.8

a Foreign debt is debt owed to non-residents and repayable in foreign currency; the figures shown include liabilities of government, public and private sectors. Longer-established developed countries have been excluded.

Highest foreign debt[a]
As % of exports of goods and services, 2019

1	Sudan	988.0	15	Chile	227.6
2	Venezuela	901.0	16	Uruguay	227.2
3	Mongolia	335.6	17	Kazakhstan	226.6
4	Mozambique	327.8	18	Laos	226.4
5	Zambia	324.8	19	Sierra Leone	219.2
6	Argentina	324.2	20	Sri Lanka	212.4
7	Panama	320.5	21	Colombia	207.7
8	Ethiopia	296.0	22	Brazil	197.4
9	Lebanon	260.2	23	Qatar	197.0
10	Rwanda	246.2	24	Niger	195.7
11	Montenegro	245.1	25	Mauritania	192.6
12	Kenya	235.2	26	Tanzania	190.0
13	Central African Rep.	231.8	27	Pakistan	189.0
14	Bahrain	229.3	28	Zimbabwe	183.6

Highest debt service ratio[b]
Average, %, 2019

1	Mongolia	125.1	15	Turkey	34.3
2	Zambia	82.7	16	Panama	30.3
3	Syria	64.0	17	Kenya	29.5
4	Lebanon	56.7	18	Colombia	28.8
5	Brazil	52.6	19	Ecuador	27.8
6	Hungary	49.0	20	Zimbabwe	26.1
7	Argentina	48.9	21	Croatia	25.7
8	Kazakhstan	47.7	22	Armenia	25.6
9	Bahrain	41.8	23	Poland	25.3
10	El Salvador	40.5	24	Serbia	24.5
11	Jamaica	38.5	25	Sri Lanka	23.8
12	Indonesia	37.3	26	Angola	23.7
13	Namibia	36.4	27	Ethiopia	23.3
14	Chile	35.1	28	Venezuela	23.1

Household debt[c]
As % of net disposable income, 2019

1	Denmark	256.7	14	France	122.1
2	Netherlands	235.7	15	Belgium	116.8
3	Switzerland	222.6	16	Japan[d]	107.0
4	Australia	209.7	17	Spain	105.0
5	South Korea	190.6	18	Greece	97.8
6	Luxembourg[d]	190.1	19	Germany	96.2
7	Sweden	188.1	20	Austria	89.8
8	Canada	186.2	21	Italy	88.2
9	Finland	148.2	22	Slovakia	79.0
10	United Kingdom	141.7	23	Estonia	76.4
11	Ireland	130.7	24	Czech Republic	76.3
12	New Zealand[d]	126.0	25	Chile[d]	73.0
13	Portugal	122.3	26	Poland	60.8

b Debt service is the sum of interest and principal repayments (amortisation) due on outstanding foreign debt. The debt service ratio is debt service as a percentage of exports of goods, non-factor services, primary income and workers' remittances.
c OECD countries.   d 2018

Aid

Largest recipients of bilateral and multilateral aid
$bn, 2019

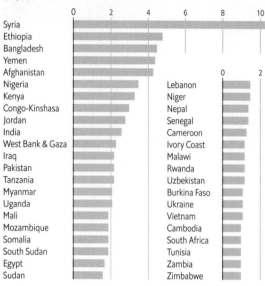

Syria	Lebanon
Ethiopia	Niger
Bangladesh	Nepal
Yemen	Senegal
Afghanistan	Cameroon
Nigeria	Ivory Coast
Kenya	Malawi
Congo-Kinshasa	Rwanda
Jordan	Uzbekistan
India	Burkina Faso
West Bank & Gaza	Ukraine
Iraq	Vietnam
Pakistan	Cambodia
Tanzania	South Africa
Myanmar	Tunisia
Uganda	Zambia
Mali	Zimbabwe
Mozambique	
Somalia	
South Sudan	
Egypt	
Sudan	

$ per person, 2019

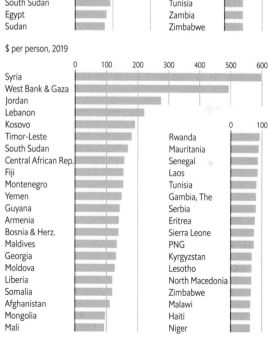

Syria	Rwanda
West Bank & Gaza	Mauritania
Jordan	Senegal
Lebanon	Laos
Kosovo	Tunisia
Timor-Leste	Gambia, The
South Sudan	Serbia
Central African Rep.	Eritrea
Fiji	Sierra Leone
Montenegro	PNG
Yemen	Kyrgyzstan
Guyana	Lesotho
Armenia	North Macedonia
Bosnia & Herz.	Zimbabwe
Maldives	Malawi
Georgia	Haiti
Moldova	Niger
Liberia	
Somalia	
Afghanistan	
Mongolia	
Mali	

Largest bilateral and multilateral donors[a]

2019		$bn	As % of GNI				$bn	As % of GNI
1	United States	33.5	0.2		15	Denmark	2.6	0.7
2	Germany	24.2	0.6		16	South Korea	2.5	0.1
3	United Kingdom	19.4	0.7			United Arab Emirates	2.5	0.5
4	Japan	15.6	0.3		18	Belgium	2.2	0.4
5	France	12.2	0.4		19	Saudi Arabia	2.1	0.2
6	Turkey	8.7	1.2		20	Austria	1.2	0.3
7	Netherlands	5.3	0.6			Russia	1.2	0.1
8	Sweden	5.2	1.0		22	Finland	1.1	0.4
9	Canada	4.7	0.3		23	Ireland	1.0	0.3
10	Italy	4.4	0.2		24	Poland	0.8	0.1
11	Norway	4.3	1.0		25	New Zealand	0.6	0.3
12	Switzerland	3.1	0.4			Qatar	0.6	0.3
13	Australia	2.9	0.2					
	Spain	2.9	0.2					

Biggest changes to aid

2019 compared with 2015, $m

Increases			Decreases		
1	Syria	5,331.8	1	Vietnam	-2,072.8
2	Yemen	2,618.1	2	Pakistan	-1,592.8
3	Bangladesh	1,924.8	3	Turkey	-1,314.6
4	Ethiopia	1,571.1	4	Ghana	-834.2
5	Nigeria	1,099.3	5	Egypt	-783.9
6	Myanmar	911.4	6	Morocco	-758.4
7	Kenya	787.4	7	Brazil	-713.0
8	Iraq	729.0	8	Indonesia	-602.2
9	Uzbekistan	705.4	9	India	-563.7
10	Cameroon	671.1	10	Liberia	-497.1
11	Mali	661.9	11	Colombia	-453.4
12	Jordan	656.4	12	South Africa	-448.8
13	Sudan	654.3	13	Tanzania	-431.7
14	Niger	620.2	14	Thailand	-396.9
15	Somalia	605.0	15	Sierra Leone	-351.6
16	Senegal	575.0	16	Angola	-330.5
17	Lebanon	560.0	17	Kyrgyzstan	-326.0
18	Ivory Coast	549.6	18	Haiti	-319.4
19	Tunisia	488.4	19	Albania	-306.7
20	Uganda	462.7	20	Ukraine	-301.1
21	West Bank & Gaza	447.2	21	China	-283.6
22	Congo-Kinshasa	426.5	22	Sri Lanka	-247.7
23	Philippines	390.4	23	Dominican Rep.	-145.5
24	Cambodia	305.0	24	Kosovo	-92.5
25	Central African Rep.	267.1	25	Honduras	-83.0
26	Serbia	258.2	26	Bolivia	-75.2
27	Venezuela	247.4	27	North Macedonia	-72.5
28	Burundi	222.4	28	Nicaragua	-68.7
29	El Salvador	215.9	29	Tajikistan	-65.5
30	Mexico	214.7	30	Cuba	-58.3

a Countries that report figures to the OECD.

Industry and services

Largest industrial output
$bn, 2019

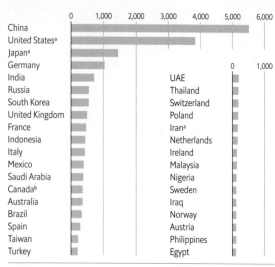

China	
United States[a]	
Japan[a]	
Germany	
India	UAE
Russia	Thailand
South Korea	Switzerland
United Kingdom	Poland
France	Iran[a]
Indonesia	Netherlands
Italy	Ireland
Mexico	Malaysia
Saudi Arabia	Nigeria
Canada[b]	Sweden
Australia	Iraq
Brazil	Norway
Spain	Austria
Taiwan	Philippines
Turkey	Egypt

Highest growth in industrial output
Average annual % increase in real terms, 2009–19

1	Timor-Leste	23.3	11	Congo-Kinshasa	12.8
2	Ethiopia	22.5	12	Maldives	11.3
3	Ghana	16.1		Moldova	11.3
4	Liberia	15.3	14	Papua New Guinea[c]	11.1
5	Cambodia	15.2	15	Zimbabwe[c]	10.3
6	Mongolia	14.6	16	Tanzania[d]	9.9
7	Laos	14.4	17	Kenya	9.3
8	Panama	14.2	18	West Bank & Gaza[c]	9.2
9	Myanmar[c]	13.8	19	China	8.9
10	Bangladesh	13.2			

Lowest growth in industrial output
Average annual % change in real terms, 2009–19

1	Sudan	-30.7	12	Iran[c]	-1.1
2	South Sudan[e]	-9.5		Italy	-1.1
3	Equatorial Guinea	-6.9	14	Brazil	-1.0
4	Greece	-4.4	15	Netherlands	-0.9
5	Yemen	-3.6	16	Central African Rep.	-0.8
6	Tunisia	-3.1	17	Portugal	-0.7
7	Cyprus	-2.6	18	Azerbaijan	-0.6
	Spain	-2.6		France	-0.6
9	Suriname	-1.9	20	Algeria	-0.4
10	Croatia	-1.8	21	Isle of Man[f]	-0.3
11	Norway	-1.2	22	Afghanistan	0.0

a 2018 b 2016 c 2009–18 d 2009–17 e 2009–15 f 2012–18

Largest manufacturing output
$bn, 2019

1	China	3,823	21	Netherlands	99
2	United States[a]	2,317		Poland	99
3	Japan[a]	1,028		Saudi Arabia	99
4	Germany	738	24	Australia	79
5	South Korea	417	25	Malaysia	78
6	India	391	26	Austria	74
7	Italy	298		Singapore	74
8	France	267	28	Philippines	70
9	United Kingdom	243	29	Sweden	69
10	Russia	223	30	Belgium	65
11	Indonesia	221	31	Iran[a]	61
12	Mexico	220	32	Argentina	58
13	Taiwan	190	33	Bangladesh	57
14	Brazil	174	34	Czech Republic	56
15	Spain	155	35	Nigeria	52
16	Canada[b]	152	36	Egypt	48
17	Turkey	139	37	Puerto Rico	47
18	Thailand	138	38	Denmark	46
19	Switzerland	132	39	Israel[a]	44
20	Ireland	120		Romania	44

Largest services output
$bn, 2019

1	United States[a]	15,824	27	Austria	279
2	China	7,750	28	Singapore	262
3	Japan[a]	3,434	29	Israel[a]	259
4	Germany	2,418	30	Argentina	242
5	United Kingdom	2,016	31	Norway	233
6	France	1,906	32	Philippines	230
7	India	1,417	33	Denmark	227
8	Italy	1,329	34	United Arab Emirates	224
9	Brazil	1,164	35	Nigeria	223
10	Canada[a]	1,039	36	Ireland	220
11	Spain	942	37	South Africa	215
12	South Korea	940	38	Malaysia	198
13	Australia	922	39	Colombia	186
14	Russia	918	40	Chile	166
15	Mexico	760	41	Finland	162
16	Netherlands	633	42	Bangladesh	160
17	Switzerland	499	43	Portugal	157
18	Indonesia	495	44	Egypt	153
19	Turkey	430	45	Pakistan	150
20	Saudi Arabia	400	46	Romania	145
21	Taiwan	383	47	Czech Republic	143
22	Belgium	371		Greece	143
23	Sweden	346	49	New Zealand[c]	134
24	Poland	343	50	Peru	124
25	Hong Kong[a]	321	51	Iraq	114
26	Thailand	319	52	Vietnam	109

a 2018   b 2016   c 2017

Agriculture and fisheries

Largest agricultural output
$bn, 2019

1	China	1,020.1	16	Italy	38.3
2	India	459.5	17	Vietnam	36.6
3	United States[a]	177.9	18	Spain	36.4
4	Indonesia	142.3	19	Egypt	33.5
5	Nigeria	98.2	20	Philippines	33.3
6	Brazil	81.6	21	Kenya	32.6
7	Japan[a]	61.4	22	Ethiopia	32.2
8	Pakistan	61.3	23	Australia	29.6
9	Russia	58.6	24	Canada[b]	28.5
10	Turkey	48.9	25	Germany	27.9
11	Iran[a]	45.1	26	Argentina	27.1
12	France	43.4	27	South Korea	26.7
	Thailand	43.4	28	Malaysia	26.5
14	Mexico	43.0	29	Venezuela[c]	24.2
15	Bangladesh	38.4	30	Colombia	21.8

Most economically dependent on agriculture
% of GDP from agriculture, 2019

1	Sierra Leone	54.3	15	Malawi	25.5
2	Guinea-Bissau	52.5		Uzbekistan	25.5
3	Chad	42.6	17	Nepal	24.3
4	Liberia	39.1	18	Guinea	23.6
5	Niger	37.8	19	Rwanda	23.5
6	Mali	37.3	20	Madagascar	23.3
7	Kenya	34.1	21	Uganda	23.1
8	Ethiopia	33.5	22	Togo	22.5
9	Central African Rep.	32.4	23	Pakistan	22.0
10	Burundi	28.9	24	Nigeria	21.9
11	Tanzania[a]	28.7	25	Gambia, The	21.8
12	Benin	26.9	26	Myanmar[a]	21.4
13	Mozambique	26.0	27	North Korea	21.2
14	Afghanistan	25.8			

Least economically dependent on agriculture
% of GDP from agriculture, 2019

1	Macau	0.0		Belgium	0.6
	Singapore	0.0		United Kingdom	0.6
3	Hong Kong[a]	0.1	16	Germany	0.7
	Liechtenstein[d]	0.1		Malta	0.7
5	Bermuda	0.2		Puerto Rico	0.7
	Luxembourg	0.2		Switzerland	0.7
	Qatar	0.2		United Arab Emirates	0.7
8	Bahrain	0.3	21	Ireland	0.9
9	Cayman Islands[a]	0.4		United States[a]	0.9
	Curaçao[a]	0.4	23	Brunei	1.0
	Isle of Man	0.4	24	Austria	1.1
12	Kuwait	0.5		Israel[a]	1.1
13	Bahamas	0.6		Trinidad & Tobago	1.1

a 2018   b 2016   c 2014   d 2017

Fisheries and aquaculture production

Fish, crustaceans and molluscs, million tonnes, 2019

1	China	62.2		South Korea	2.0
2	Indonesia	13.4	17	Mexico	1.8
3	India	13.3	18	Malaysia	1.7
4	Vietnam	7.9	19	Morocco	1.5
5	United States	5.3	20	Brazil	1.3
6	Russia	5.2		Ecuador	1.3
7	Peru	5.0		Iran	1.3
8	Bangladesh	4.4	23	Spain	1.2
9	Japan	3.8	24	Nigeria	1.1
	Norway	3.8	25	Cambodia	1.0
11	Chile	3.4		Taiwan	1.0
12	Myanmar	3.0	27	Canada	0.9
13	Philippines	2.9		Iceland	0.9
14	Thailand	2.5	29	Turkey	0.8
15	Egypt	2.0		United Kingdom	0.8

Biggest producers

'000 tonnes, 2018

Cereals

1	China	608,894	6	Indonesia	89,454
2	United States	439,710	7	Argentina	70,591
3	India	321,556	8	Ukraine	69,111
4	Russia	109,832	9	France	61,839
5	Brazil	103,261	10	Bangladesh	58,812

Meat

1	China	86,582	6	Germany	8,025
2	United States	46,823	7	Mexico	7,041
3	Brazil	28,115	8	Spain	6,958
4	Russia	10,629	9	Argentina	5,935
5	India	8,029	10	France	5,462

Fruit

1	China	225,969	6	Turkey	21,848
2	India	100,666	7	Indonesia	20,434
3	Brazil	39,344	8	Spain	19,336
4	United States	23,521	9	Italy	17,166
5	Mexico	22,207	10	Philippines	16,802

Vegetables

1	China	586,913	6	Vietnam	16,310
2	India	131,342	7	Egypt	16,068
3	United States	32,575	8	Nigeria	16,059
4	Turkey	25,884	9	Russia	13,716
5	Mexico	16,749	10	Spain	13,298

Roots and tubers

1	China	150,127	5	Ghana	30,316
2	Nigeria	114,185	6	Thailand	29,885
3	India	57,760	7	Brazil	22,596
4	Congo-Kinshasa	40,732	8	Ukraine	22,504

Commodities

Wheat

Top 10 producers, 2019–20
'000 tonnes

1	EU28	154,951
2	China	133,593
3	India	103,600
4	Russia	73,610
5	United States	52,581
6	Canada	32,670
7	Ukraine	29,171
8	Pakistan	24,349
9	Argentina	19,750
10	Turkey	19,000

Top 10 consumers, 2019–20
'000 tonnes

1	China	128,000
2	EU28	126,500
3	India	98,000
4	Russia	39,500
5	United States	30,024
6	Pakistan	25,400
7	Turkey	20,400
8	Egypt	19,700
9	United Kingdom	16,400
10	Iran	12,100

Rice[a]

Top 10 producers, 2019–20
'000 tonnes

1	China	146,730
2	India	118,870
3	Bangladesh	35,850
4	Indonesia	34,700
5	Vietnam	27,100
6	Thailand	17,655
7	Myanmar	12,700
8	Philippines	11,927
9	Japan	7,611
10	Brazil	7,602

Top 10 consumers, 2019–20
'000 tonnes

1	China	145,230
2	India	105,984
3	Indonesia	36,000
4	Bangladesh	35,500
5	Vietnam	21,250
6	Philippines	14,300
7	Thailand	12,300
8	Myanmar	10,400
9	Japan	8,350
10	Brazil	7,300

Sugar[b]

Top 10 producers, 2019
'000 tonnes

1	India	29,660
2	Brazil	29,170
3	EU28	16,650
4	Thailand	14,050
5	China	10,570
6	United States	7,220
7	Russia	7,200
8	Mexico	6,180
9	Pakistan	5,330
10	Australia	4,250

Top 10 consumers, 2019
'000 tonnes

1	India	25,510
2	EU28	18,110
3	China	16,200
4	Brazil	10,550
5	United States	10,240
6	Indonesia	6,950
7	Russia	5,950
8	Pakistan	5,350
9	Mexico	4,090
10	Egypt	3,190

Coarse grains[c]

Top 5 producers, 2019–20
'000 tonnes

1	United States	359,983
2	China	268,606
3	EU28	163,415
4	Brazil	106,353
5	Argentina	64,927

Top 5 consumers, 2019–20
'000 tonnes

1	United States	320,817
2	China	299,430
3	EU28	164,226
4	Brazil	76,013
5	Mexico	51,016

a Milled. b Raw. c Includes: maize (corn), barley, sorghum, oats, rye, millet, triticale and other. d Tonnes at 65 degrees brix.

Tea

Top 10 producers, 2019		*Top 10 consumers, 2019*	
'000 tonnes		*'000 tonnes*	
1 China	2,777	**1** China	2,469
2 India	1,390	**2** India	1,153
3 Kenya	459	**3** Turkey	325
4 Sri Lanka	300	**4** EU28	217
5 Vietnam	269	**5** Pakistan	192
6 Turkey	261	**6** Russia	135
7 Indonesia	138	**7** United States	115
8 Myanmar	132	**8** Japan	108
9 Bangladesh	91	**9** Egypt	96
Iran	91	**10** Bangladesh	95

Coffee

Top 10 producers, 2019		*Top 10 consumers, 2019–20*	
'000 tonnes		*'000 tonnes*	
1 Brazil	3,711	**1** EU28	2,619
2 Vietnam	1,829	**2** United States	1,599
3 Colombia	846	**3** Brazil	1,320
4 Indonesia	701	**4** Japan	441
5 Ethiopia	441	**5** Indonesia	288
6 Honduras	356	**6** Russia	278
7 Uganda	331	**7** Canada	236
8 India	298	**8** Ethiopia	227
9 Mexico	238	**9** Philippines	195
10 Peru	230	**10** Vietnam	159

Cocoa

Top 10 producers, 2019–20		*Top 10 consumers, 2019–20*	
'000 tonnes		*'000 tonnes*	
1 Ivory Coast	2,105	**1** EU28	1,476
2 Ghana	800	**2** Ivory Coast	614
3 Ecuador	328	**3** Netherlands	600
4 Cameroon	280	**4** Indonesia	480
5 Nigeria	250	**5** Germany	430
6 Brazil	201	**6** United States	380
7 Indonesia	200	**7** Malaysia	318
8 Peru	153	**8** Ghana	292
9 Dominican Rep.	75	**9** Brazil	221
10 Colombia	64	**10** France	140

Orange juice[d]

Top 5 producers, 2019–20		*Top 5 consumers, 2019–20*	
'000 tonnes		*'000 tonnes*	
1 Brazil	965	**1** EU28	701
2 United States	297	**2** United States	552
3 Mexico	90	**3** China	89
4 EU28	82	**4** Canada	83
5 South Africa	49	**5** Brazil	63

Copper

Top 10 producers[a], 2019
'000 tonnes

1	Chile	5,787
2	Peru	2,455
3	China	1,601
4	Congo-Kinshasa	1,433
5	United States	1,257
6	EU28	926
7	Australia	925
8	Russia	791
9	Zambia	790
10	Mexico	770

Top 10 consumers[b], 2019
'000 tonnes

1	China	12,800
2	EU28	3,132
3	United States	1,829
4	Germany	1,017
5	Japan	1,011
6	South Korea	633
7	Italy	556
8	India	527
9	Turkey	464
10	Mexico	442

Lead

Top 10 producers[a], 2019
'000 tonnes

1	China	2,405
2	Australia	510
3	Peru	308
4	United States	274
5	Mexico	259
6	EU28	222
7	Russia	220
8	India	201
9	Bolivia	88
10	Turkey	72

Top 10 consumers[b], 2019
'000 tonnes

1	China	5,915
2	EU28	1,797
3	United States	1,637
4	South Korea	623
5	India	610
6	Germany	390
7	Mexico	330
8	Spain	290
9	Japan	252
10	Brazil	242

Zinc

Top 10 producers[a], 2019
'000 tonnes

1	China	4,646
2	Peru	1,404
3	EU28	786
4	United States	753
5	India	713
6	Mexico	701
7	Bolivia	528
8	Kazakhstan	370
9	Canada	323
10	Russia	300

Top 10 consumers[c], 2019
'000 tonnes

1	China	6,821
2	EU28	1,871
3	United States	950
4	India	646
5	South Korea	638
6	Japan	517
7	Germany	389
8	Italy	276
9	Belgium	265
10	Turkey	252

Tin

Top 5 producers[a], 2019
'000 tonnes

1	China	134.3
2	Indonesia	86.4
3	Myanmar	45.0
4	Peru	19.7
5	Bolivia	17.2

Top 5 consumers[b], 2019
'000 tonnes

1	China	177.9
2	EU28	54.4
3	United States	31.3
4	Japan	24.9
5	Germany	18.4

Nickel

Top 10 producers[a], 2019
'000 tonnes

1	Indonesia	917.6
2	Philippines	341.3
3	Russia	225.7
4	New Caledonia	208.2
5	Canada	187.1
6	Australia	158.8
7	China	104.7
8	Brazil	55.7
9	EU28	53.0
10	Cuba	52.0

Top 10 consumers[b], 2019
'000 tonnes

1	China	1,304.3
2	EU28	304.0
3	Indonesia	181.9
4	Japan	154.7
5	South Korea	113.0
6	United States	105.6
7	Taiwan	84.1
8	India	58.5
9	Germany	57.3
10	Italy	45.0

Aluminium

Top 10 producers[d], 2019
'000 tonnes

1	China	36,447
2	Russia	3,896
3	India	3,524
4	Canada	2,854
5	United Arab Emirates	2,579
6	EU28	2,113
7	Australia	1,570
8	Vietnam	1,374
9	Bahrain	1,365
10	Norway	1,279

Top 10 consumers[e], 2019
'000 tonnes

1	China	36,648
2	EU28	6,881
3	United States	4,926
4	Germany	1,988
5	India	1,829
6	Japan	1,765
7	Vietnam	1,405
8	South Korea	1,157
9	Turkey	971
10	Italy	938

Precious metals

Gold[a]
Top 10 producers, 2019
tonnes

1	China	380.2
2	Australia	326.3
3	Russia	305.1
4	United States	200.4
5	Canada	182.8
6	Ghana	142.4
7	Peru	128.4
8	Mexico	109.0
9	Indonesia	108.7
10	South Africa	105.2

Silver[a]
Top 10 producers, 2019
tonnes

1	Mexico	5,840
2	Peru	3,860
3	China	3,443
4	EU28	2,215
5	Poland	1,469
6	Australia	1,325
7	Russia	1,319
8	Chile	1,309
9	Bolivia	1,153
10	Kazakhstan	1,022

Platinum
Top 3 producers, 2019
tonnes

1	South Africa	130.0
2	Russia	22.0
3	Zimbabwe	15.0

Palladium
Top 3 producers, 2019
tonnes

1	Russia	86.0
2	South Africa	80.0
3	Canada	20.0

a Mine production.   b Refined consumption.   c Slab consumption.
d Primary refined production.   e Primary refined consumption.

Rubber (natural and synthetic)

Top 10 producers, 2019			*Top 10 consumers, 2019*		
'000 tonnes			*'000 tonnes*		
1	Thailand	5,210	1	China	9,892
2	China	3,922	2	EU28	3,711
3	Indonesia	3,100	3	United States	2,883
4	EU28	2,389	4	India	1,802
5	United States	2,228	5	Japan	1,553
6	South Korea	1,565	6	Thailand	1,418
7	Russia	1,538	7	Malaysia	1,076
8	Japan	1,531	8	Brazil	822
9	Vietnam	1,222	9	Russia	643
10	India	1,093	10	Indonesia	625

Cotton

Top 10 producers, 2019–20			*Top 10 consumers, 2019–20*		
'000 tonnes			*'000 tonnes*		
1	India	6,205	1	China	7,250
2	China	5,800	2	India	4,453
3	United States	4,336	3	Pakistan	1,984
4	Brazil	3,002	4	Bangladesh	1,500
5	Pakistan	1,320	5	Turkey	1,477
6	Turkey	815	6	Vietnam	1446
7	Uzbekistan	631	7	Uzbekistan	661
8	Mexico	368	8	Brazil	610
9	Greece	355	9	Indonesia	549
10	Argentina	335	10	United States	468

Major oil seeds[a]

Top 5 producers, 2019–20			*Top 5 consumers, 2019–20*		
'000 tonnes			*'000 tonnes*		
1	Brazil	140,433	1	China	163,390
2	United States	122,421	2	United States	72,032
3	China	64,965	3	Brazil	53,708
4	Argentina	52,076	4	EU28	53,288
5	India	38,397	5	Argentina	51,396

Major vegetable oils[b]

Top 5 producers, 2019–20			*Top 5 consumers, 2019–20*		
'000 tonnes			*'000 tonnes*		
1	Indonesia	43,500	1	China	35,438
2	China	24,186	2	EU28	24,413
3	Malaysia	19,107	3	India	19,325
4	EU28	16,472	4	Indonesia	15,095
5	United States	12,681	5	United States	14,957

---

a Soyabeans, rapeseed (canola), cottonseed, sunflowerseed and groundnuts
(peanuts). b Palm, soyabean and sunflowerseed oil.
c Includes crude oil, shale oil, oil sands and natural gas liquids. d Opec member.
e Opec membership suspended 30 November 2016.

Oil[c]

Top 10 producers, 2020 '000 barrels per day		*Top 10 consumers, 2020* '000 barrels per day	
1	United States	16,476	1	United States	17,178
2	Saudi Arabia[d]	11,039	2	China	14,225
3	Russia	10,667	3	India	4,669
4	Canada	5,135	4	Saudi Arabia[d]	3,544
5	Iraq[d]	4,114	5	Japan	3,268
6	China	3,901	6	Russia	3,238
7	United Arab Emirates[d]	3,657	7	South Korea	2,560
8	Iran[d]	3,084	8	Brazil	2,323
9	Brazil	3,026	9	Canada	2,282
10	Kuwait[d]	2,686	10	Germany	2,045

Natural gas

Top 10 producers, 2020 Billion cubic metres		*Top 10 consumers, 2020* Billion cubic metres	
1	United States	914.6	1	United States	832.0
2	Russia	638.5	2	Russia	411.4
3	Iran[d]	250.8	3	China	330.6
4	Qatar	171.3	4	Iran[d]	233.1
5	Canada	165.2	5	Canada	112.6
6	China	194.0	6	Saudi Arabia[d]	112.1
7	Norway	111.5	7	Japan	104.4
8	Saudi Arabia[d]	112.1	8	Germany	86.5
9	Australia	142.5	9	Mexico	86.3
10	Algeria[d]	81.5	10	United Kingdom	72.5

Coal

Top 10 producers, 2020 Exajoules		*Top 10 consumers, 2020* Exajoules	
1	China	80.91	1	China	82.27
2	Indonesia[e]	13.88	2	India	17.54
3	India	12.68	3	United States	9.20
4	Australia	12.42	4	Japan	4.57
5	United States	10.71	5	South Africa	3.48
6	Russia	8.37	6	Russia	3.27
7	South Africa	5.97	7	Indonesia[e]	3.26
8	Kazakhstan	2.04	8	Germany	1.84
9	Poland	1.68	9	Australia	1.69
10	Colombia	1.46	10	Poland	1.67

Oil reserves[c]

Top proved reserves, end 2020
% of world total

1	Venezuela[d]	17.5	6	Russia	6.2
2	Saudi Arabia[d]	17.2	7	Kuwait[d]	5.9
3	Canada	9.7	8	United Arab Emirates[d]	5.6
4	Iran[d]	9.1	9	United States	4.0
5	Iraq[d]	8.4	10	Libya[d]	2.8

Energy

Largest producers
Million tonnes of oil equivalent, 2018

1	China	2,971	16	Kuwait	174
2	United States	2,415	17	Algeria	169
3	Russia	1,600	18	Mexico	159
4	Saudi Arabia	745	19	Nigeria	150
5	Canada	597	20	South Africa	149
6	Iran	456	21	United Kingdom	138
7	India	434	22	France	133
8	Australia	422	23	Colombia	128
9	Indonesia	399	24	Venezuela	125
10	Brazil	306	25	Germany	121
11	Iraq	258	26	Malaysia	114
12	United Arab Emirates	253	27	Angola	96
13	Qatar	252		Egypt	96
14	Norway	239	29	Turkmenistan	90
15	Kazakhstan	211	30	Oman	86

Largest consumers
Million tonnes of oil equivalent, 2018

1	China	3,722		Mexico	202
2	United States	2,551	16	Italy	172
3	Russia	840	17	Turkey	161
4	India	790	18	Australia	150
5	Japan	485	19	Spain	148
6	Canada	383	20	South Africa	142
7	Germany	349	21	Thailand	139
8	Brazil	322	22	United Arab Emirates	117
9	South Korea	312	23	Taiwan	114
10	Iran	295	24	Poland	111
11	France	260	25	Egypt	102
12	Saudi Arabia	257	26	Netherlands	97
13	United Kingdom	209	27	Malaysia	96
14	Indonesia	202			

Energy efficiency[a]
GDP per unit of energy use, 2018

Most efficient			Least efficient		
1	Chad	68.2	1	Trinidad & Tobago[b]	1.8
2	Macau	65.3	2	Turkmenistan	2.1
3	Rwanda	49.5		Virgin Islands (US)[b]	2.1
4	Somalia	41.0	4	Iceland[b]	3.2
5	Burundi	38.6	5	Kyrgyzstan	3.6
6	Burkina Faso	36.5	6	Bahrain	3.8
7	Uganda	36.3	7	Iran	3.9
8	South Sudan	35.9	8	Oman	4.2
9	Madagascar	31.6	9	Kuwait	4.3
	Mali	31.6		Venezuela	4.3
11	Niger	30.6			
12	Sierra Leone	30.4			
13	Guinea-Bissau	29.9			

a 2015 PPP $ per kg of oil equivalent. b 2017 c Coal, gas and oil.

Net energy importers

% of energy use, 2018

Highest

1	Benin	100.0
	Bermuda	100.0
	Macau	100.0
	West Bank & Gaza	100.0
5	Hong Kong	99.9
	Maldives	99.9
7	Togo	99.8
	Virgin Islands (US)	99.8
9	Liberia	99.8
10	Gambia, The	99.7
11	Guinea-Bissau	99.6
12	Guyana	99.5

Lowest

1	Timor-Leste	-3,252.5
2	Chad	-2,033.8
3	South Sudan	-1,419.0
4	Angola	-874.9
5	Congo-Brazzaville	-805.5
6	Equatorial Guinea	-753.6
7	Gabon	-648.7
8	Qatar	-410.0
9	Norway	-399.1
10	Mongolia	-395.0
11	Papua New Guinea	-345.5
12	Kuwait	-320.1

Largest consumption per person

Kg of oil equivalent, 2018

1	Qatar	17,459.6
2	Iceland	17,063.7
3	Singapore	16,257.8
4	Trinidad & Tobago	16,144.3
5	United Arab Emirates	11,950.8
6	Bahrain	11,098.0
7	Brunei	10,613.8
8	Canada	10,248.9
9	Kuwait	9,858.9
10	Norway	8,894.2
11	Virgin Islands (US)	8,143.3

12	Luxembourg	7,814.7
13	United States	7,752.9
14	Malta	7,569.6
15	Saudi Arabia	7,487.9
16	Turkmenistan	7,385.1
17	Oman	6,836.4
18	New Caledonia	6,785.9
19	South Korea	6,099.6
20	Australia	5,945.9
21	Belgium	5,856.2
22	Russia	5,757.8

Sources of electricity

% of total, 2018

Fossil fuels[c]

1	Bermuda	100.0
	Macau	100.0
3	Oman	99.9
	Turkmenistan	99.9
5	Libya	99.8

Nuclear power

1	France	71.3
2	Slovakia	55.0
3	Ukraine	53.4
4	Hungary	48.9
5	Sweden	40.4

Hydropower

1	Albania	100.0
2	Lesotho	99.8
3	Congo-Kinshasa	99.6
4	Central African Rep.	99.3
5	Paraguay	98.8

Renewables excl. hydropower

1	Lithuania	73.6
2	Denmark	71.9
3	Uruguay	53.0
4	Nicaragua	51.5
5	Kenya	51.4

Wind power

1	Denmark	46.6
2	Lithuania	45.3
3	Uruguay	32.6
4	Ireland	29.4
5	Portugal	22.3

Biomass and waste

1	Eswatini	28.1
2	Lithuania	25.0
3	Denmark	22.1
4	Finland	19.7
5	Guatemala	19.2

Labour markets

Labour-force participation

% of working-age population[a] working or looking for work, 2020 or latest

Highest		Lowest	
Qatar		Jordan	
Madagascar		Puerto Rico	
Tanzania		Yemen	
UAE		Tajikistan	
Zimbabwe		Moldova	
Rwanda		Algeria	
Cambodia		Iraq	
North Korea		Iran	
Burundi		Morocco	
Laos		Syria	
Nepal		West Bank & Gaza	
Ethiopia		Egypt	
Mozambique		Senegal	
Vietnam		Mauritania	
Angola		Lebanon	
Malawi		Tunisia	
Cameroon		Bosnia & Herz.	
Zambia		India	
Eritrea		PNG	
Iceland		Sudan	
Liberia		Afghanistan	
Bahrain		Somalia	
Kenya		Libya	
Niger		Suriname	
Bahamas		Italy	
Kuwait		Armenia	
Macau		Pakistan	
CAR		Cuba	
Paraguay		Turkey	
Benin		Eswatini	

Women on boards[b]

OECD countries, %, 2019

1	France	45.1		18	Ireland	28.8
2	Iceland	44.4			South Africa	28.8
3	New Zealand	42.3		20	United States	28.2
4	Norway	40.4		21	Portugal	26.6
5	Belgium	38.4		22	Switzerland	26.1
	Italy	38.4		23	Latvia	25.6
7	Sweden	38.0		24	Israel	24.3
8	Netherlands	36.6		25	Slovenia	22.9
9	Germany	36.3		26	Poland	22.8
10	Finland	35.1		27	Luxembourg	18.2
11	United Kingdom	34.7		28	Turkey	17.5
12	Australia	34.0		29	Czech Republic	17.2
13	Denmark	33.6		30	India	16.6
14	Austria	31.5		31	Lithuania	14.3
15	Slovakia	31.4		32	Brazil	13.7
16	Canada	31.3		33	China	13.0
17	Spain	29.3			Greece	13.0

a Aged 15 and over.   b Largest publically listed companies.

Highest rate of unemployment
% of labour force[a], 2019

1	South Africa	28.7	26	Brazil	13.7
2	West Bank & Gaza	27.4		Iraq	13.7
3	Lesotho	24.7	28	Yemen	13.4
4	Eswatini	23.4	29	Somalia	13.1
5	Gabon	20.5	30	Algeria	12.8
6	Namibia	20.4		Barbados	12.8
7	Armenia	20.2	32	South Sudan	12.7
8	Libya	19.4		Uruguay	12.7
9	Jordan	18.5	34	Zambia	12.2
10	North Macedonia	18.4	35	Georgia	12.1
11	Botswana	17.7	36	Virgin Islands (US)	11.8
	Sudan	17.7	37	Afghanistan	11.7
13	Costa Rica	17.1		Albania	11.7
14	Bosnia & Herz.	16.9		Argentina	11.7
	Greece	16.9	40	Chile	11.5
16	Tunisia	16.7	41	Puerto Rico	11.2
17	New Caledonia	16.5	42	Iran	11.0
18	Montenegro	15.9	43	Mauritania	10.7
19	Guyana	15.8	44	Egypt	10.5
20	Spain	15.7	45	Congo-Brazzaville	10.3
21	Colombia	15.4	46	Morocco	10.2
22	Haiti	14.5		Panama	10.2
23	Bahamas	14.4	48	Gambia, The	9.6
24	Turkey	13.9	49	Canada	9.5
25	French Polynesia	13.8		Ukraine	9.5

Highest rate of youth unemployment
% of labour force[a] aged 15–24, 2019

1	South Africa	57.5	21	Georgia	29.9
2	Libya	49.5	22	Algeria	29.7
3	Eswatini	46.2		Haiti	29.7
4	West Bank & Gaza	40.0	24	Saudi Arabia	29.6
5	New Caledonia	39.3	25	Uruguay	29.4
6	French Polynesia	37.8	26	Italy	29.2
	Namibia	37.8	27	Brazil	27.5
8	Jordan	37.3	28	Serbia	27.1
9	Tunisia	35.8	29	Albania	27.0
10	Botswana	35.6	30	Egypt	26.5
	North Macedonia	35.6	31	Guyana	26.2
12	Gabon	35.5	32	Argentina	26.0
13	Greece	35.1	33	Iran	25.5
14	Lesotho	34.4	34	Montenegro	25.3
15	Bosnia & Herz.	34.0	35	Iraq	25.2
16	Armenia	33.5	36	Turkey	24.6
17	Spain	32.6	37	Bahamas	24.5
18	Sudan	32.1	38	Yemen	24.2
19	Costa Rica	31.8	39	Mauritius	23.8
20	Barbados	30.2	40	India	23.0

a ILO definition.

Average hours worked
Per employed person per week, 2019 or latest[a]

Men			Women		
1	Mauritania	56.0	1	Egypt	53.0
2	Bangladesh	54.1	2	Qatar	51.0
3	Mongolia	53.6	3	Mauritania	50.9
4	Burkina Faso	53.5	4	Lesotho	48.6
5	Egypt	53.0	5	Mongolia	48.1
6	Belize	52.0	6	Belize	46.0
7	Lesotho	51.9		Macau	46.0
8	Lebanon	51.3		Myanmar	46.0
9	Kenya	50.9	9	Brunei	45.3
10	Botswana	49.8	10	Burkina Faso	45.1
11	Sri Lanka	49.4	11	Botswana	44.5
12	Iran	49.3	12	Jordan	44.1
13	Jordan	49.2	13	Kenya	43.9
14	Qatar	49.0	14	Malaysia	43.7
15	Eswatini	48.9	15	Namibia	43.3
16	Guyana	48.7	16	Samoa	43.2
	Mexico	48.7	17	Eswatini	43.0
	Turkey	48.7		Vietnam	43.0
19	Myanmar	48.1	19	Laos	42.2
20	Colombia	47.9		Montenegro	42.2
	Nepal	47.9	21	Singapore	41.7
22	Brunei	47.8	22	Guyana	41.5
23	Peru	47.6		Serbia	41.5
24	Togo	47.2		Uganda	41.5

Working hours lost
Due to covid-19 crisis[b], % 2020

Most			Least		
1	Peru	27.5	1	Burundi	-0.1
2	Honduras	24.3	2	New Zealand	0.8
3	Panama	23.5	3	Niger	1.1
4	Argentina	21.0	4	Belarus	1.3
5	Colombia	20.9		Finland	1.3
6	Bolivia	20.5		Yemen	1.3
7	El Salvador	19.4	7	Papua New Guinea	1.8
8	Ecuador	17.6		Tanzania	1.8
9	Costa Rica	17.5	9	Macau	1.9
10	Nepal	17.4	10	Mongolia	2.5
11	Armenia	16.8		Norway	2.5
12	Chile	16.7		Somalia	2.5
13	Guatemala	16.4	13	Burkina Faso	2.6
	Kuwait	16.4		Zambia	2.6
15	Dominican Rep.	15.5	15	Timor-Leste	2.7
16	Brazil	14.9	16	Benin	3.2
17	Bahamas	14.8		Tajikistan	3.2
18	Eritrea	14.7	18	Denmark	3.3
	Turkey	14.7		Latvia	3.3
20	Cyprus	14.6		Mali	3.3

a 2015–19   b ILO estimate.

Business costs and foreign direct investment

Office rents

Prime rent change on a year earlier, Q4 2020, %[a]

Increase			Decrease		
1	Moscow, Russia	31.0	1	Hong Kong	17.4
2	Stockholm, Sweden	10.0	2	New York (Midtown South), US	12.6
3	Birmingham, UK	7.3	3	Houston, US	12.4
4	Paris, France	5.7	4	Chicago, US	9.5
5	Luxembourg	4.0	5	San Francisco, US	9.0
6	Calgary, Canada	3.4	6	Dublin, Ireland	7.9
7	Canberra, Australia	3.2	7	London (West End), UK	7.7
	Hamburg, Germany	3.2	8	Beijing, China	7.0
9	Edinburgh, UK	2.9	9	Montreal, Canada	6.3
	Geneva, Switzerland	2.9	10	Tokyo, Japan	5.7
11	Berlin, Germany	2.7	11	Singapore	5.2
	Manchester, UK	2.7	12	Guangzhou, China	4.9
13	Taipei, Taiwan	2.5		Mexico City, Mexico	4.9
14	Wellington, New Zealand	2.1	14	London (City), UK	4.1
15	New York (Midtown), US	2.0	15	Washington, DC, US	4.0
16	Seoul, South Korea	1.9	16	Vancouver, Canada	3.4
17	Bucharest, Romania	1.4	17	Auckland, New Zealand	3.1
18	Adelaide, Australia	1.3	18	Shanghai, China	3.0
19	Sydney, Australia	0.5	19	Brisbane, Australia	2.9
20	Dallas, US	0.2			

Foreign direct investment[b]

Inflows, $m, 2019

	Inflows, $m, 2019			Outflows, $m, 2019	
1	United States	246,215	1	Japan	226,648
2	China	141,225	2	United States	124,899
3	Singapore	92,081	3	Netherlands	124,652
4	Netherlands	84,216	4	China	117,120
5	Ireland	78,234	5	Germany	98,700
6	Brazil	71,989	6	Canada	76,602
7	Hong Kong	68,379	7	Hong Kong	59,279
8	United Kingdom	59,137	8	France	38,663
9	India	50,553	9	South Korea	35,531
10	Canada	50,332	10	Singapore	33,283
11	Germany	36,359	11	United Kingdom	31,480
12	Australia	36,156	12	Italy	24,934
13	Cayman Islands	34,690	13	Spain	24,135
14	France	33,965	14	Sweden	22,814
15	Mexico	32,921	15	Russia	22,530
16	Russia	31,735	16	Belgium	19,707
17	Italy	26,569	17	Ireland	18,103
18	Cyprus	24,248	18	Denmark	16,045
19	Indonesia	23,429	19	United Arab Emirates	15,901
20	Sweden	20,568	20	Brazil	15,515
21	Israel	18,224	21	Cyprus	14,053
22	Vietnam	16,120	22	Saudi Arabia	13,185
23	Japan	14,552	23	India	12,104
24	Colombia	14,493	24	Taiwan	11,861

a Reflects the rate of change in local prime net rent over the preceding 12 months.
b Investment in companies in a foreign country.

Business creativity and research

Entrepreneurial activity
Percentage of population aged 18–64 who are either a nascent entrepreneur[a] or owner-manager of a new business, average 2015–20

Highest			Lowest		
1	Angola	45.2	1	Italy	3.7
2	Senegal	38.6		Pakistan	3.7
3	Botswana	33.2	3	Bosnia & Herz.	4.0
4	Togo	32.9	4	Bulgaria	4.5
5	Ecuador	32.8	5	France	5.1
6	Burkina Faso	28.8		Japan	5.1
7	Chile	26.9	7	Germany	5.3
8	Cameroon	26.5	8	Belarus	5.8
9	Lebanon	24.9		Spain	5.8
10	Colombia	23.9	10	Belgium	6.2
	Guatemala	23.9	11	North Macedonia	6.3
12	Peru	23.6	12	Finland	6.7
13	Sudan	22.2		Greece	6.7
14	Barbados	21.1	14	Slovenia	6.8
15	Armenia	21.0	15	Poland	7.1
16	Brazil	20.9	16	Norway	7.2
17	Madagascar	20.7	17	Morocco	7.3
18	Kuwait	19.2	18	Russia	7.4
19	Panama	18.5		Sweden	7.4
	Vietnam	18.5	20	Hungary	7.9
21	Thailand	18.1	21	United Kingdom	8.3
22	Philippines	17.2	22	Switzerland	8.4
23	Canada	17.1		Taiwan	8.4
24	Estonia	16.2	24	Georgia	8.6
25	Uruguay	16.1	25	Jordan	8.7
26	Mexico	16.0	26	Cyprus	8.8

Brain gains[b]

Highest, 2020			Lowest, 2020		
1	Singapore	6.1	1	Venezuela	1.4
	Switzerland	6.1	2	Bosnia & Herz.	1.7
3	Luxembourg	5.8	3	North Macedonia	2.0
4	United Arab Emirates	5.7	4	Croatia	2.1
5	United States	5.6		Iran	2.1
6	Saudi Arabia	5.5	6	Nicaragua	2.2
7	Bahrain	5.4		Zimbabwe	2.2
	Qatar	5.4	8	Haiti	2.3
9	Canada	5.2		Romania	2.3
	China	5.2		Serbia	2.3
	Hong Kong	5.2		Slovakia	2.3
	Malta	5.2	12	Bolivia	2.4
	Netherlands	5.2		Greece	2.4
14	Azerbaijan	5.1		Moldova	2.4
	New Zealand	5.1	15	Tunisia	2.5
16	Ireland	5.0			
	United Kingdom	5.0			

a An individual who has started a new firm which has not paid wages for over three months.
b Scores: 1=attracts no highly skilled individuals from abroad; 7=attracts many highly skilled individuals from abroad.

Total expenditure on R&D

$bn, 2019

1	United States	657.5
2	China	320.5
3	Japan	164.7
4	Germany	122.6
5	South Korea	76.4
6	France	59.5
7	United Kingdom	49.7
8	Italy	29.0
9	Canada	26.8
10	Australia[a]	25.3
11	Switzerland[a]	22.4
12	Brazil[b]	21.9
13	Taiwan	21.4
14	Netherlands	19.6
15	Israel	19.5
16	India[b]	18.1
	Sweden	18.1
18	Russia	17.5
19	Spain	17.4
20	Belgium	15.4

% of GDP, 2019

1	Israel	4.93
2	South Korea	4.64
3	Taiwan	3.49
4	Sweden	3.40
5	Switzerland[a]	3.29
6	Japan	3.20
7	Austria	3.19
8	Germany	3.18
9	United States	3.07
10	Denmark	2.96
11	Belgium	2.89
12	Finland	2.79
13	Iceland	2.33
14	China	2.24
15	France	2.19
16	Netherlands	2.16
17	Norway	2.15
18	Slovenia	2.04
19	Czech Republic	1.94

Innovation index[c]

2020, 100=maximum score

		Overall	Inputs	Outputs
1	Switzerland	66.1	69.4	62.8
2	Sweden	62.5	69.2	55.7
3	United States	60.6	68.8	52.3
4	United Kingdom	59.8	66.0	53.6
5	Netherlands	58.8	64.5	53.1
6	Denmark	57.5	66.8	48.3
7	Finland	57.0	65.6	48.5
8	Singapore	56.6	70.2	43.0
9	Germany	56.5	62.7	50.4
10	South Korea	56.1	64.8	47.4
11	Hong Kong	54.2	65.8	42.7
12	France	53.7	61.4	45.9
13	Israel	53.5	61.4	45.7
14	China	53.3	55.5	51.0
15	Ireland	53.0	59.7	46.4
16	Japan	52.7	63.6	41.8
17	Canada	52.3	64.8	39.7
18	Luxembourg	50.8	57.2	44.4
19	Austria	50.1	61.2	39.1
20	Norway	49.3	62.7	35.9
21	Iceland	49.2	57.3	41.2
22	Belgium	49.1	59.6	38.6

a 2017   b 2018
c The innovation index measures countries' capacity for and success in innovation, based on 79 indicators. Inputs include political and business environment, human capital and research and infrastructure; outputs include knowledge creation and creative outputs.

Businesses and banks

Largest non-financial companies
By market capitalisation, $trn, end-December 2020

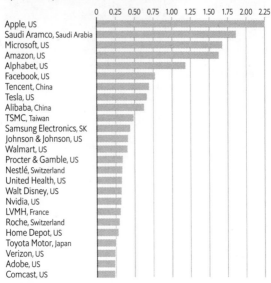

	0	0.25	0.50	0.75	1.00	1.25	1.50	1.75	2.00	2.25
Apple, US										
Saudi Aramco, Saudi Arabia										
Microsoft, US										
Amazon, US										
Alphabet, US										
Facebook, US										
Tencent, China										
Tesla, US										
Alibaba, China										
TSMC, Taiwan										
Samsung Electronics, SK										
Johnson & Johnson, US										
Walmart, US										
Procter & Gamble, US										
Nestlé, Switzerland										
United Health, US										
Walt Disney, US										
Nvidia, US										
LVMH, France										
Roche, Switzerland										
Home Depot, US										
Toyota Motor, Japan										
Verizon, US										
Adobe, US										
Comcast, US										

By net profit, $bn, 2020

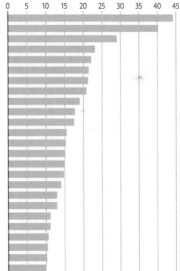

	0	5	10	15	20	25	30	35	40	45
Microsoft, US										
Alphabet, US										
Facebook, US										
Tencent, China										
Samsung Electronics, SK										
Alibaba, China										
Amazon, US										
Intel, US										
Toyota Motor, Japan										
Verizon, US										
TSMC, Taiwan										
China Mobile, China										
United Health, US										
Roche, Switzerland										
Johnson & Johnson, US										
Walmart, US										
Sanofi, France										
Nestlé, Switzerland										
Procter & Gamble, US										
Home Depot, US										
Cisco Systems, US										
Thyssenkrupp, Germany										
Comcast, US										
Surgutneftegas, Russia										
Oracle, US										

Largest banks
By market capitalisation, $bn, end December 2020

1	JPMorgan Chase	United States	387.3
2	Industrial & Commercial Bank of China	China	262.4
3	Bank of America	United States	262.2
4	China Construction Bank	China	191.9
5	China Merchants Bank	China	167.9
6	Agricultural Bank of China	China	164.8
7	Bank of China	China	131.3
8	Citigroup	United States	128.4
9	Wells Fargo	United States	124.8
10	Royal Bank of Canada	Canada	116.6
11	Commonwealth Bank of Australia	Australia	112.1
12	HDFC	India	108.3
13	HSBC	United Kingdom	105.3
14	TD Bank Group	Canada	102.3
15	U.S. Bancorp	United States	70.2

By assets, $bn, end December 2020

1	Industrial & Commercial Bank of China	China	5,109
2	China Construction Bank	China	4,310
3	Agricultural Bank of China	China	4,168
4	Bank of China	China	3,739
5	JPMorgan Chase	United States	3,386
6	Mitsubishi UFJ	Japan	3,123
7	BNP Paribas	France	3,042
8	HSBC	United Kingdom	2,984
9	Bank of America	United States	2,820
10	Crédit Agricole	France	2,397
11	Citigroup	United States	2,260
12	Sumitomo Mitsui Financial	Japan	2,040
13	Mizuho	Japan	1,992
14	Japan Post Bank	Japan	1,957
15	Wells Fargo	United States	1,955

Largest sovereign-wealth funds
By assets, $bn, April 2021

1	Government Pension Fund, Norway	1,289
2	China Investment Corporation	1,046
3	Abu Dhabi Investment Authority, UAE	649
4	Hong Kong Monetary Authority Investment Portfolio	581
5	Kuwait Investment Authority	534
6	GIC Private Limited, Singapore	453
7	Temasek Holdings, Singapore	417
8	Public Investment Fund of Saudi Arabia	399
9	National Council for Social Security Fund, China	372
10	Investment Corporation of Dubai, UAE	302
11	Qatar Investment Authority	295
12	Turkey Wealth Fund	245
13	Mubadala Investment Company, UAE	243
14	National Welfare Fund, Russia	183

Note: Countries listed refer to the company's domicile.

Stockmarkets

Largest market capitalisation
$bn, end 2020

1	NYSE – US	26,233	21	BME Spanish Exchanges	759
2	Nasdaq – US	19,060	22	Moscow Exchange	695
3	Shanghai SE	6,976	23	Singapore Exchange	653
4	Japan Exchange Group	6,718	24	Stock Exchange of	
5	Hong Kong Exchanges	6,130		Thailand	543
6	Euronext	5,444	25	Indonesia SE	496
7	Shenzhen SE	5,239	26	Bursa Malaysia	437
8	London SE Group[a]	4,046	27	Bolsa Mexicana de	
9	TMX Group	2,608		Valores	400
10	BSE India	2,570	28	Philippine SE	273
11	National Stock		29	Tel-Aviv SE	262
	Exchange of India	2,552	30	Borsa Istanbul	237
12	Saudi SE (Tadawul)	2,429	31	Abu Dhabi SE	202
13	Deutsche Börse	2,284	32	Bolsa de Comercio de	
14	Korea Exchange[b]	2,176		Santiago	185
15	Nasdaq Nordic and			Bolsa Electronica de Chile	185
	Baltics[c]	2,110	34	Warsaw SE	178
16	SIX Swiss Exchange	2,002	35	Ho Chi Minh SE	177
17	ASX Australian Securities		36	Qatar SE	165
	Exchange	1,721	37	Taipei Exchange	155
18	Taiwan SE	1,599	38	NZX Limited	132
19	Johannesburg SE	1,052		Vienna SE	132
20	B3 – Brasil Bolsa Balcão	988			

Stockmarket gains and losses
$ terms, % change December 31st 2019 to December 31st 2020

	Best performance			Worst performance	
1	China (Shenzhen comp)	44.0	1	Egypt (EGX 30)	-20.7
2	United States (NAScomp)	43.6	2	Brazil (BVSP)	-20.3
3	Denmark (OMXCB)	40.1	3	Argentina (MERV)	-12.5
4	South Korea (KOSPI)	39.2	4	United Kingdom	
5	Taiwan (TWI)	31.0		(FTSE 100)	-11.6
6	Japan (NIKKEI 225)	22.1	5	Russia (RTS)	-10.4
7	China (Shanghai comp)	21.3	6	Singapore (STI)	-10.2
8	Sweden (OMXS30)	20.6	7	Hungary (BUX)	-9.2
9	United States (S&P 500)	16.3	8	Thailand (SET)	-8.3
10	India BSE (SENSEX 30)	13.1	9	Spain (IBEX 35)	-7.8
11	Germany (DAX)[d]	12.9	10	Peru (IGBVL)	-7.1
12	Netherlands (AEX)	12.6	11	Indonesia (IDX)	-6.2
13	Australia (ASX)	10.4	12	Chile (IGPA)	-5.0
	Japan (TOPIX)	10.4	13	Austria (ATX)	-4.9
	Switzerland (SMI)	10.4	14	Mexico (IPC)	-4.1
16	United States (DJIA)	7.3	15	Greece (ATHEX comp)	-3.8
17	Euro area		16	Czech Republic (SE PX)	-2.9
	(FTSE EURO 100)	5.1		Hong Kong (Hang Seng)	-2.9
18	Israel (TA 125)	4.3	18	Belgium (BEL 20)	-0.2
19	Malaysia (KLCI)	4.2	19	Poland (WIG)	0.2
	Norway (OSEAX)	4.2	20	France (CAC 40)	1.2

a Includes Borsa Italiana.   b Includes Kosdaq.   c Armenia, Copenhagen, Helsinki, Iceland, Riga, Stockholm, Tallinn and Vilnius stock exchanges.   d Total return index.

Number of listed companies[a]

End 2020

1	National Equities Exchange and Quotations – China	8,187	**20**	Warsaw SE	806
2	BSE India	5,155	**21**	Taipei Exchange	782
3	Japan Exchange Group	3,758	**22**	Stock Exchange of Thailand	743
4	TMX Group	3,394	**23**	Indonesia SE	713
5	Nasdaq – US	2,933	**24**	Singapore Exchange	696
6	BMESpanishExchanges	2,738	**25**	Deutsche Börse	485
7	Hong Kong Exchanges	2,538	**26**	Tel-Aviv SE	455
8	Shenzhen SE	2,354	**27**	Ho Chi Minh SE	392
9	London SE Group[b]	2,347	**28**	Borsa Istanbul	372
10	Korea Exchange[c]	2,340	**29**	Tehran SE	367
11	NYSE – US	2,094	**30**	Hanoi SE	353
12	Australian Securities Exchange	2,049	**31**	B3 – Brasil Bolsa Balcão	349
13	National Stock Exchange of India	1,959	**32**	Johannesburg SE	331
14	Shanghai SE	1,800	**33**	Dhaka SE	329
15	Euronext	1,493	**34**	Chittagong SE	299
16	Nasdaq Nordic and Baltics	1,071	**35**	Bolsa de Comercio de Santiago	294
17	Taiwan SE	961	**36**	Colombo SE	283
18	Bursa Malaysia	934	**37**	Philippine SE	271
19	Vienna SE	809	**38**	Moscow Exchange	270
			39	Bolsa Electronica de Chile	265
			40	Bulgarian SE	259

Cryptocurrencies

Market capitalisation, \$bn[d], at December 31st 2020

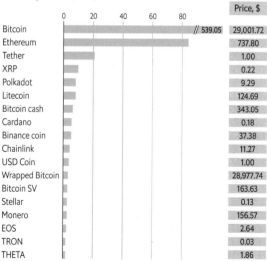

	Price, \$
Bitcoin // 539.05	29,001.72
Ethereum	737.80
Tether	1.00
XRP	0.22
Polkadot	9.29
Litecoin	124.69
Bitcoin cash	343.05
Cardano	0.18
Binance coin	37.38
Chainlink	11.27
USD Coin	1.00
Wrapped Bitcoin	28,977.74
Bitcoin SV	163.63
Stellar	0.13
Monero	156.57
EOS	2.64
TRON	0.03
THETA	1.86

a Domestic and foreign. b Includes Borsa Italiana. c Includes Kosdaq.
d Total market value of circulating supply.

Public finance

Government debt
As % of GDP, 2019

1	Japan[a]	238.7	16	Israel[a]	71.7
2	Greece	200.2	17	Finland	69.8
3	Italy	154.5	18	Ireland	68.8
4	Portugal	136.0	19	Germany	68.2
5	United States	135.0	20	Poland	63.5
6	France	124.0	21	Slovakia	63.1
7	Belgium	120.3	22	Netherlands	62.5
8	Spain	117.3	23	Mexico	59.3
9	United Kingdom	117.2	24	Sweden	55.6
10	Canada	106.7	25	Denmark	51.4
11	Austria	88.9	26	Latvia	47.2
12	Hungary	83.5	27	Norway	46.7
13	Colombia	82.8	28	Lithuania	44.5
14	Slovenia	80.9	29	Switzerland	41.0
15	Australia	75.9	30	Czech Republic	37.7

Government spending
As % of GDP, 2019

1	France	55.6	16	Luxembourg	42.3
2	Finland	53.3	17	Spain	42.1
3	Belgium	52.0	18	Netherlands	42.0
4	Norway	51.5	19	Poland	41.8
5	Sweden	49.3	20	Czech Republic	41.3
6	Denmark	49.2	21	United Kingdom	41.0
7	Italy	48.6	22	Canada	39.9
8	Austria	48.4		Israel	39.9
9	Greece	47.5	24	Estonia	38.9
10	Hungary	45.6		Japan[a]	38.9
11	Germany	45.2	26	Australia[a]	38.6
12	Iceland	43.4	27	Latvia	38.4
13	Slovenia	43.3	28	United States	38.1
14	Slovakia	42.7	29	Lithuania	34.6
15	Portugal	42.5	30	Switzerland	32.7

Tax revenue
As % of GDP, 2019

1	Denmark	46.3	14	Iceland	36.1
2	France	45.4	15	Hungary	35.8
3	Belgium	42.9	16	Poland	35.4
	Sweden	42.9	17	Czech Republic	34.9
5	Austria	42.4	18	Portugal	34.8
	Italy	42.4	19	Slovakia	34.7
7	Finland	42.2	20	Spain	34.6
8	Norway	39.9	21	Canada	33.5
9	Netherlands	39.3	22	Estonia	33.1
10	Luxembourg	39.2	23	United Kingdom	33.0
11	Germany	38.8	24	New Zealand	32.3
	Greece	38.7	25	Japan[a]	32.0
	Slovenia	37.7	26	Latvia	31.2

Democracy

Democracy index
Most democratic=10, 2020

Most

1	Norway	9.81	1	North Korea	1.08
2	Iceland	9.37	2	Congo-Kinshasa	1.13
3	Sweden	9.26	3	Central African Rep.	1.32
4	New Zealand	9.25	4	Syria	1.43
5	Canada	9.24	5	Chad	1.55
6	Finland	9.20	6	Turkmenistan	1.72
7	Denmark	9.15	7	Laos	1.77
8	Ireland	9.05	8	Equatorial Guinea	1.92
9	Australia	8.96	9	Tajikistan	1.94
	Netherlands	8.96	10	Libya	1.95
11	Taiwan	8.94		Yemen	1.95
12	Switzerland	8.83	12	Saudi Arabia	2.08
13	Luxembourg	8.68	13	Uzbekistan	2.12
14	Germany	8.67	14	Burundi	2.14
15	Uruguay	8.61	15	Eritrea	2.15
16	United Kingdom	8.54	16	Iran	2.20
17	Chile	8.28	17	China	2.27
18	Austria	8.16	18	Bahrain	2.49
	Costa Rica	8.16	19	Sudan	2.54
20	Mauritius	8.14	20	Belarus	2.59

Parliamentary seats
Population per parliamentarian, lower or single house, April 2021

Most

1	India	1,657,030	1	Liechtenstein	1,480
2	United States	597,998	2	Monaco	1,583
3	China	465,676	3	Iceland	5,238
4	Bangladesh	460,574	4	Malta	6,585
5	Indonesia	448,977	5	Equatorial Guinea	6,912
6	Pakistan	428,464	6	Bahamas	7,036
7	Nigeria	386,316	7	Montenegro	7,753
8	Brazil	357,244	8	Gabon	9,190
9	Philippines	310,110	9	Brunei	9,289
10	Iran	273,655	10	Luxembourg	9,450

Women in parliament
Lower or single house, women as % of total seats, April 2021

1	Rwanda	61.3	12	Norway	44.4
2	Cuba	53.4	13	Namibia	44.2
3	United Arab Emirates	50.0	14	Spain	44.0
4	New Zealand	48.3	15	Senegal	43.0
5	Mexico	48.2	16	Argentina	42.4
6	Sweden	47.0		Mozambique	42.4
7	South Africa	46.5	18	Belgium	42.0
8	Andorra	46.4		Switzerland	42.0
9	Bolivia	46.2	20	Belarus	40.0
10	Finland	46.0		Portugal	40.0
11	Costa Rica	45.6	22	Austria	39.9

Education

Primary enrolment
Number enrolled as % of relevant age group

Highest			Lowest		
1	Malawi	145	1	Niger	66
2	Sierra Leone	144	2	Eritrea	68
3	Nepal	142	3	Mali	76
4	Madagascar	134	4	Sudan	79
5	Rwanda	131	5	Jordan	82
6	Sweden	129		Senegal	82
7	Togo	126	7	Liberia	85
8	Namibia	124		Nigeria	85
9	Lesotho	121	9	Bulgaria	87
10	Burundi	119		Romania	87
11	Congo-Kinshasa	118	11	Cayman Islands	88
	Turkmenistan	118		Kuwait	88
13	Benin	117	13	Chad	89
			14	Moldova	90
			15	Honduras	91

Highest secondary enrolment
Number enrolled as % of relevant age group

1	Belgium	156	12	Iceland	118
2	Finland	155	13	Estonia	117
	Ireland	155		Norway	117
4	Sweden	152	15	New Zealand	115
5	Costa Rica	141		Thailand	115
6	Netherlands	134	17	Canada	114
7	Australia	133		Slovenia	114
8	Denmark	130	19	Kazakhstan	113
9	Spain	126	20	Liechtenstein	112
10	Portugal	121		Poland	112
	Uruguay	121		Saudi Arabia	112

Highest tertiary enrolment[a]
Number enrolled as % of relevant age group

1	Greece	143		Belarus	87
2	Turkey	113		Netherlands	87
3	Puerto Rico	109	14	Russia	85
4	Australia	108	15	New Zealand	83
5	Latvia	93		Norway	83
6	Chile	91	17	Cyprus	81
	Spain	91		Denmark	81
8	Argentina	90		Hong Kong	81
	Finland	90	20	Belgium	79
10	Singapore	89	21	Ireland	77
11	Austria	87		Slovenia	77

Notes: Latest available year 2016–20. The gross enrolment ratios shown are the actual number enrolled as a percentage of the number of children in the official age group. They may exceed 100 when children outside the age group are receiving that level of education.
a Tertiary education includes all levels of post-secondary education including courses leading to awards not equivalent to a university degree, courses leading to a first university degree and postgraduate courses.

Literacy rate
% adult population[a]

1	Chad	22.3	**19**	Malawi	62.1
2	South Sudan	34.5	**20**	Togo	63.7
3	Niger	35.0	**21**	Nepal	67.9
4	Mali	35.5	**22**	Timor-Leste	68.1
5	Burkina Faso	41.2	**23**	Burundi	68.4
6	Benin	42.4	**24**	Rwanda	73.2
7	Afghanistan	43.0	**25**	Morocco	73.8
8	Sierra Leone	43.2	**26**	India	74.4
9	Liberia	48.3	**27**	Bangladesh	74.7
10	Gambia, The	50.8	**28**	Madagascar	74.8
11	Ethiopia	51.8	**29**	Myanmar	75.6
12	Senegal	51.9	**30**	Uganda	76.5
13	Mauritania	53.5	**31**	Eritrea	76.6
14	Pakistan	59.1	**32**	Cameroon	77.1
15	Mozambique	60.7	**33**	Tanzania	77.9
	Sudan	60.7	**34**	Ghana	79.0
17	Haiti	61.7	**35**	Cambodia	80.5
18	Nigeria	62.0			

Education spending
% of GDP[a]

Highest			Lowest		
1	Norway	7.9	**1**	Bangladesh	1.3
2	Denmark	7.8	**2**	Bermuda	1.5
3	Iceland	7.7		Congo-Kinshasa	1.5
	Sierra Leone	7.7		Monaco	1.5
5	Sweden	7.6		South Sudan	1.5
6	Costa Rica	7.0	**6**	Mauritania	1.9
	Lesotho	7.0		Myanmar	1.9
8	Timor-Leste	6.8		Papua New Guinea	1.9
9	Tunisia	6.6	**9**	Sri Lanka	2.1
10	South Africa	6.5		Uganda	2.1
11	Belgium	6.4	**11**	Cambodia	2.2
	Finland	6.4	**12**	Bahrain	2.3
13	Brazil	6.3		Guinea	2.3
	New Zealand	6.3	**14**	Azerbaijan	2.5
15	Honduras	6.1		Chad	2.5
	Israel	6.1	**16**	Liberia	2.6
17	Kyrgyzstan	6.0	**17**	Armenia	2.7
18	Zimbabwe	5.9		Qatar	2.7
19	Cyprus	5.8	**19**	Haiti	2.8
20	France	5.5		Madagascar	2.8
	Guyana	5.5	**21**	Benin	2.9
	Mozambique	5.5		Kazakhstan	2.9
23	Austria	5.4		Pakistan	2.9
	Burkina Faso	5.4	**24**	Cameroon	3.1
	Chile	5.4		Jordan	3.1
	Togo	5.4		Romania	3.1
	Ukraine	5.4		Rwanda	3.1
				United Arab Emirates	3.0

a Latest year 2015–19.

Marriage and divorce

Highest marriage rates
Number of marriages per 1,000 population, 2019 or latest

1	Fiji	9.8		United States	6.9
2	Egypt	9.6	22	Latvia	6.8
3	Bahamas	9.5		Turkey	6.8
4	Tajikistan	9.3	24	Barbados	6.7
	Uzbekistan	9.3		Iran	6.7
6	West Bank & Gaza	9.0	26	North Macedonia	6.5
7	Albania	8.1	27	Belarus	6.4
8	Cyprus	7.8		Malaysia	6.4
	Kyrgyzstan	7.8	29	Azerbaijan	6.3
10	Mauritius	7.7		Liechtenstein	6.3
11	Guam	7.5		Singapore	6.3
	Kazakhstan	7.5	32	Georgia	6.2
	Moldova	7.5	33	Jamaica	6.1
	Sri Lanka	7.5		Mongolia	6.1
15	Bermuda	7.4	35	Brunei	6.0
	Cayman Islands	7.4	36	Hong Kong	5.9
	Romania	7.4		Ukraine	5.9
18	Vietnam	7.2	38	Malta	5.8
19	Lithuania	7.0		Trinidad & Tobago	5.8
20	Jordan	6.9			

Lowest marriage rates
Number of marriages per 1,000 population, 2019 or latest

1	Qatar	1.4		New Zealand	3.9
2	Panama	2.1		Puerto Rico	3.9
3	French Guiana	2.4	26	Finland	4.0
4	Venezuela	2.6		Mexico	4.0
5	Uruguay	2.7	28	Bulgaria	4.1
6	Argentina	2.8	29	Andorra	4.3
	Guadeloupe	2.8		Guatemala	4.3
	Martinique	2.8		Ireland	4.3
9	Peru	2.9		Norway	4.3
10	Luxembourg	3.1	33	Greece	4.4
11	Italy	3.2		United Kingdom	4.4
	New Caledonia	3.2	35	Costa Rica	4.5
13	Suriname	3.3	36	Japan	4.6
14	Chile	3.4	37	South Korea	4.7
	Portugal	3.4	38	Australia	4.8
	Réunion	3.4		Monaco	4.8
17	France	3.5		Switzerland	4.8
	Kuwait	3.5	41	Croatia	4.9
	Slovenia	3.5	42	Armenia	5.0
	Spain	3.5		Dominican Rep.	5.0
21	Curaçao	3.6		Estonia	5.0
22	Netherlands	3.7		French Polynesia	5.0
23	Belgium	3.9		Sweden	5.0

Note: The data are based on latest available figures (no earlier than 2014) and hence will be affected by the population age structure at the time. Marriage rates refer to registered marriages only and, therefore, reflect the customs surrounding registry and efficiency of administration.

Highest divorce rates
Number of divorces per 1,000 population, 2019 or latest[a]

1	Moldova	4.0	14	Dominican Rep.	2.5
2	Belarus	3.5		Sweden	2.5
3	Guam	3.4		United States	2.5
4	Kazakhstan	3.2	17	Ecuador	2.4
5	Latvia	3.1		Estonia	2.4
	Lithuania	3.1		Finland	2.4
7	Ukraine	3.0	20	Czech Republic	2.3
8	Costa Rica	2.8	21	Cyprus	2.2
	Georgia	2.8		South Korea	2.2
10	Cuba	2.7	23	Egypt	2.1
11	Curaçao	2.6		Iran	2.1
	Denmark	2.6		Jordan	2.1
	Puerto Rico	2.6		Macau	2.1

Lowest divorce rates
Number of divorces per 1,000 population, 2019 or latest[a]

1	Vietnam	0.3	15	Slovenia	1.1
2	Guatemala	0.4	16	Brunei	1.2
	Qatar	0.4		Jamaica	1.2
4	Peru	0.5		Mexico	1.2
5	Ireland	0.7		Tajikistan	1.2
	Malta	0.7	20	Armenia	1.3
	Panama	0.7		Mongolia	1.3
	Venezuela	0.7	22	Montenegro	1.4
9	French Guiana	0.8		Serbia	1.4
	North Macedonia	0.8	24	Azerbaijan	1.5
11	Bosnia & Herz.	0.9		Bulgaria	1.5
	Uruguay	0.9		Croatia	1.5
	Uzbekistan	0.9		Italy	1.5
14	Martinique	1.0		Suriname	1.5

Mean age of women at first marriage
Years, 2018 or latest[b]

Youngest			Oldest		
1	Barbados	17.0	1	Slovenia	34.0
2	Niger	17.2	2	French Polynesia	33.8
3	Central African Rep.	17.3	3	Estonia	33.6
4	South Sudan	18.4	4	Andorra	32.9
5	Mozambique	18.7		Hungary	32.9
6	Bangladesh	18.8	6	New Caledonia	32.8
	Chad	18.8	7	Lithuania	32.7
	Mali	18.8	8	Bulgaria	32.6
9	Guyana	19.2	9	Czech Republic	32.4
10	Guinea	19.8		Iceland	32.4
11	Burkina Faso	20.0		Ireland	32.4
12	Nepal	20.1		Netherlands	32.4
13	Malawi	20.4	13	Italy	32.2
14	Equatorial Guinea	20.5	14	Norway	32.1

a No earlier than 2014.   b No earlier than 2010.

Households, living costs and giving

Number of households
Biggest, m, 2019 or latest

1	China	480.2	21	Turkey	24.2
2	India	299.6	22	Ethiopia	21.9
3	United States	132.7	23	South Korea	20.5
4	Indonesia	69.9	24	Congo-Kinshasa	19.2
5	Brazil	66.5	25	Spain	18.7
6	Russia	57.7	26	South Africa	18.5
7	Japan	54.4	27	Ukraine	17.0
8	Nigeria	42.9	28	Canada	15.6
9	Germany	40.9	29	Poland	14.9
10	Bangladesh	38.0	30	Argentina	14.5
11	Mexico	35.2		Colombia	14.5
12	Pakistan	32.5	32	Kenya	13.1
13	France	30.0	33	Myanmar	13.0
14	United Kingdom	29.5	34	Tanzania	11.9
15	Vietnam	26.9	35	French Guiana	11.6
16	Italy	26.0	36	Australia	9.3
17	Philippines	25.9	37	Uganda	9.2
18	Iran	25.8	38	Ghana	8.9
19	Thailand	24.7	39	Peru	8.7
20	Egypt	24.5	40	Algeria	8.3

Average household size, people

Biggest, 2019 or latest

1	Senegal	8.4
2	Gambia, The	8.3
3	Afghanistan	8.0
4	Maldives	7.5
5	Pakistan	6.7
6	Yemen	6.5
7	Bahrain	6.4
	Guinea	6.4
9	Tajikistan	6.3
10	Niger	5.9
11	United Arab Emirates	5.8
12	Chad	5.7
	Sierra Leone	5.7
14	Burkina Faso	5.6
	Mali	5.6
	Saudi Arabia	5.6
17	Liberia	5.3
	Timor-Leste	5.3
19	Algeria	5.2

Smallest, 2019 or latest

1	Sweden	1.9
2	Finland	2.0
	Germany	2.0
4	Estonia	2.1
	Lithuania	2.1
6	Bermuda	2.2
	Czech Republic	2.2
	France	2.2
	Latvia	2.2
	Malta	2.2
	Netherlands	2.2
	Norway	2.2
	Switzerland	2.2
14	Austria	2.3
	Guadeloupe	2.3
	Hungary	2.3
	Isle of Man	2.3
	Italy	2.3
	Japan	2.3
	Martinique	2.3
	Slovenia	2.3
	United Kingdom	2.3

a The cost of living index shown is compiled by the Economist Intelligence Unit for use by companies in determining expatriate compensation: it is a comparison of the cost of maintaining a typical international lifestyle in the country rather than a comparison of the purchasing power of a citizen of the country. The index is based on typical urban prices an international executive and family will face abroad. The prices

Cost of living[a]

December 2020, US = 100

Highest			Lowest		
1	France	103	1	Syria	22
	Hong Kong	103	2	Uzbekistan	29
3	Singapore	102	3	Venezuela	30
4	Israel	101		Zambia	30
5	Switzerland	100	5	Kazakhstan	33
6	Denmark	96	6	Argentina	35
7	Japan	95		Pakistan	35
8	Norway	90	8	Algeria	39
	South Korea	90	9	Paraguay	41
10	Austria	88	10	India	42
11	Australia	86		Nigeria	42
	Finland	86	12	Brazil	43
13	Ireland	85	13	Romania	45
14	United Kingdom	84	14	Nepal	46
15	Jordan	80		South Africa	46
16	Spain	78		Sri Lanka	46
17	Belgium	77	17	Turkey	47
	Italy	77	18	Panama	49
	Netherlands	77	19	Colombia	50
	New Caledonia	77		Hungary	50
	New Zealand	77	21	Morocco	52
22	China	75		Russia	52
	Germany	75			
24	Canada	74			
	Thailand	74			

World Giving Index[b]

Top givers, % of population, 2020

1	Indonesia	69		Ukraine	43
2	Kenya	58		United States	43
3	Nigeria	52		Zambia	43
4	Myanmar	51	21	Paraguay	41
5	Australia	49		South Africa	41
6	Ghana	47		United Kingdom	41
	New Zealand	47	24	Georgia	40
8	Kosovo	46		Ireland	40
	Thailand	46		Malaysia	40
	Uganda	46		Nepal	40
11	Bahrain	45		Tanzania	40
	Tajikistan	45		Uzbekistan	40
13	Ethiopia	44		Vietnam	40
	India	44	31	Chile	39
	Mongolia	44		Dominican Rep.	39
	United Arab Emirates	44		Iran	39
17	Cameroon	43		Iraq	39

a are for products of international comparable quality found in a supermarket or department store. Prices found in local markets and bazaars are not used unless the available merchandise is of the specified quality and the shopping area itself is safe for executive and family members. New York City prices are used as the base, so United States = 100.
b Three criteria are used to assess giving: in the previous month those surveyed either gave money to charity, gave time to those in need or helped a stranger.

Transport: roads and cars

Longest road networks
Km, 2019 or latest

1	United States	6,853,024	26	Pakistan	263,942
2	India	5,903,293	27	Malaysia	238,823
3	China	5,012,500	28	Argentina	231,374
4	Brazil	2,000,000	29	Colombia	219,159
5	Russia	1,529,373	30	Philippines	217,456
6	Canada	1,409,008	31	Hungary	210,791
7	Japan	1,226,559	32	Nigeria	198,233
8	France	1,090,222	33	Uzbekistan	183,496
9	South Africa	891,932	34	Kenya	177,800
10	Australia	872,848	35	Peru	173,209
11	Thailand	702,210	36	Egypt	167,774
12	Spain	683,175	37	Ukraine	163,028
13	Germany	644,480	38	Myanmar	157,000
14	Sweden	573,134	39	Belgium	155,357
15	Vietnam	570,448	40	Congo-Kinshasa	154,633
16	Indonesia	544,474	41	Uganda	146,000
17	Italy	494,844	42	Netherlands	139,691
18	Finland	454,000	43	Mali	139,107
19	Turkey	438,633	44	Austria	137,039
20	Poland	423,997	45	Czech Republic	130,671
21	United Kingdom	422,310	46	Algeria	127,000
22	Mexico	398,148	47	Ethiopia	120,171
23	Bangladesh	369,105	48	Greece	117,000
24	Iran	291,014	49	Sri Lanka	114,093
25	Saudi Arabia	274,861	50	Mongolia	113,200

Densest road networks
Km of road per sq km land area, 2019 or latest

1	Monaco	38.5		Trinidad & Tobago	1.9
2	Macau	14.3	25	Denmark	1.8
3	Malta	9.7		Germany	1.8
4	Bermuda	8.3		Sri Lanka	1.8
5	Bahrain	5.3		Switzerland	1.8
6	Belgium	5.1		Vietnam	1.8
7	Singapore	4.9	30	Austria	1.7
8	Netherlands	4.1		Czech Republic	1.7
9	Barbados	4.0		Italy	1.7
10	Liechtenstein	3.9		United Kingdom	1.7
11	Japan	3.4	34	Finland	1.5
12	Puerto Rico	3.0	35	Estonia	1.4
13	Bangladesh	2.8		Ireland	1.4
14	Hungary	2.3		Poland	1.4
15	Cyprus	2.2		Spain	1.4
	Luxembourg	2.2		Sweden	1.4
	Slovenia	2.2		Thailand	1.4
18	Lebanon	2.1	41	Lithuania	1.3
19	France	2.0	42	Mauritius	1.2
	Hong Kong	2.0	43	Latvia	1.1
	India	2.0		South Korea	1.1
	Jamaica	2.0		Taiwan	1.1
23	Guam	1.9			

Speed cameras
Number of cameras per 1,000km of road, 2020 or latest

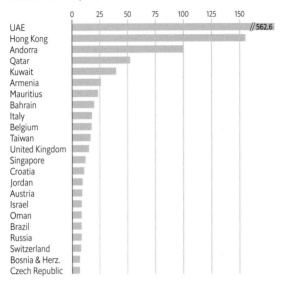

UAE	// 562.6
Hong Kong	
Andorra	
Qatar	
Kuwait	
Armenia	
Mauritius	
Bahrain	
Italy	
Belgium	
Taiwan	
United Kingdom	
Singapore	
Croatia	
Jordan	
Austria	
Israel	
Oman	
Brazil	
Russia	
Switzerland	
Bosnia & Herz.	
Czech Republic	

Most road deaths
Fatalities per 100,000 population, 2018

1	Dominican Rep.	53.5	24	Guinea	29.7
2	Zimbabwe	40.6		Uganda	29.7
3	Venezuela	38.2	26	Congo-Brazzaville	29.2
4	Liberia	37.9		Vietnam	29.2
5	Eritrea	37.4	28	Gambia, The	29.1
6	Central African Rep.	36.0	29	Madagascar	29.0
7	South Sudan	35.7	30	Togo	28.8
8	Burundi	35.2	31	Yemen	28.4
9	Namibia	34.0	32	Kenya	28.0
10	Saudi Arabia	33.2	33	Ethiopia	27.6
11	Malawi	33.1	34	Somalia	27.4
12	Congo-Kinshasa	33.0	35	Iraq	27.1
	Eswatini	33.0	36	Benin	26.9
14	Thailand	32.3	37	Equatorial Guinea	26.3
15	Sierra Leone	32.2	38	Sudan	26.1
16	Guinea-Bissau	32.1	39	Angola	26.0
17	Lesotho	31.6	40	Botswana	25.7
18	Tanzania	31.0		Niger	25.7
19	Burkina Faso	30.8	42	Mauritania	25.6
20	Chad	30.6	43	Ghana	25.3
21	Mozambique	30.1	44	North Korea	24.1
22	Cameroon	29.9	45	Ivory Coast	23.9
	Rwanda	29.9	46	Gabon	23.8

Highest car ownership
Number of cars per 1,000 population, 2019

1	Puerto Rico	921	26	Finland	481
2	Brunei	803	27	Bulgaria	477
3	New Zealand	693	28	Sweden	476
4	Iceland	686	29	Portugal	454
5	Malta	660	30	Denmark	429
6	Luxembourg	645	31	Cyprus	427
7	Italy	625	32	Lithuania	419
8	Canada	613	33	Ireland	417
9	Poland	593	34	Malaysia	413
10	Australia	560	35	Kuwait	407
11	Austria	545	36	Slovakia	402
12	Estonia	540	37	Croatia	364
	Germany	540	38	United States	360
	Switzerland	540	39	Libya	354
15	Slovenia	533	40	Belarus	348
16	Norway	505	41	South Korea	345
	United Kingdom	505	42	Bahrain	336
18	Czech Republic	504		Latvia	336
19	Netherlands	503	44	Hungary	335
20	Greece	500	45	Russia	334
21	Guam	499	46	Israel	330
22	Belgium	498	47	Barbados	325
23	France	497	48	Bermuda	318
24	Japan	488	49	Syria	301
25	Spain	484	50	Suriname	287

Lowest car ownership
Number of cars per 1,000 population, 2019

1	Ethiopia	0.8		Kenya	18.3
2	Sudan	1.2		Togo	18.3
3	Burundi	1.9	25	Nicaragua	18.8
4	Bangladesh	2.5	26	India	18.9
5	Malawi	3.5	27	Benin	19.1
6	Haiti	3.7	28	Cuba	21.0
7	Uganda	3.8	29	Ghana	21.1
8	Honduras	4.5	30	Yemen	22.4
	Liberia	4.5	31	Senegal	23.5
10	Mauritania	4.9	32	Vietnam	24.1
	Tanzania	4.9	33	Angola	26.2
12	Madagascar	8.4	34	Philippines	31.5
13	Mali	9.7	35	Sri Lanka	34.1
14	Cameroon	10.8	36	Afghanistan	35.5
15	Burkina Faso	11.1	37	Guatemala	43.5
	Mozambique	11.1	38	Egypt	48.1
17	Congo-Kinshasa	13.2	39	Iraq	48.6
18	Zambia	13.9	40	Peru	49.8
19	Pakistan	14.0	41	Jamaica	52.8
20	Nigeria	16.5	42	Indonesia	56.7
21	Ivory Coast	18.0	43	Zimbabwe	60.4
22	El Salvador	18.3	44	Paraguay	60.7

Car production
Number of cars produced, '000, 2019

1	China	21,360	23	Canada	461
2	Japan	8,329	24	Poland	435
3	Germany	4,661	25	Morocco	360
4	India	3,623	26	South Africa	349
5	South Korea	3,613	27	Portugal	282
6	United States	2,513	28	Sweden	279
7	Brazil	2,448	29	Uzbekistan	271
8	Spain	2,248	30	Vietnam	250
9	France	1,675	31	Belgium	247
10	Russia	1,524	32	Slovenia	199
11	Czech Republic	1,428	33	Taiwan	190
12	Mexico	1,383	34	Netherlands	176
13	United Kingdom	1,303	35	Austria	158
14	Slovakia	1,100	36	Pakistan	157
15	Indonesia	1,046	37	Finland	115
16	Turkey	983	38	Argentina	108
17	Thailand	795	39	Algeria	60
18	Iran	770		Colombia	60
19	Italy	542	41	Kazakhstan	44
20	Malaysia	534	42	Serbia	35
21	Hungary	498	43	Belarus	20
22	Romania	490	44	Egypt	19

Cars sold
New car registrations, '000, 2019

1	China	21,472	26	Austria	320
2	United States	4,720	27	Switzerland	311
3	Japan	4,301	28	Argentina	282
4	Germany	3,607	29	Chile	261
5	India	2,962	30	Philippines	259
6	United Kingdom	2,311	31	Czech Republic	250
7	Brazil	2,262	32	Israel	240
8	France	2,214	33	Vietnam	230
9	Italy	1,917	34	Denmark	226
10	Russia	1,568	35	Portugal	224
11	South Korea	1,497	36	Colombia	221
12	Spain	1,258	37	United Arab Emirates	199
13	Australia	799	38	Pakistan	163
14	Indonesia	786	39	Romania	162
15	Mexico	764	40	Taiwan	159
16	Poland	556	41	Hungary	158
17	Belgium	550	42	Morocco	148
	Malaysia	550		Uzbekistan	148
19	Canada	497	44	Norway	134
20	Thailand	469	45	Egypt	127
21	Saudi Arabia	460	46	Ireland	117
22	Netherlands	446	47	Peru	115
23	Turkey	387	48	Finland	114
24	Sweden	356		Greece	114
25	South Africa	355	50	New Zealand	104

Transport: planes and trains

Most air travel
Passengers carried, m, 2019

1	United States	926.7		16	Thailand	78.2
2	China	659.6		17	Australia	76.9
3	Ireland	170.2		18	France	71.3
4	India	167.5		19	Mexico	69.9
5	United Kingdom	142.4		20	Malaysia	63.6
6	Japan	130.2		21	Vietnam	53.2
7	Russia	115.5		22	Philippines	47.8
8	Turkey	111.0		23	Austria	46.5
9	Germany	109.6			Hong Kong	46.5
10	Brazil	102.9		25	Netherlands	46.4
11	Canada	93.4		26	Singapore	43.1
12	United Arab Emirates	92.8		27	Hungary	39.8
13	South Korea	92.4		28	Saudi Arabia	39.4
14	Indonesia	91.3		29	Colombia	37.0
15	Spain	88.2		30	Qatar	33.0

Busiest airports

Total passengers, m, 2020

1	Guangzhou Baiyun, Intl	43.8
2	Atlanta, Hartsfield	42.9
3	Chengdu Shuangliu, Intl	40.7
4	Dallas, Ft Worth	39.4
5	Shenzhen Bao'an, Intl	37.9
6	Chongqing Jiangbei, Intl	34.9
7	Beijing, Capital	34.5
8	Denver Int.	33.7
9	Kunming Changshui, Intl	33.0
10	Shanghai, Hongqiao Intl	31.2
11	Xi'an Xianyang, Intl	31.1
12	Tokyo Intl. (Haneda)	31.0
13	Chicago, O'Hare	30.9
14	Shanghai, Pudong Intl.	30.5
15	Los Angeles, Intl.	28.8

Total cargo, m tonnes, 2020

1	Memphis, Intl.	4.6
2	Hong Kong, Intl.	4.5
3	Shanghai, Pudong Intl.	3.7
4	Louisville, Muhammad Ali Intl.	2.9
5	Seoul, Incheon	2.8
6	Dubai Intl.	2.5
7	Miami International Airport	2.4
8	Taiwan, Taoyuan Intl.	2.3
9	Chicago, O'Hare	2.1
10	Tokyo, Narita	2.0
11	Guangzhou Baiyun, Intl	1.8
12	Singapore, Changi	1.5

Average daily aircraft movements, take-offs and landings, 2020

1	Atlanta, Hartsfield	1,501
2	Chicago, O'Hare	1,475
3	Dallas, Ft Worth	1,410
4	Denver Int.	1,213
5	Charlotte/Douglas, Intl.	1,090
6	Los Angeles, Intl.	1,039
7	Dubai Intl.	1,023
	Guangzhou Baiyun, Intl	1,023
9	Shanghai, Pudong Intl.	892
10	Shenzhen Bao'an, Intl	878
11	Chengdu Shuangliu, Intl	854
12	Phoenix, Skyharbor Intl.	850
13	Seattle–Tacoma International Airport	811
14	Beijing, Capital	799
15	Chongqing Jiangbei, Intl	752
	Kunming Changshui, Intl	752
17	George Bush Intercontinental Airport	733
18	Xi'an Xianyang, Intl	700
19	Miami International Airport	689
20	Hangzhou Xiaoshan Intl.	650
21	San Francisco International Airport	633
22	Paris, Charles de Gaulle	627
23	Amsterdam Airport Schiphol	623
24	Shanghai, Hongqiao Intl	601

Longest railway networks
'000 km, 2019 or latest

1	United States	150.5	21	Sweden	9.7
2	Russia	85.5	22	Czech Republic	9.4
3	India	68.2	23	Iran	9.1
4	China	68.1	24	Pakistan	7.8
5	Canada	47.7	25	Turkmenistan	7.7
6	Germany	33.4	26	Hungary	7.6
7	Australia	32.9	27	Indonesia	6.1
8	France	28.2	28	Finland	5.9
9	Ukraine	21.6	29	Belarus	5.5
10	South Africa	21.0	30	Egypt	5.2
11	Japan	19.1	31	Austria	4.9
12	Poland	18.5	32	Uzbekistan	4.6
13	Argentina	17.9	33	Sudan	4.3
14	Italy	16.8	34	Norway	4.2
15	United Kingdom	16.3	35	South Korea	4.1
16	Kazakhstan	16.1		Thailand	4.1
17	Spain	15.7	37	Algeria	4.0
18	Mexico	14.4		Bulgaria	4.0
19	Romania	10.8	39	Serbia	3.7
20	Turkey	10.4	40	Congo-Kinshasa	3.6

Most rail passengers
Km per person per year, 2019 or latest

1	Japan	3,448	13	China	939
2	Switzerland	2,429	14	Italy	916
3	South Korea	1,756	15	Russia	888
4	France	1,657	16	Belgium	881
5	Austria	1,475	17	India	850
6	Sweden	1,373	18	Norway	842
7	United Kingdom	1,192	19	Finland	820
8	Germany	1,173	20	Hungary	802
9	Denmark	1,153	21	Slovakia	717
10	Netherlands	1,105	22	Australia	698
11	Kazakhstan	1,030	23	Belarus	658
12	Czech Republic	962	24	Ukraine	652

Most rail freight
Million tonne-km per year, 2019 or latest

1	China	2,882,100	13	France	31,829
2	Russia	2,602,493	14	Poland	25,234
3	United States	2,364,144	15	Uzbekistan	22,860
4	India	654,285	16	Sweden	22,717
5	Canada	433,139	17	Austria	21,736
6	Kazakhstan	219,927	18	Italy	21,309
7	Ukraine	181,844	19	Japan	20,117
8	Germany	113,114	20	Mongolia	17,384
9	Mexico	89,049	21	United Kingdom	17,206
10	Australia	66,361	22	Lithuania	16,181
11	Belarus	48,205	23	Czech Republic	16,180
12	Iran	34,859	24	Indonesia	15,573

Transport: shipping

Merchant fleets
Number of vessels, by country of domicile, January 2021

1	China	6,869	**16**	India	1,042
2	Greece	4,648	**17**	Taiwan	990
3	Japan	3,910	**18**	United Arab Emirates	970
4	Singapore	2,861	**19**	Denmark	946
5	Germany	2,504	**20**	France	912
6	Indonesia	2,208	**21**	Italy	678
7	Norway	2,043	**22**	Malaysia	620
8	United States	1,933	**23**	Bermuda	542
9	Russia	1,742	**24**	Philippines	499
10	Hong Kong	1,690	**25**	Thailand	401
11	South Korea	1,615	**26**	Brazil	396
12	Turkey	1,528	**27**	Canada	381
13	United Kingdom	1,364	**28**	Ukraine	333
14	Netherlands	1,192	**29**	Cyprus	306
15	Vietnam	1,060			

Ships' flags
Registered fleet, 2020

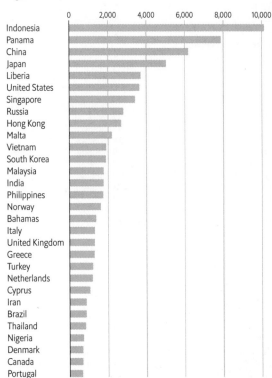

Crime and punishment

Murders

Homicides per 100,000 pop., 2018 or latest

1	El Salvador	52.0
2	Jamaica	43.9
3	Lesotho	43.6
4	Honduras	38.9
5	Venezuela	36.7
6	South Africa	36.4
7	Nigeria	34.5
8	Bahamas	32.0
9	Trinidad & Tobago	30.6
10	Mexico	29.1
11	Brazil	27.4
12	Colombia	25.3
13	Guatemala	22.5
14	Puerto Rico	21.1
15	Central African Rep.	20.1
16	Guyana	14.2
17	Uruguay	12.1
18	Eswatini	11.6
19	Costa Rica	11.3
20	Uganda	10.5

Robberies

Per 100,000 pop., 2018 or latest

1	Costa Rica	1,588
2	Argentina	923
3	Uruguay	867
4	Brazil	696
5	Chile	639
6	Ecuador	420
7	South Africa	332
8	Mexico	258
9	Colombia	244
10	Panama	243
11	Peru	223
12	Trinidad & Tobago	180
13	Bahamas	165
14	France	154
15	Belgium	142
16	Guyana	140
17	Morocco	135
18	Bolivia	132
19	Spain	129
20	Honduras	127

Prisoners

Total prison pop., 2021 or latest

1	United States	2,094,000
2	China	1,710,000
3	Brazil	759,518
4	India	478,600
5	Russia	477,515
6	Thailand	307,910
7	Turkey	281,094
8	Indonesia	262,480
9	Mexico	215,232
10	Philippines	215,000
11	Iran	189,000
12	South Africa	147,922
13	Vietnam	123,697
14	Egypt	120,000
15	Ethiopia	110,000
16	Argentina	103,209
17	Colombia	97,936
18	Peru	96,440
19	Myanmar	92,000
20	Morocco	86,384
21	Bangladesh	83,107
22	United Kingdom[a]	77,859
23	Pakistan	77,275
24	Poland	71,297
25	Malaysia	68,603
26	Saudi Arabia	68,056

Per 100,000 pop., 2021 or latest

1	United States	639
2	El Salvador	562
3	Turkmenistan	552
4	Rwanda	511
5	Cuba	510
6	Maldives	499
7	Thailand	443
8	Bahamas	442
9	Panama	420
10	Guam	411
11	Virgin Islands (US)	394
12	Costa Rica	374
13	Brazil	357
14	Belarus	345
15	Uruguay	337
16	Turkey	335
17	Nicaragua	332
18	Russia	330
19	Cayman Islands	312
20	Namibia	295
21	Peru	290
22	Bermuda	278
	Eswatini	278
	Puerto Rico	278
25	Trinidad & Tobago	276
26	Fiji	274

a England and Wales.

War and terrorism

Defence spending
As % of GDP, 2020

1	Oman	12.0		Jordan	4.9
2	Afghanistan	10.6	**14**	Mali	4.5
3	Lebanon	10.5	**15**	Qatar	4.4
4	Kuwait	7.1	**16**	Trinidad & Tobago	4.2
	Saudi Arabia	7.1	**17**	Bahrain	4.1
6	Algeria	6.7		Brunei	4.1
7	Iraq	5.8	**19**	Cambodia	3.9
8	United Arab Emirates	5.6	**20**	Botswana	3.6
9	Azerbaijan	5.4		Colombia	3.6
10	Morocco	5.3		Pakistan	3.6
11	Israel	5.2		United States	3.6
12	Armenia	4.9	**24**	Namibia	3.4

Defence spending
$bn, 2020

			Per person, $, 2020		
1	United States	738.0	**1**	Qatar	2,645
2	China	193.3	**2**	Kuwait	2,593
3	India	64.1	**3**	United States	2,219
4	United Kingdom	61.5	**4**	Oman	2,059
5	France	55.0	**5**	United Arab Emirates	1,984
6	Germany	51.3	**6**	Israel[b]	1,918
7	Japan	49.7	**7**	Singapore	1,753
8	Saudi Arabia	48.5	**8**	Saudi Arabia	1,420
9	Russia[a]	43.2	**9**	Australia	1,230
10	South Korea	40.4	**10**	Norway	1,188
11	Australia	31.3	**11**	Brunei	942
12	Italy	29.3	**12**	United Kingdom	936
13	Brazil	22.1	**13**	Bahrain	934
14	Canada	20.0	**14**	Denmark	836
15	United Arab Emirates	19.8	**15**	France	811

Armed forces
'000, 2021

		Regulars	Reserves				Regulars	Reserves
1	China	2,035	510	**16**	Colombia	293	35
2	India	1,459	1,155	**17**	Sri Lanka	255	6
3	United States	1,388	845	**18**	Japan	247	56
4	North Korea	1,280	600	**19**	Saudi Arabia	227	0
5	Russia	900	2,000	**20**	Mexico	216	82
6	Pakistan	652	0	**21**	Ukraine	209	900
7	Iran	610	350	**22**	France	203	41
8	South Korea	599	3,100	**23**	Eritrea	202	120
9	Vietnam	482	5,000	**24**	Morocco	196	150
10	Egypt	439	479	**25**	Iraq	193	0
11	Myanmar	406	0	**26**	South Sudan	185	0
12	Indonesia	396	400	**27**	Germany	184	30
13	Brazil	367	1,340	**28**	Afghanistan	179	0
14	Thailand	361	200	**29**	Israel	170	465
15	Turkey	355	379	**30**	Syria	169	0

a National defence budget only.   b Includes US Foreign Military Assistance.

Arms exporters

$m, 2020

1	United States	9,372
2	Russia	3,203
3	France	1,995
4	Germany	1,232
5	Spain	1,201
6	South Korea	827
7	Italy	806
8	China	760
9	Netherlands	488
10	United Kingdom	429
11	Australia	396
12	Israel	345
13	Sweden	286
14	Canada	200
15	United Arab Emirates	191

Arms importers

$m, 2020

1	India	2,799
2	Saudi Arabia	2,466
3	Australia	1,658
4	South Korea	1,317
5	Egypt	1,311
6	China	811
7	Qatar	783
8	United Kingdom	764
9	Pakistan	759
10	Japan	724
11	United States	687
12	Netherlands	610
13	Algeria	549
14	Israel	474
15	Norway	450

Active paramilitary forces

'000, 2021

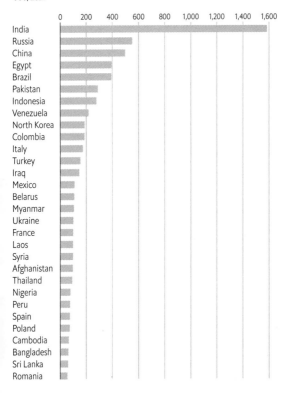

Space and peace

Orbital launches

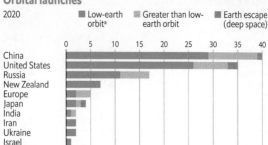

2020

- ■ Low-earth orbit[a]
- ■ Greater than low-earth orbit
- ■ Earth escape (deep space)

China
United States
Russia
New Zealand
Europe
Japan
India
Iran
Ukraine
Israel

Satellites in space

By country of ownership[b], 2020

1	United States	1,878		Saudi Arabia	13
2	China	405	18	Netherlands	12
3	Russia	174	19	Brazil	11
4	United Kingdom	166	20	United Arab Emirates	10
5	Japan	82	21	Indonesia	9
6	India	60	22	Finland	8
7	Canada	43		Singapore	8
8	Germany	40	24	Norway	7
9	Luxembourg	36		Turkey	7
10	Argentina	28	26	Kazakhstan	6
11	Spain	21		Thailand	6
12	South Korea	17	28	Algeria	5
13	Israel	16		Denmark	5
14	Australia	13		Egypt	5
	France	13		Malaysia	5
	Italy	13		Switzerland	5

Global Peace Index[c]

Most peaceful, 2021			*Least peaceful, 2021*		
1	Iceland	1.100	1	Afghanistan	3.631
2	New Zealand	1.253	2	Yemen	3.407
3	Denmark	1.256	3	Syria	3.371
4	Portugal	1.267	4	South Sudan	3.363
5	Slovenia	1.315	5	Iraq	3.257
6	Austria	1.317	6	Somalia	3.211
7	Switzerland	1.323	7	Congo Kinshasa	3.196
8	Ireland	1.326	8	Libya	3.166
9	Czech Republic	1.329	9	Central African Rep.	3.131
10	Canada	1.330	10	Russia	2.993
11	Singapore	1.347	11	Sudan	2.936
12	Japan	1.373	12	Venezuela	2.934
13	Finland	1.402	13	North Korea	2.923
14	Norway	1.438	14	Pakistan	2.868
15	Sweden	1.460	15	Turkey	2.843

a Up to 2,000km. b Excludes multi-country/agency.
c Ranks 163 countries using 23 indicators which gauge the level of safety and security in society, the extent of domestic or international conflict and the degree of militarisation.

Environment

Biggest emitters of carbon dioxide
Million tonnes, 2017

1	China	10,253.6	21	Thailand	303.5
2	United States	5,130.6	22	Spain	301.3
3	India	2,227.7	23	Kazakhstan	295.9
4	Russia	1,763.1	24	United Arab Emirates	281.3
5	Japan	1,257.7	25	Taiwan	267.1
6	Germany	844.3	26	Netherlands	241.9
7	South Korea	825.1	27	Singapore	237.7
8	Iran	680.3	28	Egypt	234.6
9	Canada	607.8	29	Malaysia	224.7
10	Saudi Arabia	584.2	30	Vietnam	211.1
11	Indonesia	493.5	31	Pakistan	198.6
12	Brazil	479.3	32	Ukraine	197.4
13	Mexico	475.2	33	Argentina	195.2
14	South Africa	474.4	34	Iraq	140.4
15	United Kingdom	420.1	35	Algeria	137.7
16	Turkey	408.0	36	Belgium	137.4
17	Australia	400.4	37	Venezuela	134.6
18	France	368.8	38	Philippines	127.1
19	Italy	354.9	39	Qatar	113.0
20	Poland	326.3	40	Czech Republic	108.7

Largest amount of carbon dioxide emitted per person
Tonnes, 2017

1	Singapore	41.0	13	Turkmenistan	16.8
2	Qatar	39.9	14	Canada	16.6
3	Trinidad & Tobago	34.5	15	Australia	16.3
4	United Arab Emirates	29.9		Kazakhstan	16.3
5	Bahrain	26.0	17	South Korea	16.1
6	Brunei	24.6	18	United States	15.8
7	Virgin Islands (US)	24.4	19	Netherlands	14.2
8	Kuwait	22.1	20	Oman	14.0
9	Malta	22.0	21	Hong Kong	13.2
10	Luxembourg	17.8	22	Belgium	12.1
11	New Caledonia	17.4		Russia	12.1
12	Saudi Arabia	17.0	24	Iceland	11.9

Change in carbon emissions
Million tonnes, 2017 compared with 2007

Biggest increases			Biggest decreases		
1	China	3,189.1	1	United States	-872.5
2	India	915.0	2	Ukraine	-175.0
3	Saudi Arabia	235.9	3	United Kingdom	-158.4
4	Iran	230.0	4	Italy	-114.4
5	South Korea	191.9	5	Japan	-108.7
6	Indonesia	170.1	6	Spain	-86.1
7	Russia	146.9	7	France	-58.8
8	Turkey	126.8	8	North Korea	-45.6
9	Brazil	118.0	9	Greece	-32.0
10	Vietnam	112.7	10	Germany	-30.2
11	Singapore	96.8	11	Netherlands	-26.6

Worst air pollution
Mean annual concentration of PM.2.5[a] weighted by total population, 2017

1	Nepal	99.7	27	South Sudan	45.6
2	Niger	94.1	28	Congo-Kinshasa	44.9
3	Qatar	91.2	29	Gabon	44.4
4	India	90.9	30	Turkey	44.3
5	Saudi Arabia	87.9	31	Syria	43.8
6	Egypt	87.0	32	Rwanda	43.2
7	Cameroon	72.8	33	Burkina Faso	42.9
8	Nigeria	71.8	34	Oman	41.1
9	Bahrain	70.8	35	United Arab Emirates	40.9
10	Chad	66.0	36	Senegal	40.7
11	Iraq	61.6	37	Mongolia	40.1
12	Bangladesh	60.8	38	Benin	39.0
13	Kuwait	60.7		Ethiopia	39.0
14	Pakistan	58.3		Iran	39.0
15	Afghanistan	56.9	41	Algeria	38.9
16	Central African Rep.	56.8		Burundi	38.9
17	Sudan	55.4	43	Mali	38.5
18	Libya	54.3	44	Tunisia	37.7
19	Equatorial Guinea	53.2	45	Togo	35.7
20	China	52.7	46	Myanmar	35.6
21	Uganda	50.5	47	Ghana	34.7
	Yemen	50.5	48	Gambia, The	34.0
23	Eritrea	48.0	49	West Bank & Gaza	33.2
24	Mauritania	47.4	50	Jordan	33.0
25	Congo-Brazzaville	46.6	51	Morocco	32.6
26	Tajikistan	46.2	52	Armenia	32.5

Population living in slums[b]
%, 2018

1	Central African Rep.	95.4	20	Moldova	59.2
2	South Sudan	91.4	21	Sierra Leone	59.1
3	Sudan	88.4	22	Benin	58.8
4	Chad	86.9		Niger	58.8
5	Congo-Kinshasa	77.5	24	Burkina Faso	57.1
6	Mozambique	77.2		Jamaica	57.1
7	Guinea-Bissau	74.4	26	Myanmar	56.1
8	Mauritania	73.2	27	Zambia	54.6
9	Somalia	72.1	28	Togo	54.3
10	Afghanistan	70.7	29	Nigeria	53.9
11	Liberia	70.3	30	Lesotho	53.6
12	Yemen	66.2	31	Uzbekistan	52.2
13	Haiti	65.9	32	Guinea	50.1
14	Malawi	65.1	33	Nepal	49.3
15	Equatorial Guinea	64.9	34	Angola	48.6
16	Ethiopia	64.3	35	Bolivia	48.5
17	Madagascar	61.2	36	Uganda	48.3
18	Lebanon	61.1	37	Congo-Brazzaville	47.8
19	Ivory Coast	60.1	38	Burundi	47.7

a Per cubic meter particulates less than 2.5 microns in diameter.   b Households with either no access to basic amenities (like clean water), lack of housing durability or insecure tenancy.

Open defecation[a]
Prevalence among population, %, 2017

1	Niger	67.8	15	Lesotho	27.3
2	Chad	67.0	16	India	25.7
	Eritrea[b]	67.0		Ivory Coast	25.7
4	South Sudan	62.8	18	Zimbabwe	24.9
5	Benin	53.8	19	Sudan	24.3
6	Namibia	48.7	20	Central African Rep.[b]	23.7
7	Togo	47.7	21	Ethiopia	22.4
8	Burkina Faso	46.7	22	Nepal	21.5
9	Madagascar	44.6	23	Laos	20.7
10	Liberia	39.6	24	Angola	19.9
11	Mauritania	31.9		Haiti	19.9
12	Cambodia	31.7	26	Nigeria	19.8
13	Somalia	27.5	27	Yemen	19.6
14	Mozambique	27.4	28	Timor-Leste	19.5

Handwashing
Lowest access to basic facilities, such as soap and water, 2017
% of total population, 2017

1	Liberia	1.2	15	Burkina Faso	11.9
2	Lesotho	2.1	16	Zambia	13.9
3	Congo-Kinshasa	4.5	17	Guinea	17.4
4	Rwanda	4.6	18	Sierra Leone	19.3
5	Chad	5.8	19	Ivory Coast	19.4
6	Burundi	6.1	20	Uganda	21.2
7	Guinea-Bissau	6.4	21	Haiti	22.9
8	Gambia, The	7.9	22	Sudan	23.4
9	Ethiopia	8.0	23	Eswatini	24.1
10	Malawi	8.7		Senegal	24.1
11	Cameroon	9.4	25	Kenya	24.7
12	Somalia	9.8	26	Bolivia	25.4
13	Togo	10.5	27	Angola	26.7
14	Benin	11.0	28	Timor-Leste	28.2

Lowest access to basic sanitation
% of population, 2017

1	Ethiopia	7.3	15	Congo-Kinshasa	20.5
2	Chad	8.3		Guinea-Bissau	20.5
3	Madagascar	10.5	17	Guinea	22.7
4	South Sudan	11.3	18	Malawi	26.2
5	Papua New Guinea	12.9	19	Zambia	26.4
6	Niger	13.6	20	Kenya	29.1
7	Sierra Leone	15.7	21	Mozambique	29.4
8	Togo	16.1	22	Tanzania	29.9
9	Benin	16.5	23	Ivory Coast	32.1
10	Liberia	17.0	24	Namibia	34.5
11	Ghana	18.5	25	Haiti	34.7
	Uganda	18.5	26	Zimbabwe	36.2
13	Burkina Faso	19.4	27	Sudan	36.6
14	Congo-Brazzaville	20.2	28	Somalia	38.3

a Includes in fields, bushes, open water, beaches.   b 2016

Largest forested land
Sq km, 2017

1	Russia	8,153,116		24	Gabon	235,662
2	Brazil	5,000,916		25	Finland	224,090
3	Canada	3,470,391		26	Central African Rep.	223,930
4	United States	3,097,950		27	Nigeria	221,169
5	China	2,143,395		28	Congo-Brazzaville	219,910
6	Australia	1,340,174		29	Turkey	217,525
7	Congo-Kinshasa	1,294,594		30	Cameroon	205,085
8	Indonesia	939,498		31	Thailand	199,810
9	Peru	728,348		32	Malaysia	192,645
10	India	713,608		33	Sudan	188,760
11	Angola	682,726		34	Spain	185,593
12	Mexico	660,754		35	Guyana	184,430
13	Colombia	597,398		36	Chile	178,419
14	Bolivia	514,922		37	Zimbabwe	175,828
15	Tanzania	471,520		38	Ethiopia	172,875
16	Venezuela	464,282		39	South Africa	171,593
17	Zambia	453,787		40	France	170,028
18	Mozambique	374,066		41	Paraguay	169,403
19	Papua New Guinea	359,564		42	Laos	166,990
20	Myanmar	294,130		43	Botswana	156,096
21	Argentina	288,990		44	Suriname	152,330
22	Sweden	279,800		45	Vietnam	144,154
23	Japan	249,350		46	Mongolia	141,761

Forests

Biggest change in forested areas, '000 sq km, 2007–17

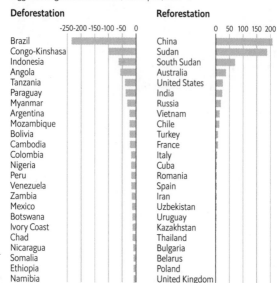

Deforestation

-250 -200 -150 -100 -50 0

Brazil
Congo-Kinshasa
Indonesia
Angola
Tanzania
Paraguay
Myanmar
Argentina
Mozambique
Bolivia
Cambodia
Colombia
Nigeria
Peru
Venezuela
Zambia
Mexico
Botswana
Ivory Coast
Chad
Nicaragua
Somalia
Ethiopia
Namibia

Reforestation

0 50 100 150 200

China
Sudan
South Sudan
Australia
United States
India
Russia
Vietnam
Chile
Turkey
France
Italy
Cuba
Romania
Spain
Iran
Uzbekistan
Uruguay
Kazakhstan
Thailand
Bulgaria
Belarus
Poland
United Kingdom

Protected land and waters as % of total territory
2018

Highest

1	Monaco	99.5
2	New Caledonia	96.0
3	Slovenia	55.1
4	Hong Kong	48.9
5	Luxembourg	40.9
6	Germany	38.8
7	Poland	38.1
8	Zambia	37.9
9	Slovakia	37.6
10	Venezuela	36.9
11	Congo-Brazzaville	36.8
12	France	33.2
13	Tanzania	31.0
14	Bolivia	30.9
15	New Zealand	30.5

Lowest

1	Barbados	0.0
	Bermuda	0.0
	French Polynesia	0.0
	Mauritius	0.0
5	Afghanistan	0.1
	Cayman Islands	0.1
	Guam	0.1
	Maldives	0.1
9	Turkey	0.2
10	Curaçao	0.3
	Lesotho	0.3
	Libya	0.3
13	Haiti	0.4
14	Yemen	0.6

Number of plant species under threat
2018

1	Ecuador	1,859
2	Madagascar	1,111
3	Malaysia	727
4	Tanzania	644
5	China	593
6	Brazil	558
7	Cameroon	555
8	United States	510
9	Mexico	484
10	Indonesia	458

11	India	396
12	New Caledonia	350
13	Peru	328
14	Sri Lanka	297
15	Colombia	268
16	Philippines	254
17	Spain	247
18	Kenya	243
19	Vietnam	231
20	Jamaica	215

Number of mammal species under threat
2018

1	Indonesia	191
2	Madagascar	121
3	Mexico	96
4	India	93
5	Brazil	80
6	China	73
7	Malaysia	71
8	Australia	63
9	Thailand	59
10	Colombia	58
11	Vietnam	56
12	Peru	53
13	Myanmar	49
14	Ecuador	47
15	Cameroon	46
16	Laos	45
17	Papua New Guinea	41
	Tanzania	41

19	United States	40
20	Cambodia	39
21	Argentina	38
	Philippines	38
23	Bangladesh	37
24	Venezuela	35
25	Ethiopia	34
	Russia	34
27	Brunei	33
28	Congo-Kinshasa	32
29	Ivory Coast	31
	Nigeria	31
	Uganda	31
32	Guinea	30
	Kenya	30
	South Africa	30
	Sri Lanka	30

Life expectancy

Highest life expectancy
Years, 2020–25

1	Monaco[a]	89.4		New Zealand	82.8
2	Hong Kong	85.3	26	Guadeloupe	82.7
3	Japan	85.0		Portugal	82.7
4	Macau	84.7	28	Finland	82.5
5	Switzerland	84.3	29	Liechtenstein[a]	82.4
6	Singapore	84.1	30	Belgium	82.2
7	Italy	84.0	31	Austria	82.1
	Spain	84.0	32	Germany	81.9
9	Australia	83.9		Slovenia	81.9
10	Channel Islands	83.6	34	Bermuda[a]	81.8
11	Iceland	83.5		Cayman Islands[a]	81.8
	Israel	83.5		Isle of Man[a]	81.8
	South Korea	83.5		United Kingdom	81.8
14	Sweden	83.3	38	Réunion	81.6
15	Andorra[a]	83.2	39	Cyprus	81.5
16	France	83.1	40	Denmark	81.4
	Malta	83.1	41	Virgin Islands (US)	81.2
	Martinique	83.1	42	Taiwan	81.0
19	Canada	83.0	43	Costa Rica	80.9
20	Norway	82.9	44	Chile	80.7
21	Greece	82.8		Guam	80.7
	Ireland	82.8		Puerto Rico	80.7
	Luxembourg	82.8		Qatar	80.7
	Netherlands	82.8	48	French Guiana	80.5

Highest male life expectancy
Years, 2020–25

1	Monaco[a]	85.6	10	Channel Islands	81.8
2	Hong Kong	82.4	11	Macau	81.7
	Switzerland	82.4		Sweden	81.7
4	Iceland	82.2	13	Malta	81.4
5	Australia	82.1	14	Ireland	81.3
	Singapore	82.1		Spain	81.3
7	Israel	82.0	16	Canada	81.2
8	Italy	81.9		Netherlands	81.2
	Japan	81.9		New Zealand	81.2

Highest female life expectancy
Years, 2020–25

1	Monaco[a]	93.4		Switzerland	86.0
2	Hong Kong	88.2	11	Guadeloupe	85.9
3	Japan	88.1	12	Australia	85.8
4	Macau	87.6		France	85.8
5	Spain	86.7	14	Andorra[a]	85.6
6	South Korea	86.4	15	Channel Islands	85.3
7	Singapore	86.2		Portugal	85.3
8	Martinique	86.1	17	Finland	85.2
9	Italy	86.0		Liechtenstein[a]	85.2

a 2021 estimate.

Lowest life expectancy

Years, 2020–25

1	Central African Rep.	54.4	25	Uganda	64.4
2	Chad	55.2	26	Zambia	64.7
3	Lesotho	55.6	27	Ghana	64.9
4	Nigeria	55.8		Namibia	64.9
5	Sierra Leone	55.9		South Africa	64.9
6	Somalia	58.3	30	Haiti	65.0
7	South Sudan	58.7		Liberia	65.0
8	Ivory Coast	58.8	32	Congo-Brazzaville	65.2
9	Guinea-Bissau	59.4		Papua New Guinea	65.2
10	Equatorial Guinea	59.8	34	Malawi	65.6
11	Cameroon	60.3		Mauritania	65.6
12	Mali	60.5	36	Afghanistan	66.0
13	Eswatini	61.0	37	Sudan	66.1
14	Congo-Kinshasa	61.6	38	Tanzania	66.4
15	Mozambique	62.1		Yemen	66.4
	Togo	62.1	40	Gabon	67.0
17	Angola	62.2	41	Eritrea	67.5
	Zimbabwe	62.2		Kenya	67.5
19	Guinea	62.6	43	Ethiopia	67.8
20	Burundi	62.7		Myanmar	67.8
21	Benin	62.8		Pakistan	67.8
22	Burkina Faso	63.0	46	Fiji	67.9
23	Gambia, The	63.3	47	Madagascar	68.2
24	Niger	63.6	48	Turkmenistan	68.6

Lowest male life expectancy

Years, 2020–25

1	Central African Rep.	52.2	11	Equatorial Guinea	58.8
2	Lesotho	52.5	12	Cameroon	59.0
3	Chad	53.7	13	Mozambique	59.1
4	Nigeria	54.8	14	Angola	59.5
5	Sierra Leone	55.0	15	Mali	59.7
6	Somalia	56.6	16	Congo-Kinshasa	60.0
7	Eswatini	57.0	17	Zimbabwe	60.4
8	South Sudan	57.2	18	Burundi	60.8
9	Guinea-Bissau	57.3	19	Benin	61.2
10	Ivory Coast	57.5		Togo	61.2

Lowest female life expectancy

Years, 2020–25

1	Central African Rep.	56.6	11	Mali	61.4
2	Chad	56.7	12	Cameroon	61.7
3	Nigeria	56.8	13	Togo	63.1
	Sierra Leone	56.8	14	Congo-Kinshasa	63.2
5	Lesotho	58.9	15	Guinea	63.3
6	Ivory Coast	60.1	16	Zimbabwe	63.7
	Somalia	60.1	17	Burkina Faso	63.8
8	South Sudan	60.3	18	Benin	64.5
9	Equatorial Guinea	61.1	19	Burundi	64.6
10	Guinea-Bissau	61.3	20	Gambia, The	64.7

Death rates and infant mortality

Highest death rates
Number of deaths per 1,000 population, 2020–25

1	Bulgaria	15.6	49	Curaçao	9.4
2	Ukraine	15.2		Ivory Coast	9.4
3	Latvia	15.0		South Africa	9.4
4	Lithuania	14.4	52	Barbados	9.3
5	Lesotho	13.4	53	Netherlands	9.2
	Romania	13.4		United States	9.2
7	Croatia	13.3	55	Mauritius	9.1
	Serbia	13.3		Sweden	9.1
9	Russia	13.1	57	Bermuda[a]	9.0
10	Hungary	13.0		Malta	9.0
11	Georgia	12.7		Trinidad & Tobago	9.0
12	Belarus	12.6	60	Eswatini	8.9
13	Estonia	12.2		Guinea-Bissau	8.9
14	Moldova	12.0	62	Congo-Kinshasa	8.8
15	Germany	11.7		Guadeloupe	8.8
16	Bosnia & Herz.	11.5	64	Albania	8.7
	Japan	11.5	65	Fiji	8.6
18	Greece	11.4		Mali	8.6
19	Central African Rep.	11.3	67	Cameroon	8.5
	Chad	11.3	68	Equatorial Guinea	8.4
21	Portugal	11.1		Myanmar	8.4
22	Nigeria	11.0	70	Haiti	8.3
23	Czech Republic	10.9		Thailand	8.3
	Italy	10.9	72	Benin	8.2
25	Montenegro	10.8		Switzerland	8.2
	Sierra Leone	10.8	74	Taiwan	8.1
27	Poland	10.7	75	Channel Islands	8.0
28	Monaco[a]	10.5	76	Andorra[a]	7.9
	North Macedonia	10.5		Canada	7.9
	Slovenia	10.5		Guyana	7.9
31	Slovakia	10.4		Liechtenstein[a]	7.9
32	Puerto Rico	10.3		Norway	7.9
33	Isle of Man[a]	10.2		Togo	7.9
	Somalia	10.2	82	China	7.8
35	Finland	10.1	83	Guinea	7.7
36	Austria	10.0		Jamaica	7.7
	Denmark	10.0	85	Argentina	7.6
38	South Sudan	9.9		Mozambique	7.6
39	Belgium	9.8		Suriname	7.6
40	Armenia	9.7		Zimbabwe	7.6
	Cuba	9.7	89	Angola	7.4
	Martinique	9.7		Cyprus	7.4
43	North Korea	9.6		India	7.4
	Virgin Islands (US)	9.6		Namibia	7.4
45	France	9.5		Niger	7.4
	Spain	9.5	94	Burundi	7.3
	United Kingdom	9.5		Kazakhstan	7.3
	Uruguay	9.5		Venezuela	7.3

Note: Both death and, in particular, infant mortality rates can be underestimated in certain countries where not all deaths are officially recorded.   a 2021 estimates.

Highest infant mortality
Number of deaths per 1,000 live births, 2020–25

1	Central African Rep.	71		Guinea	45
2	Sierra Leone	70		Mozambique	45
3	Chad	67	24	Togo	43
4	Somalia	63	25	Yemen	42
5	Congo-Kinshasa	60	26	Turkmenistan	40
6	South Sudan	59	27	Niger	39
7	Equatorial Guinea	58		Uganda	39
8	Mali	57		Zambia	39
9	Pakistan	56	30	Gambia, The	38
10	Nigeria	55		Sudan	38
11	Benin	54	32	Burundi	37
	Cameroon	54		Papua New Guinea	37
	Ivory Coast	54	34	Kosovo[a]	36
14	Angola	53	35	Eswatini	35
15	Guinea-Bissau	50	36	Tanzania	34
	Lesotho	50		Zimbabwe	34
17	Haiti	48	38	Laos	33
	Mauritania	48		Malawi	33
19	Liberia	47		Myanmar	33
20	Afghanistan	45	41	Timor-Leste	32
	Burkina Faso	45			

Lowest death rates
No. of deaths per 1,000 pop., 2020–25

1	Qatar	1.5
2	United Arab Emirates	1.8
3	Oman	2.5
4	Bahrain	2.6
5	Maldives	2.7
6	French Guiana	3.1
7	Kuwait	3.3
8	West Bank & Gaza	3.5
9	Saudi Arabia	3.7
10	Jordan	4.0
11	Syria	4.1
12	Macau	4.3
13	Honduras	4.5
14	Tajikistan	4.6
15	Algeria	4.7
	Guatemala	4.7
	Iraq	4.7
18	Iran	4.8
19	Lebanon	4.9
	Rwanda	4.9
21	Brunei	5.0
22	Morocco	5.1
	Nicaragua	5.1

Lowest infant mortality
No. of deaths per 1,000 live births, 2020–25

1	Finland	1
	Hong Kong	1
	Iceland	1
	Singapore	1
5	Austria	2
	Belarus	2
	Belgium	2
	Bermuda[a]	2
	Czech Republic	2
	Estonia	2
	Germany	2
	Greece	2
	Ireland	2
	Israel	2
	Italy	2
	Japan	2
	Luxembourg	2
	Macau	2
	Monaco[a]	2
	Montenegro	2
	Netherlands	2
	Norway	2
	Portugal	2
	Slovenia	2
	South Korea	2
	Spain	2
	Sweden	2

Death and disease

Diabetes

Prevalence in pop. aged 20–79, %, 2019 age-standardised estimate[a]

1	Sudan	22.1
2	Mauritius	22.0
3	New Caledonia	21.8
4	Pakistan	19.9
5	French Polynesia	19.5
6	Guam	18.7
7	Papua New Guinea	17.9
8	Egypt	17.2
9	Malaysia	16.7
10	United Arab Emirates	16.3
11	Saudi Arabia	15.8
12	Bahrain	15.6
	Qatar	15.6
14	Fiji	14.7
15	Puerto Rico	13.7

Ischaemic heart disease

Deaths per 100,000 population, 2019, age-standardised estimate[a]

1	Tajikistan	390
2	Azerbaijan	388
3	Uzbekistan	355
4	Ukraine	306
5	Afghanistan	302
	Oman	302
7	Mongolia	284
8	Belarus	282
9	Moldova	280
	Syria	280
11	Turkmenistan	279
	Yemen	279
13	Egypt	268
14	Kyrgyzstan	246
	Monaco	246
16	Morocco	242

Cancer

Deaths per 100,000 pop., 2019, age standardised estimate[a]

1	Mongolia	194
2	Zimbabwe	167
3	Hungary	162
4	Serbia	158
5	Slovakia	157
6	Papua New Guinea	156
7	Uruguay	153
8	North Macedonia	149
9	Croatia	148
	Poland	148
11	Malawi	147
12	Kenya	144
	Latvia	144
14	Lithuania	142
15	Jamaica	141
	Lebanon	141
	Romania	141
18	Barbados	140
19	Turkey	138
20	Bosnia & Herz.	136
21	Slovenia	135
22	Brunei	134
	China	134
	South Africa	134
25	Burundi	132

Pollution

Deaths attributable to ambient and household air pollution per 100,000 population, 2016, age-standardised estimate[a]

1	Sierra Leone	324
2	Nigeria	307
3	Chad	280
4	Ivory Coast	269
5	Niger	252
6	Togo	250
7	Guinea	243
8	Gambia, The	237
9	Guinea-Bissau	215
10	Somalia	213
11	Central African Rep.	212
12	Afghanistan	211
13	Mali	209
14	Cameroon	208
15	North Korea	207
16	Burkina Faso	206
17	Benin	205
18	Ghana	204
19	Nepal	194
	Yemen	194
21	Laos	189
22	Philippines	185
	Sudan	185

a Assumes that every country and region has the same age profile.
Note: Statistics are not available for all countries. The number of cases diagnosed and reported depends on the quality of medical practice and administration and can be under-reported in a number of countries.

Measles immunisation
Lowest % of children aged 12–23 months, 2019

1	Papua New Guinea	37
2	Chad	41
3	Montenegro	42
4	Somalia	46
5	Guinea	47
6	Central African Rep.	49
	South Sudan	49
8	Angola	51
9	Equatorial Guinea	53
10	Nigeria	54
11	Congo-Kinshasa	57
12	Ethiopia	58
13	Syria	59
14	Cameroon	60
15	Gabon	62
16	Afghanistan	64
	Suriname	64

DPT[a] immunisation
Lowest % of children aged 12–23 months, 2019

1	Papua New Guinea	35
2	Somalia	42
3	Central African Rep.	47
	Guinea	47
5	South Sudan	49
6	Chad	50
7	Haiti	51
8	Equatorial Guinea	53
9	Syria	54
10	Angola	57
	Congo-Kinshasa	57
	Nigeria	57
13	Venezuela	64
14	Philippines	65
15	Afghanistan	66
16	Cameroon	67
17	Laos	68

HIV/AIDS prevalence
Prevalence in adults aged 15+, %, 2019

1	Eswatini	27.1
2	Lesotho	23.1
3	Botswana	22.2
4	South Africa	17.3
5	Zimbabwe	13.4
6	Namibia	12.7
7	Mozambique	12.1
	Zambia	12.1
9	Malawi	9.5
10	Equatorial Guinea	7.0
11	Uganda	6.1
12	Tanzania	5.1
13	Kenya	4.8
14	Central African Rep.	3.6
	Gabon	3.6
16	Guinea-Bissau	3.4
17	Cameroon	3.2
18	Congo-Brazzaville	3.1
19	Rwanda	2.9
20	Ivory Coast	2.7
21	South Sudan	2.4
22	Togo	2.3
23	Gambia, The	2.0
24	Haiti	1.9
25	Angola	1.8
26	Ghana	1.7

AIDS
Deaths per 100,000 population, 2019

1	Lesotho	235
2	Eswatini	207
3	Botswana	206
4	Mozambique	161
5	Equatorial Guinea	132
6	Zimbabwe	127
7	South Africa	125
8	Namibia	120
9	Zambia	97
10	Congo-Brazzaville	84
11	Central African Rep.	81
12	Guinea-Bissau	76
13	South Sudan	71
14	Malawi	70
15	Cameroon	54
16	Gabon	52
	Ivory Coast	52
18	Uganda	51
19	Tanzania	49
20	Gambia, The	48
21	Ghana	46
22	Kenya	44
23	Angola	40
	Liberia	40
25	Togo	38
26	Jamaica	36
27	Sierra Leone	33

a Diphtheria, pertussis and tetanus.

Health

Highest health spending
As % of GDP, 2018

1	United States	16.9
2	Sierra Leone	16.1
3	Switzerland	11.9
4	Germany	11.4
5	France	11.3
6	Cuba	11.2
7	Central African Rep.	11.0
	Japan	11.0
9	Sweden	10.9
10	Canada	10.8
11	Austria	10.3
	Belgium	10.3
13	Denmark	10.1
	Norway	10.1
15	Armenia	10.0
	Netherlands	10.0
	United Kingdom	10.0
18	Argentina	9.6
19	Brazil	9.5
20	Afghanistan	9.4
	Maldives	9.4
	Portugal	9.4
23	Australia	9.3
	Lesotho	9.3
	Malawi	9.3
26	New Zealand	9.2
	Uruguay	9.2

Lowest health spending
As % of GDP, 2018

1	Monaco	1.6
2	Congo-Brazzaville	2.1
3	Bangladesh	2.3
	Laos	2.3
5	Brunei	2.4
	Papua New Guinea	2.4
7	Benin	2.5
	Qatar	2.5
9	Angola	2.6
10	Gabon	2.8
11	Indonesia	2.9
	Kazakhstan	2.9
13	Equatorial Guinea	3.0
14	Gambia, The	3.1
15	Pakistan	3.2
16	Congo-Kinshasa	3.3
	Ethiopia	3.3
18	Fiji	3.4
19	Azerbaijan	3.5
	Cameroon	3.5
	Ghana	3.5
	India	3.5
23	Tanzania	3.6
	Venezuela	3.6
25	Malaysia	3.8
	Mongolia	3.8
	Sri Lanka	3.8
	Thailand	3.8

Out-of-pocket health spending
$ per person at PPP, 2017

Highest

1	Liberia	5,408
2	Switzerland	2,094
3	Malta	1,371
4	Singapore	1,347
5	Cyprus	1,138
6	United States	1,123
7	Austria	1,086
8	Belgium	1,007
9	South Korea	956
10	Norway	946
11	Portugal	921
12	Turkmenistan	909
13	Trinidad & Tobago	889
14	Italy	850
15	Australia	848
16	Armenia	841
17	Finland	827
18	Greece	798
19	Sweden	794

Lowest

1	Papua New Guinea	9
2	Mozambique	11
3	Malawi	13
4	Burundi	15
	Congo-Kinshasa	15
6	Rwanda	16
7	Madagascar	21
8	Gambia, The	22
	Zambia	22
10	Ethiopia	23
11	Tanzania	26
12	Timor-Leste	27
13	Eritrea	28
	South Sudan	28
15	Mali	30
16	Central African Rep.	31
17	Botswana	33
18	Benin	36
19	Niger	37

Burden of obesity
Years lost due to overweight, average 2020–50

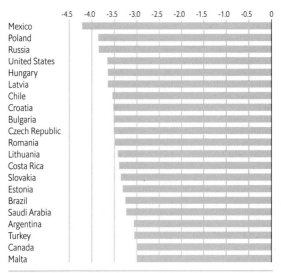

Premature mortality
Annual premature deaths due to overweight, per 100,000 population, 2020–50

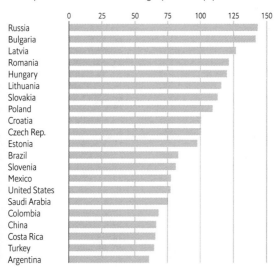

Telephones and the internet

Mobile telephones
Subscribers per 100 population, 2019

1	Macau[a]	345.3	26	Iran	142.4
2	Hong Kong	288.5	27	Vietnam	141.2
3	United Arab Emirates	200.6	28	Suriname	140.0
4	Thailand	186.2	29	Malaysia	139.6
5	Montenegro	183.3	30	Gambia, The[a]	139.5
6	Kuwait	174.2		Nepal[a]	139.5
7	Costa Rica	169.4	32	Kazakhstan	138.6
8	Lithuania	168.8	33	Qatar	138.3
9	South Africa	165.6	34	Oman	138.2
10	Russia	164.4	35	Uruguay	138.1
11	Turkmenistan[a]	162.9	36	Gabon	137.8
12	Botswana	162.6	37	Israel	137.3
13	Maldives	156.0	38	Mongolia	137.0
14	Singapore	155.6	39	Luxembourg	135.8
15	Trinidad & Tobago	155.1	40	Slovakia	135.6
16	Philippines	154.8	41	New Zealand[a]	134.9
17	Cayman Islands[a]	152.5	42	Georgia	134.7
18	Estonia	147.2	43	South Korea	134.5
19	Japan	147.0		United States	134.5
	Mauritius	147.0	45	Kyrgyzstan	134.4
21	El Salvador[a]	146.9	46	Ghana	134.3
22	Ivory Coast	145.3	47	Brunei	132.7
23	Sri Lanka	144.3	48	Chile	132.2
24	Malta	144.1	49	Panama	131.9
25	Cyprus	143.8	50	Colombia	131.7

Landline telephones
Per 100 population, 2019

1	Monaco	113.2	22	Israel	36.9
2	Malta	58.3	23	Ireland	36.2
3	France	58.0	24	Liechtenstein	36.1
4	Cayman Islands[a]	54.9		Mauritius	36.1
5	Taiwan	54.6		Switzerland	36.1
6	Hong Kong	54.2	27	Canada	35.5
7	Andorra	51.4	28	Iran	34.9
8	Portugal	49.8	29	Bermuda[a]	34.7
9	Japan	49.5	30	Belgium	34.1
10	Germany	48.4	31	Slovenia	34.0
11	South Korea	48.3	32	Uruguay	33.7
12	United Kingdom	47.8	33	Singapore	32.9
13	Belarus	47.1	34	United States	32.7
14	Greece	46.0	35	French Polynesia	32.5
15	Barbados	44.6		Netherlands	32.5
16	Luxembourg	43.4	37	Croatia	32.3
17	Spain	42.0	38	Italy	32.2
18	Austria	41.6	39	Hungary	31.5
19	Cyprus	37.5	40	Australia	31.0
20	New Zealand[a]	37.1	41	Montenegro	30.0
21	Iceland	37.0	42	Serbia	29.2

a 2018

Broadband

Fixed-broadband subscribers per 100 population, 2019

1	Monaco	52.6	26	Australia	34.7
2	Cayman Islands[a]	49.3		New Zealand[a]	34.7
3	Andorra	47.1		United States	34.7
4	Switzerland	46.9	29	Belarus	34.0
5	Malta	46.0	30	Japan	33.5
6	France	45.7	31	Spain	33.4
7	Liechtenstein	45.2	32	Hungary	32.9
8	Denmark	43.9	33	Curaçao	32.6
9	Netherlands	43.6	34	Estonia	32.5
10	South Korea	42.8		Finland	32.5
11	Germany	42.0	36	China	31.3
	Norway	42.0	37	United Arab Emirates	31.2
13	Iceland	41.1	38	Macau[a]	30.6
14	Canada	40.8	39	Slovenia	30.2
15	Sweden	40.2	40	Ireland	30.0
16	Belgium	39.8	41	Uruguay	29.2
17	United Kingdom	39.7	42	Israel	29.1
18	Greece	39.6	43	Slovakia	29.0
19	Portugal	38.8	44	Italy	28.9
20	Cyprus	37.8	45	Bulgaria	28.8
21	Hong Kong	37.7	46	Lithuania	28.7
22	Luxembourg	37.4	47	Montenegro	28.5
23	Barbados	37.2	48	Austria	28.1
24	Bermuda[a]	36.2	49	Croatia	28.0
25	Czech Republic	35.0	50	Romania	27.3

Broadband speeds

Average download speed, Mbps, 2019

1	Taiwan	85.0	23	Canada	28.8
2	Singapore	70.9	24	Slovenia	27.8
3	Sweden	55.2	25	Germany	24.6
4	Denmark	49.2	26	Poland	24.4
5	Japan	42.8	27	Ireland	23.9
6	Luxembourg	41.7		Malaysia	23.9
7	Netherlands	40.2	29	Czech Republic	23.3
8	Switzerland	38.9	30	Portugal	22.7
9	Norway	38.5	31	Madagascar	22.6
10	Andorra	38.3	32	United Kingdom	22.4
11	Spain	36.1	33	Iceland	22.1
12	Belgium	35.7	34	Liechtenstein	22.0
13	United States	32.9	35	Romania	21.8
14	Latvia	32.7	36	Monaco	20.2
	New Zealand	32.7	37	Austria	19.3
16	Estonia	31.5	38	Macau	19.2
17	Hong Kong	31.4		Serbia	19.2
18	Hungary	31.1		South Korea	19.2
19	Lithuania	30.7	41	Malta	18.2
20	France	30.4		Thailand	18.2
21	Slovakia	29.5	43	Italy	17.3
22	Finland	29.3	44	Croatia	17.2

The press

Media manipulation

Organisational form and prevalence of social media manipulation, 2020[a]

Legend:
- ■ Government agencies
- ■ Politicians & parties
- ■ Private contractors
- ■ Civil society organisations
- ■ Citizens & influencers

Israel	Venezuela	Ukraine
Kuwait	Angola	UAE
Libya	Argentina	Vietnam
Malaysia	Australia	Zimbabwe
Philippines	Bahrain	Croatia
Poland	Belarus	Cuba
Russia	Bolivia	Czech Rep.
UK	Bosnia & H.	Germany
US	Cambodia	Italy
Armenia	Colombia	Lebanon
Azerbaijan	Ecuador	North Korea
Brazil	Egypt	N. Macedonia
China	Ethiopia	Pakistan
Costa Rica	Georgia	Qatar
El Salvador	Ghana	Serbia
Guatemala	Greece	Tajikistan
Hungary	Honduras	Thailand
India	Iran	Uzbekistan
Indonesia	Kyrgyzstan	Yemen
Iraq	Malta	Austria
Kazakhstan	Mexico	Eritrea
Kenya	Nigeria	Moldova
Rwanda	South Korea	Myanmar
Saudi Arabia	Spain	Netherlands
South Africa	Sudan	Oman
Taiwan	Syria	Sri Lanka
Turkey	Tunisia	Sweden

Trust in news

% population that agree they can trust most news most of the time, 2020[b]

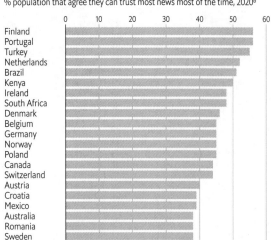

Finland, Portugal, Turkey, Netherlands, Brazil, Kenya, Ireland, South Africa, Denmark, Belgium, Germany, Norway, Poland, Canada, Switzerland, Austria, Croatia, Mexico, Australia, Romania, Sweden

a Types of political actors using social media influence operations, and where examples of those organisations found.
b News sources including news used by individuals, news in search, and news in social media.

Press freedom[a]

Scores, 1=best, 100=worst, 2020

Most free

			Least free		
1	Norway	7.8	1	North Korea	85.8
2	Finland	7.9	2	Turkmenistan	85.4
3	Denmark	8.1	3	Eritrea	83.5
4	Sweden	9.3	4	China	78.5
5	Netherlands	10.0	5	Vietnam	74.7
6	Costa Rica	10.5	6	Syria	72.6
	Jamaica	10.5	7	Iran	64.8
8	Switzerland	10.6	8	Laos	64.3
9	New Zealand	10.7	9	Cuba	63.8
10	Portugal	11.8	10	Saudi Arabia	62.1
11	Germany	12.2	11	Bahrain	60.1
12	Belgium	12.6	12	Azerbaijan	58.5
	Estonia	12.6	13	Yemen	58.3
	Ireland	12.6	14	Egypt	56.8
15	Iceland	15.1	15	Equatorial Guinea	56.4

Index of abuse against journalists[b]

2020, 100=worst

1	Syria	82.1	17	Yemen	55.2
2	China	80.4	18	Russia	53.4
3	Eritrea	72.4	19	Honduras	53.3
4	Egypt	68.9	20	Libya	51.9
5	Turkey	68.3		North Korea	51.9
6	Iran	66.4	22	Morocco	50.9
	Saudi Arabia	66.4	23	Thailand	50.8
8	Vietnam	64.8	24	United Arab Emirates	49.1
9	Pakistan	62.5	25	Congo-Kinshasa	48.0
10	Mexico	61.8	26	Nigeria	47.7
11	Afghanistan	61.2	27	Ghana	47.0
12	Iraq	58.4	28	Ukraine	46.1
13	Azerbaijan	58.1	29	Colombia	46.0
14	Somalia	57.4	30	Chad	45.3
15	Laos	56.7		Haiti	45.3
16	Philippines	56.1			

Number of journalists in prison

As of end 2019

1	China	49	10	Azerbaijan	6
2	Turkey	46		Bahrain	6
3	Egypt	26	12	Burundi	4
	Saudi Arabia	26		Morocco	4
5	Eritrea	16		Rwanda	4
6	Iran	12		Syria	4
	Vietnam	12	16	Algeria	3
8	Cameroon	7	17	India	2
	Russia	7			

a Based on 87 questions on topics such as media independence, censorship and transparency in 2019.
b Based on the intensity of abuse and violence against the media in 2019.

Arts and entertainment

Cinema attendances

Total visits, m, 2019			*Visits per person, 2019*		
1	China	1,727.0	1	South Korea	4.4
2	India	1,592.0	2	Iceland	3.7
3	United States	1,163.0	3	United States	3.5
4	Mexico	350.1	4	Australia	3.4
5	South Korea	226.7		New Zealand	3.4
6	Russia	219.4	6	France	3.2
7	France	208.9		Hong Kong	3.2
8	Japan	194.9		Singapore	3.2
9	United Kingdom	176.1	9	Ireland	3.1
10	Brazil	172.2	10	Estonia	2.8
11	Indonesia	145.7	11	Mexico	2.6
12	Germany	118.6		United Kingdom	2.6
13	Spain	105.5	13	Canada	2.5
14	Italy	97.6	14	Malaysia	2.4
15	Canada	92.6	15	Denmark	2.3
16	Philippines	89.8		Spain	2.3
17	Australia	85.3		United Arab Emirates	2.3
18	Malaysia	77.8	18	Netherlands	2.2
19	Colombia	73.1	19	Luxembourg	2.1
20	Poland	60.2		Norway	2.1
21	Turkey	59.6	21	Israel	2.0
22	Vietnam	54.6	22	Taiwan	1.9
23	Peru	53.6	23	Austria	1.7
24	Argentina	48.7		Belgium	1.7
25	South Africa	45.4		Czech Republic	1.7
26	Taiwan	44.8		Hungary	1.7
27	Thailand	40.1	27	Chile	1.6
28	Netherlands	38.0		Italy	1.6
29	Chile	29.5		Peru	1.6
30	Ukraine	28.9		Poland	1.6
				Sweden	1.6

Oscars award for best foreign-language film

Most awards			*Most nominations*		
1	Italy	11	1	France	38
2	France	9	2	Italy	28
3	Spain	4	3	Spain	20
4	Denmark	3	4	Sweden	16
	Netherlands	3	5	Japan	13
	Sweden	3	6	Denmark	12
	USSR	3	7	Germany	11
8	Argentina	2		Poland	11
	Austria	2	9	Hungary	10
	Czechoslovakia	2		Israel	10
	Germany	2	11	Mexico	9
	Hungary	2		USSR	9
	Iran	2	13	West Germany	8
	Switzerland	2			

Nobel prize winners: 1901–2020

Peace

1	United States	19
2	United Kingdom	12
3	France	9
4	Sweden	5
5	Belgium	4
	Germany	4

Medicine

1	United States	60
2	United Kingdom	26
3	Germany	15
4	France	8
5	Sweden	7

Literature

1	France	17
2	United States	14
3	United Kingdom	11
4	Germany	8
5	Sweden	7

Economics[a]

1	United States	43
2	United Kingdom	9
3	France	2
	Norway	2
	Sweden	2

Physics

1	United States	58
2	United Kingdom	22
3	Germany	20
4	France	11
5	Japan	7

Chemistry

1	United States	54
2	United Kingdom	26
3	Germany	17
4	France	8
5	Switzerland	7

Nobel prize winners: 1901–2020

By country of birth

1	United States	282		Egypt	6
2	United Kingdom	105		Israel	6
3	Germany	84	26	Finland	5
4	France	57		Ireland	5
5	Sweden	29		Ukraine	5
6	Japan	27	29	Argentina	4
7	Poland	26		Belarus	4
	Russia	26		Romania	4
9	Canada	19	32	Lithuania	3
	Italy	19		Mexico	3
	Switzerland	19		New Zealand	3
12	Austria	18		Pakistan	3
	Netherlands	18	36	Algeria	2
14	China	12		Bosnia & Herz.	2
	Norway	12		Chile	2
16	Denmark	11		Colombia	2
17	Australia	10		Guatemala	2
18	Belgium	9		Iran	2
	Hungary	9		Liberia	2
	India	9		Luxembourg	2
	South Africa	9		Portugal	2
22	Spain	7		South Korea	2
23	Czech Republic	6		Turkey	2

Notes: Prizes by country of residence at time awarded. When prizes have been shared in the same field, one credit given to each country. a Since 1969.

Vices

Beer drinkers
Consumption, litres per person, 2019

1	Czech Republic	188.6	11	Estonia	80.5
2	Austria	107.8	12	Slovenia	80.0
3	Romania	100.3	13	Netherlands	79.3
4	Germany	99.0	14	Bulgaria	78.7
5	Poland	97.7	15	Panama	78.3
6	Namibia	95.5	16	Slovakia	76.1
7	Ireland	92.9	17	Australia	75.1
8	Spain	88.8	18	Lithuania	74.4
9	Croatia	85.5	19	Hungary	73.7
10	Latvia	81.4	20	United States	72.7

Prevalence of tobacco use
15 years and older[a], 2018, %

1	Myanmar	45.5	23	Georgia	29.7
2	Chile	44.7		Lesotho	29.7
3	Lebanon	42.6	25	Turkey	29.3
4	Serbia	40.6	26	Albania	29.2
5	Bangladesh	39.1	27	Austria	29.1
	Greece	39.1	28	Madagascar	28.9
7	Bulgaria	38.9	29	Sweden	28.8
8	Bosnia & Herz.	38.3	30	Russia	28.3
9	Timor-Leste	38.2	31	Germany	28.0
10	Indonesia	37.9	32	Kyrgyzstan	27.9
11	Laos	37.8		Portugal	27.9
12	Cyprus	36.7		Spain	27.9
	Latvia	36.7	35	Mongolia	27.6
14	Croatia	36.6	36	Cuba	27.1
15	France	34.6		Lithuania	27.1
16	Andorra	33.8	38	India	27.0
17	Slovakia	32.3	39	Mauritius	26.9
18	Nepal	31.9	40	Armenia	26.7
19	Czech Republic	31.5		Fiji	26.7
20	South Africa	31.4	42	Belarus	26.6
21	Hungary	30.6	43	Poland	26.0
22	Estonia	30.5		Tunisia	26.0

Gambling losses
$ per adult, 2020

1	Australia	993	11	United States	367
2	Hong Kong	709	12	Iceland	364
3	Singapore	657	13	Ireland	341
4	Canada	495	14	Sweden	338
5	New Zealand	484	15	Denmark	332
6	Norway	437	16	United Kingdom	330
7	Finland	403	17	Italy	296
8	Bermuda	399	18	Cyprus	282
9	Japan	392	19	Slovenia	248
10	Malta	383	20	Switzerland	247

a Age-standardised rate.

Tourism

Most tourist arrivals
Number of arrivals, '000, 2019

1	France[a]	89,322	21	Macau	18,633
2	Spain	83,509	22	Vietnam	18,009
3	United States	79,256	23	India	17,910
4	China	65,700	24	Saudi Arabia	17,526
5	Italy	64,513	25	South Korea	17,503
6	Turkey	51,192	26	Croatia	17,353
7	Mexico	45,024	27	Hungary	16,937
8	Thailand	39,797	28	United Arab Emirates	16,730
9	Germany	39,563	29	Indonesia	15,455
10	United Kingdom	39,418	30	Singapore	15,119
11	Japan	32,182	31	Ukraine	13,438
12	Austria	31,884	32	Denmark	13,285
13	Greece	31,348	33	Egypt	13,026
14	Malaysia	26,101	34	Morocco	12,932
15	Portugal	24,600	35	Taiwan	11,864
16	Russia	24,419	36	Switzerland	11,818
17	Hong Kong	23,752	37	Ireland	10,951
18	Canada	22,145	38	South Africa	10,229
19	Poland	21,155	39	Australia	9,466
20	Netherlands	20,128	40	Tunisia	9,429

Biggest tourist spenders
$bn, 2019

1	China	250.7	13	India	28.6
2	United States	182.4	14	Brazil	21.2
3	Germany	99.9	15	Switzerland	21.1
4	United Kingdom	69.0	16	Belgium	21.0
5	France	60.7	17	Sweden	18.1
6	Australia	41.4	18	Norway	18.0
7	Russia	40.6	19	Kuwait	17.1
8	Italy	37.9	20	Thailand	16.9
9	Canada	35.8	21	Nigeria	16.4
10	South Korea	34.8		Saudi Arabia	16.4
11	United Arab Emirates	33.4	23	Indonesia	14.5
12	Japan	29.1	24	Austria	13.8

Largest tourist receipts
$bn, 2019

1	United States	214.1	12	India	30.0
2	Spain	79.7	13	Turkey	29.8
3	France	63.8	14	Hong Kong	29.0
4	Thailand	60.5	15	Canada	27.0
5	United Kingdom	52.7	16	Mexico	24.6
6	Italy	49.6	17	Austria	22.9
7	Japan	46.1	18	United Arab Emirates	21.8
8	Australia	45.7	19	South Korea	21.6
9	Germany	41.6	20	Portugal	20.6
10	Macau	39.5	21	Greece	20.4
11	China	35.8	22	Singapore	20.1

a 2018

Covid-19

Tests per 1,000 population
Year to March 31st 2021

1	Slovakia	4,715		25	France	845
2	Cyprus	4,136		26	Russia	823
3	Luxembourg	3,825		27	Italy	816
4	Denmark	3,788		28	Ireland	805
5	United Arab Emirates	3,777		29	Spain	777
6	Austria	2,602		30	Canada	727
7	Andorra	2,177		31	Finland	720
8	Bahrain	2,094		32	Mongolia	684
9	United Kingdom	1,826		33	Switzerland	657
10	Malta	1,814		34	Greece	625
11	Israel	1,721		35	Australia	612
12	Hong Kong	1,493		36	Germany	601
13	Singapore	1,461		37	Qatar	593
14	Maldives	1,188		38	Chile	586
15	Czech Republic	1,163		39	Jordan	580
16	United States	1,150		40	Belarus	563
17	Latvia	967		41	Serbia	503
18	Belgium	963		42	Slovenia	500
19	Liechtenstein	885		43	Panama	497
20	Portugal	884		44	Kuwait	482
21	Lithuania	874		45	Kazakhstan	460
22	Estonia	855		46	Netherlands	457
23	Iceland	847		47	Turkey	456
	Norway	847		48	Saudi Arabia	433

Cases per million population
Year to March 31st 2021

1	Andorra	150,392		25	Croatia	65,932
2	Montenegro	145,041		26	Malta	65,328
3	Czech Republic	142,761		27	Armenia	64,817
4	Slovenia	103,304		28	United Kingdom	63,580
5	Israel	95,510		29	North Macedonia	62,239
6	Luxembourg	94,769		30	Qatar	62,175
7	United States	91,352		31	Poland	61,278
8	Serbia	88,108		32	Brazil	59,945
9	Bahrain	84,554		33	Jordan	59,913
10	Panama	82,014		34	Austria	59,460
11	Portugal	79,778		35	Italy	57,463
12	Estonia	79,640		36	Moldova	56,971
13	Lithuania	79,201		37	Monaco	56,900
14	Sweden	79,171		38	Kuwait	54,275
15	Belgium	74,937		39	Latvia	54,033
16	Netherlands	74,650		40	Cyprus	51,997
17	Georgia	70,602		41	Argentina	51,947
18	Lebanon	68,555		42	Chile	51,914
19	Liechtenstein	68,228		43	Bosnia & Herz.	51,562
20	France	68,204		44	Romania	49,400
21	Spain	68,019		45	Bulgaria	49,250
22	Hungary	67,483		46	West Bank & Gaza	47,481
23	Switzerland	67,404		47	Colombia	47,272
24	Slovakia	66,082		48	Ireland	47,067

Deaths per million population
Year to March 31st 2021

1	Czech Republic	2,464	25	Sweden	1,288
2	Hungary	2,145	26	Colombia	1,246
3	Montenegro	2,025	27	Argentina	1,235
4	Bosnia & Herz.	2,007	28	Moldova	1,228
5	Slovenia	1,939	29	Romania	1,219
6	Belgium	1,914	30	Chile	1,209
7	Bulgaria	1,898	31	Armenia	1,185
8	United Kingdom	1,824	32	Luxembourg	1,145
9	North Macedonia	1,810	33	Switzerland	1,138
10	Slovakia	1,780	34	Bolivia	1,049
11	United States	1,649	35	Austria	1,021
12	Portugal	1,634	36	Latvia	1,007
13	Italy	1,591	37	Kosovo	965
14	Mexico	1,576	38	Ecuador	950
	Peru	1,576	39	Georgia	947
16	Brazil	1,511	40	Ireland	932
17	Liechtenstein	1,468	41	Lebanon	911
18	Croatia	1,447	42	Netherlands	905
19	Spain	1,413	43	Germany	903
20	Panama	1,410	44	South Africa	891
21	Poland	1,400	45	Malta	888
22	France	1,336	46	Ukraine	787
23	Lithuania	1,311	47	Serbia	776
24	Andorra	1,307	48	Greece	772

Population vaccinated[a]
As of May 31st 2021, %

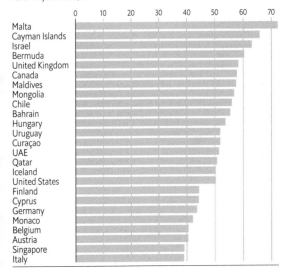

a   Received at least one dose of a covid vaccine.

Country profiles

ALGERIA

Area, sq km	2,381,741	Capital	Algiers
Arable as % of total land	3.2	Currency	Algerian dinar (AD)

People

Population, m	43.1	Life expectancy: men	76.3 yrs
Pop. per sq km	18.1	women	78.8 yrs
Average annual rate of change		Adult literacy	81.4
in pop. 2020–25, %	1.6	Fertility rate (per woman)	2.8
Pop. aged 0–19, 2025, %	38.1	Urban population, %	73.2
Pop. aged 65 and over, 2025, %	7.7		per 1,000 pop.
No. of men per 100 women	102.1	Crude birth rate	20.5
Human Development Index	74.8	Crude death rate	4.7

The economy

GDP	$171bn	GDP per head	$3,974
GDP	AD20,428bn	GDP per head in purchasing	
Av. ann. growth in real		power parity (USA=100)	18.4
GDP 2014–19	2.0%	Economic freedom index	49.7

Origins of GDP		**Components of GDP**	
	% of total		% of total
Agriculture	12.4	Private consumption	43.5
Industry, of which:	37.4	Public consumption	16.9
manufacturing	23.8	Investment	46.0
Services	46.2	Exports	22.8
		Imports	-29.2

Structure of employment

	% of total		% of labour force
Agriculture	9.6	Unemployed 2020	12.8
Industry	30.4	Av. ann. rate 2010–20	11.0
Services	60.0		

Energy

	m TOE		
Total output	168.7	Net energy imports as %	
Total consumption	63.4	of energy use	-166
Consumption per head			
kg oil equivalent	1,473		

Inflation and finance

			% change 2019–20
Consumer price			
inflation 2020	2.4%	Narrow money (M1)	3.7
Av. ann. inflation 2015–20	4.1%	Broad money	5.1
Deposit rate, Dec. 2020	1.75%		

Exchange rates

	end 2020		December 2020
			2010 = 100
AD per $	123.13	Effective rates	
AD per SDR	190.31	– nominal	73.3
AD per €	162.14	– real	91.1

Trade

Principal exports		**Principal imports**	
	$bn fob		*$bn cif*
Hydrocarbons	32.9	Capital goods	13.8
Semi-finished goods	1.5	Intermediate goods	10.2
Capital goods	0.1	Consumer goods	9.0
Raw materials	0.1	Food	8.5
Total incl. others	**35.0**	Total incl. others	**44.0**

Main export destinations		**Main origins of imports**	
	% of total		*% of total*
Italy	22.4	China	12.2
Spain	19.1	France	8.3
France	11.9	South Africa	5.4
Netherlands	10.3	Italy	5.1

Balance of payments, reserves and debt, $bn

Visible exports fob	35.0	Change in reserves	-15.6
Visible imports fob	-44.3	Level of reserves	
Trade balance	-9.3	end Dec.	71.8
Invisibles inflows	4.4	No. months of import cover	14.5
Invisibles outflows	-15.2	Official gold holdings, m oz	5.6
Net transfers	3.0	Foreign debt	5.5
Current account balance	-17.1	– as % of GDP	3.2
– as % of GDP	-10.0	– as % of total exports	13.3
Capital balance	0.3	Debt service ratio	0.5
Overall balance	-16.9		

Health and education

Health spending, % of GDP	6.2	Education spending, % of GDP	...
Doctors per 1,000 pop.	1.7	Enrolment, %: primary	107
Hospital beds per 1,000 pop.	1.9	secondary	...
At least basic drinking water,		tertiary	51
% of pop.	93.6		

Society

No. of households, m	8.3	Cost of living, Dec. 2020	
Av. no. per household	5.2	New York = 100	39
Marriages per 1,000 pop.	...	Cars per 1,000 pop.	95
Divorces per 1,000 pop.	...	Telephone lines per 100 pop.	10.8
Religion, % of pop.		Mobile telephone subscribers	
Muslim	97.9	per 100 pop.	109.4
Non-religious	1.8	Internet access, %	49.0
Christian	0.2	Broadband subs per 100 pop.	8.3
Hindu	<0.1	Broadband speed, Mbps	1.4
Jewish	<0.1		
Other	<0.1		

ARGENTINA

| Area, sq km | 2,780,400 | Capital | Buenos Aires |
| Arable as % of total land | 14.3 | Currency | Peso (P) |

People

Population, m	44.8	Life expectancy: men	73.8 yrs
Pop. per sq km	16.1	women	80.4 yrs
Average annual rate of change		Adult literacy	99.0
in pop. 2020–25, %	0.9	Fertility rate (per woman)	2.2
Pop. aged 0–19, 2025, %	31.2	Urban population, %	92.0
Pop. aged 65 and over, 2025, %	12.0		per 1,000 pop.
No. of men per 100 women	95.3	Crude birth rate	16.2
Human Development Index	84.5	Crude death rate	7.6

The economy

GDP	$445bn	GDP per head	$9,912
GDP	P21,447bn	GDP per head in purchasing	
Av. ann. growth in real		power parity (USA=100)	35.3
GDP 2014–19	-0.3%	Economic freedom index	52.7

Origins of GDP		**Components of GDP**	
	% of total		% of total
Agriculture	7.3	Private consumption	64.6
Industry, of which:	27.9	Public consumption	15.8
manufacturing	15.5	Investment	14.5
Services	64.8	Exports	17.4
		Imports	-15.2

Structure of employment

	% of total		% of labour force
Agriculture	0.1	Unemployed 2020	11.7
Industry	21.8	Av. ann. rate 2010–20	8.3
Services	78.1		

Energy

	m TOE		
Total output	83.7	Net energy imports as %	
Total consumption	90.5	of energy use	8
Consumption per head			
kg oil equivalent	2,022		

Inflation and finance

			% change 2019–20
Consumer price			
inflation 2020	42.0%	Narrow money (M1)	78.1
Av. ann. inflation 2015–20	...	Broad money	81.7
Deposit rate, Dec. 2020	33.38%		

Exchange rates

	end 2020		December 2020
			2010 = 100
P per $	84.05	Effective rates	
P per SDR	121.05	– nominal	...
P per €	103.14	– real	...

Trade

Principal exports		**Principal imports**	
	$bn fob		*$bn cif*
Processed agricultural products	24.0	Intermediate goods	17.1
Manufactures	19.2	Capital goods	8.5
Primary products	17.5	Consumer goods	6.3
Fuels & energy	4.4	Fuels	4.4
Total	**65.1**	Total incl. others	**49.1**

Main export destinations		**Main origins of imports**	
	% of total		*% of total*
Brazil	15.9	Brazil	20.7
China	10.5	China	18.8
United States	6.2	United States	12.7
Chile	4.7	Germany	5.6

Balance of payments, reserves and debt, $bn

Visible exports fob	65.2	Change in reserves	-21.4
Visible imports fob	-46.9	Level of reserves	
Trade balance	18.2	end Dec.	44.9
Invisibles inflows	20.5	No. months of import cover	6.0
Invisibles outflows	-43.5	Official gold holdings, m oz	1.8
Net transfers	0.8	Foreign debt	279.3
Current account balance	-4.0	– as % of GDP	62.8
– as % of GDP	-0.9	– as % of total exports	324.2
Capital balance	-32.3	Debt service ratio	48.9
Overall balance	-37.6		

Health and education

Health spending, % of GDP	9.6	Education spending, % of GDP	4.9
Doctors per 1,000 pop.	4.0	Enrolment, %: primary	110
Hospital beds per 1,000 pop.	5.0	secondary	108
At least basic drinking water,		tertiary	90
% of pop.	99.1		

Society

No. of households, m	14.5	Cost of living, Dec. 2020	
Av. no. per household	3.1	New York = 100	35
Marriages per 1,000 pop.	2.8	Cars per 1,000 pop.	261
Divorces per 1,000 pop.	...	Telephone lines per 100 pop.	17.3
Religion, % of pop.		Mobile telephone subscribers	
Christian	85.2	per 100 pop.	125.8
Non-religious	12.2	Internet access, %	74.3
Other	1.1	Broadband subs per 100 pop.	19.6
Muslim	1.0	Broadband speed, Mbps	2.8
Jewish	0.5		
Hindu	<0.1		

AUSTRALIA

Area, sq km	7,741,220	Capital	Canberra
Arable as % of total land	4.0	Currency	Australian dollar (A$)

People

Population, m	25.2	Life expectancy: men	82.1 yrs
Pop. per sq km	3.3	women	85.8 yrs
Average annual rate of change		Adult literacy	...
in pop. 2020–25, %	1.1	Fertility rate (per woman)	1.8
Pop. aged 0–19, 2025, %	25.2	Urban population, %	86.1
Pop. aged 65 and over, 2025, %	17.8		per 1,000 pop.
No. of men per 100 women	99.2	Crude birth rate	12.1
Human Development Index	94.4	Crude death rate	6.7

The economy

GDP	$1,397bn	GDP per head	$55,060
GDP	A$1,953bn	GDP per head in purchasing	
Av. ann. growth in real		power parity (USA=100)	81.8
GDP 2014–19	2.5%	Economic freedom index	82.4

Origins of GDP		**Components of GDP**	
	% of total		% of total
Agriculture	2.3	Private consumption	55.3
Industry, of which:	27.1	Public consumption	24.1
manufacturing	6.0	Investment	23.2
Services	70.8	Exports	24.1
		Imports	-21.6

Structure of employment

	% of total		% of labour force
Agriculture	2.6	Unemployed 2020	6.6
Industry	19.1	Av. ann. rate 2010–20	5.6
Services	78.4		

Energy

	m TOE		
Total output	422.1	Net energy imports as %	
Total consumption	149.9	of energy use	-182
Consumption per head			
kg oil equivalent	5,946		

Inflation and finance

			% change 2019–20
Consumer price			
inflation 2020	0.9%	Narrow money (M1)	17.4
Av. ann. inflation 2015–20	1.5%	Broad money	13.7
Monetary policy rate, Dec. 2020	0.10%		

Exchange rates

	end 2020		December 2020
A$ per $	1.30	Effective rates	2010 = 100
A$ per SDR	1.87	– nominal	86.0
A$ per €	103.14	– real	85.4

Trade

Principal exports

	$bn fob
Fuels	95.0
Crude materials	87.8
Food	26.2
Machinery & transport equip.	16.3
Total incl. others	**271.0**

Principal imports

	$bn cif
Machinery & transport equip.	85.7
Misc. manufactured articles	32.2
Mineral fuels	27.0
Manufactured goods	22.5
Total incl. others	**213.8**

Main export destinations

	% of total
China	38.4
Japan	14.7
South Korea	6.4
United Kingdom	3.9

Main origins of imports

	% of total
China	27.3
United States	12.5
Japan	7.4
Thailand	5.1

Balance of payments, reserves and aid, $bn

Visible exports fob	271.4	Overall balance	3.0
Visible imports fob	-223.4	Change in reserves	4.9
Trade balance	48.0	Level of reserves	
Invisibles inflows	120.9	end Dec.	58.7
Invisibles outflows	-160.1	No. months of import cover	1.8
Net transfers	-0.7	Official gold holdings, m oz	1.6
Current account balance	8.0	Aid given	2.9
– as % of GDP	0.6	– as % of GNI	0.2
Capital balance	-3.1		

Health and education

Health spending, % of GDP	9.3	Education spending, % of GDP	5.1
Doctors per 1,000 pop.	3.7	Enrolment, %: primary	100
Hospital beds per 1,000 pop.	3.8	secondary	133
At least basic drinking water,		tertiary	108
% of pop.	100		

Society

No. of households, m	9.3	Cost of living, Dec. 2020	
Av. no. per household	2.7	New York = 100	86
Marriages per 1,000 pop.	4.8	Cars per 1,000 pop.	560
Divorces per 1,000 pop.	2.0	Telephone lines per 100 pop.	31.0
Religion, % of pop.		Mobile telephone subscribers	
Christian	67.3	per 100 pop.	110.6
Non-religious	24.2	Internet access, %	86.5
Other	4.2	Broadband subs per 100 pop.	34.7
Muslim	2.4	Broadband speed, Mbps	16.4
Hindu	1.4		
Jewish	0.5		

AUSTRIA

Area, sq km	83,879	Capital	Vienna
Arable as % of total land	16.1	Currency	Euro (€)

People

Population, m	9.0	Life expectancy: men	79.9 yrs
Pop. per sq km	107.3	women	84.2 yrs
Average annual rate of change		Adult literacy	...
in pop. 2020–25, %	0.2	Fertility rate (per woman)	1.6
Pop. aged 0–19, 2025, %	19.4	Urban population, %	58.5
Pop. aged 65 and over, 2025, %	21.0		*per 1,000 pop.*
No. of men per 100 women	97.2	Crude birth rate	9.9
Human Development Index	92.2	Crude death rate	10.0

The economy

GDP	$445bn	GDP per head	$50,138
GDP	€398bn	GDP per head in purchasing	
Av. ann. growth in real		power parity (USA=100)	92.5
GDP 2014–19	1.9%	Economic freedom index	73.9

Origins of GDP		**Components of GDP**	
	% of total		*% of total*
Agriculture	1.2	Private consumption	51.7
Industry, of which:	28.6	Public consumption	19.4
manufacturing	18.6	Investment	25.5
Services	70.2	Exports	55.6
		Imports	-52.2

Structure of employment

	% of total		*% of labour force*
Agriculture	3.6	Unemployed 2020	5.8
Industry	25.4	Av. ann. rate 2010–20	5.2
Services	71.0		

Energy

	m TOE		
Total output	13.2	Net energy imports as %	
Total consumption	36.8	of energy use	64
Consumption per head			
kg oil equivalent	4,108		

Inflation and finance

			% change 2019–20
Consumer price			
inflation 2020	1.4%	Narrow money (M1)	13.5
Av. ann. inflation 2015–20	1.6%	Broad money	10.3
Deposit rate, Dec. 2020	-0.14%		

Exchange rates

	end 2020		*December 2020*
€ per $	0.81	Effective rates	*2010 = 100*
€ per SDR	1.17	– nominal	102.4
		– real	103.6

Trade

Principal exports		**Principal imports**	
	$bn fob		*$bn cif*
Machinery & transport equip.	73.2	Machinery & transport equip.	68.8
Chemicals & related products	24.5	Chemicals & related products	24.8
Food, drink & tobacco	13.5	Mineral fuels & lubricants	13.7
Raw materials	5.7	Food, drink & tobacco	13.3
Total incl. others	**178.7**	Total incl. others	**184.7**

Main export destinations		**Main origins of imports**	
	% of total		*% of total*
Germany	28.8	Germany	40.8
Italy	6.2	Italy	6.4
United States	6.2	Czech Republic	4.4
Switzerland	4.9	Netherlands	4.4
EU28	70.8	EU28	78.0

Balance of payments, reserves and aid, $bn

Visible exports fob	170.8	Overall balance	-0.2
Visible imports fob	-167.5	Change in reserves	0.4
Trade balance	3.3	Level of reserves	
Invisibles inflows	110.1	end Dec.	23.5
Invisibles outflows	-96.9	No. months of import cover	1.1
Net transfers	-3.9	Official gold holdings, m oz	9.0
Current account balance	12.7	Aid given	1.2
– as % of GDP	2.8	– as % of GNI	0.3
Capital balance	-19.5		

Health and education

Health spending, % of GDP	10.3	Education spending, % of GDP	5.4
Doctors per 1,000 pop.	5.2	Enrolment, %: primary	103
Hospital beds per 1,000 pop.	7.3	secondary	100
At least basic drinking water,		tertiary	87
% of pop.	100		

Society

No. of households, m	3.9	Cost of living, Dec. 2020	
Av. no. per household	2.3	New York = 100	88
Marriages per 1,000 pop.	5.3	Cars per 1,000 pop.	545
Divorces per 1,000 pop.	1.8	Telephone lines per 100 pop.	41.6
Religion, % of pop.		Mobile telephone subscribers	
Christian	80.4	per 100 pop.	119.8
Non-religious	13.5	Internet access, %	87.8
Muslim	5.4	Broadband subs per 100 pop.	28.1
Other	0.5	Broadband speed, Mbps	19.3
Jewish	0.2		
Hindu	<0.1		

BANGLADESH

Area, sq km	147,630	Capital	Dhaka
Arable as % of total land	59.7	Currency	Taka (Tk)

People

Population, m	163.0	Life expectancy: men	71.8 yrs
Pop. per sq km	1,104.1	women	75.6 yrs
Average annual rate of change		Adult literacy	74.7
in pop. 2020–25, %	0.9	Fertility rate (per woman)	1.9
Pop. aged 0–19, 2025, %	33.3	Urban population, %	37.4
Pop. aged 65 and over, 2025, %	6.0		per 1,000 pop.
No. of men per 100 women	102.2	Crude birth rate	16.7
Human Development Index	63.2	Crude death rate	5.5

The economy

GDP	$303bn	GDP per head	$1,856
GDP	Tk25,425bn	GDP per head in purchasing	
Av. ann. growth in real		power parity (USA=100)	7.6
GDP 2014–19	7.4%	Economic freedom index	56.5

Origins of GDP		**Components of GDP**	
	% of total		% of total
Agriculture	13.3	Private consumption	69.0
Industry, of which:	31.2	Public consumption	6.3
manufacturing	19.9	Investment	31.6
Services	55.5	Exports	15.3
		Imports	-21.4

Structure of employment

	% of total		% of labour force
Agriculture	38.3	Unemployed 2020	5.3
Industry	21.3	Av. ann. rate 2010–20	4.3
Services	40.4		

Energy

	m TOE		
Total output	28.3	Net energy imports as %	
Total consumption	38.9	of energy use	27
Consumption per head			
kg oil equivalent	239		

Inflation and finance

			% change 2019–20
Consumer price			
inflation 2020	5.6%	Narrow money (M1)	21.3
Av. ann. inflation 2015–20	5.7%	Broad money	13.1
Deposit rate, Dec. 2020	5.33%		

Exchange rates

	end 2020		December 2020
Tk per $	84.80	Effective rates	2010 = 100
Tk per SDR	122.13	– nominal	...
Tk per €	104.06	– real	...

Trade

Principal exports		Principal imports	
	$bn fob		*$bn cif*
Clothing	25.8	Textiles & yarns	6.4
Jute goods	0.7	Capital machinery	4.8
Fish & fish products	0.4	Iron & steel	4.8
Leather	0.1	Fuels	4.6
Total incl. others	**35.9**	Total incl. others	**55.0**

Main export destinations		Main origins of imports	
	% of total		*% of total*
United States	12.8	China	24.1
Germany	12.7	India	12.6
United Kingdom	8.5	Singapore	4.7
Spain	5.8	United States	3.5

Balance of payments, reserves and debt, $bn

Visible exports fob	38.7	Change in reserves	0.7
Visible imports fob	-54.7	Level of reserves	
Trade balance	-15.9	end Dec.	32.7
Invisibles inflows	6.4	No. months of import cover	5.9
Invisibles outflows	-12.3	Official gold holdings, m oz	0.4
Net transfers	18.9	Foreign debt	57.1
Current account balance	-2.9	– as % of GDP	18.9
– as % of GDP	-1.0	– as % of total exports	89.9
Capital balance	5.6	Debt service ratio	9.1
Overall balance	0.6		

Health and education

Health spending, % of GDP	2.3	Education spending, % of GDP	1.3
Doctors per 1,000 pop.	0.6	Enrolment, %: primary	116
Hospital beds per 1,000 pop.	...	secondary	73
At least basic drinking water,		tertiary	24
% of pop.	97.0		

Society

No. of households, m	38.0	Cost of living, Dec. 2020	
Av. no. per household	4.3	New York = 100	66
Marriages per 1,000 pop.	...	Cars per 1,000 pop.	2
Divorces per 1,000 pop.	...	Telephone lines per 100 pop.	0.9
Religion, % of pop. of pop.		Mobile telephone subscribers	
Muslim	89.8	per 100 pop.	101.5
Hindu	9.1	Internet access, %	12.9
Other	0.9	Broadband subs per 100 pop.	5.0
Christian	0.2	Broadband speed, Mbps	2.7
Jewish	<0.1		
Non-religious	<0.1		

BELGIUM

Area, sq km	30,530	Capital	Brussels
Arable as % of total land	28.1	Currency	Euro (€)

People

Population, m	11.5	Life expectancy: men	80.0 yrs
Pop. per sq km	376.7	women	84.3 yrs
Average annual rate of change		Adult literacy	...
in pop. 2020–25, %	0.3	Fertility rate (per woman)	1.7
Pop. aged 0–19, 2025, %	22.4	Urban population, %	98.0
Pop. aged 65 and over, 2025, %	21.0		per 1,000 pop.
No. of men per 100 women	98.3	Crude birth rate	10.6
Human Development Index	93.1	Crude death rate	9.8

The economy

GDP	$533bn	GDP per head	$46,421
GDP	€476bn	GDP per head in purchasing	
Av. ann. growth in real		power parity (USA=100)	86.3
GDP 2014–19	1.7%	Economic freedom index	70.1

Origins of GDP		**Components of GDP**	
	% of total		% of total
Agriculture	0.7	Private consumption	51.4
Industry, of which:	21.4	Public consumption	23.0
manufacturing	13.6	Investment	25.0
Services	77.9	Exports	81.8
		Imports	-81.2

Structure of employment

	% of total		% of labour force
Agriculture	0.9	Unemployed 2020	6.0
Industry	20.8	Av. ann. rate 2010–20	7.3
Services	78.2		

Energy

	m TOE		
Total output	11.7	Net energy imports as %	
Total consumption	67.6	of energy use	83
Consumption per head			
kg oil equivalent	5,856		

Inflation and finance

Consumer price			% change 2019–20
inflation 2020	0.4%	Narrow money (M1)	13.5
Av. ann. inflation 2015–20	1.6%	Broad money	10.3
Deposit rate, Dec. 2020	-0.35%		

Exchange rates

	end 2020		December 2020
€ per $	0.81	Effective rates	2010 = 100
€ per SDR	1.17	– nominal	104.1
		– real	101.6

Trade

Principal exports

	$bn fob
Chemicals & related products	135.5
Machinery & transport equip.	104.5
Food, drink & tobacco	42.6
Mineral fuels & lubricants	36.6
Total incl. others	**446.9**

Principal imports

	$bn cif
Machinery & transport equip.	109.8
Chemicals & related products	115.4
Mineral fuels & lubricants	50.6
Food, drink & tobacco	34.7
Total incl. others	**427.8**

Main export destinations

	% of total
Germany	17.9
France	14.1
Netherlands	12.1
United Kingdom	7.6
EU28	72.7

Main origins of imports

	% of total
Netherlands	17.3
Germany	13.3
France	9.8
United States	7.6
EU28	64.3

Balance of payments, reserves and debt, $bn

Visible exports fob	314.4	Overall balance	0.1
Visible imports fob	-310.5	Change in reserves	2.1
Trade balance	3.9	Level of reserves	
Invisibles inflows	196.0	end Dec.	28.9
Invisibles outflows	-190.0	No. months of import cover	0.7
Net transfers	-8.1	Official gold holdings, m oz	7.3
Current account balance	1.8	Aid given	2.2
– as % of GDP	0.3	– as % of GNI	0.4
Capital balance	2.5		

Health and education

Health spending, % of GDP	10.3	Education spending, % of GDP	6.4
Doctors per 1,000 pop.	3.1	Enrolment, %: primary	103
Hospital beds per 1,000 pop.	5.6	secondary	156
At least basic drinking water,		tertiary	79
% of pop.	100		

Society

No. of households, m	4.8	Cost of living, Dec. 2020	
Av. no. per household	2.4	New York = 100	77
Marriages per 1,000 pop.	3.9	Cars per 1,000 pop.	498
Divorces per 1,000 pop.	2.0	Telephone lines per 100 pop.	34.1
Religion, % of pop.		Mobile telephone subscribers	
Christian	64.2	per 100 pop.	99.7
Non-religious	29.0	Internet access, %	90.3
Muslim	5.9	Broadband subs per 100 pop.	39.8
Other	0.6	Broadband speed, Mbps	35.7
Jewish	0.3		
Hindu	<0.1		

BRAZIL

Area, sq km	8,515,770	Capital	Brasília
Arable as % of total land	6.7	Currency	Real (R)

People

Population, m	211.1	Life expectancy: men	73.0 yrs
Pop. per sq km	24.8	women	80.1 yrs
Average annual rate of change		Adult literacy	93.2
in pop. 2020–25, %	0.6	Fertility rate (per woman)	1.7
Pop. aged 0–19, 2025, %	26.3	Urban population, %	86.8
Pop. aged 65 and over, 2025, %	11.4		per 1,000 pop.
No. of men per 100 women	96.6	Crude birth rate	12.8
Human Development Index	76.5	Crude death rate	6.8

The economy

GDP	$1,840bn	GDP per head	$8,717
GDP	R7,257bn	GDP per head in purchasing	
Av. ann. growth in real		power parity (USA=100)	23.4
GDP 2014–19	-0.6%	Economic freedom index	53.4

Origins of GDP		**Components of GDP**	
	% of total		% of total
Agriculture	5.1	Private consumption	64.9
Industry, of which:	21.4	Public consumption	20.3
manufacturing	11.8	Investment	15.1
Services	73.5	Exports	14.3
		Imports	-14.7

Structure of employment

	% of total		% of labour force
Agriculture	9.1	Unemployed 2020	13.7
Industry	20.0	Av. ann. rate 2010–20	9.7
Services	70.9		

Energy

	m TOE		
Total output	306.4	Net energy imports as %	
Total consumption	321.8	of energy use	5
Consumption per head			
kg oil equivalent	1,525		

Inflation and finance

Consumer price		% change 2019–20	
inflation 2020	3.2%	Narrow money (M1)	8.0
Av. ann. inflation 2015–20	4.5%	Broad money	18.6
Deposit rate, Dec. 2020	1.94%		

Exchange rates

	end 2020		December 2020
R per $	5.20	Effective rates	2010 = 100
R per SDR	7.48	– nominal	51.5
R per €	6.38	– real	55.3

Trade

Principal exports		**Principal imports**	
	$bn fob		*$bn cif*
Primary products	119.0	Intermediate products & raw	
Manufactured goods	77.9	materials	113.1
Semi-manufactured goods	28.4	Capital goods	25.7
		Consumer goods	24.9
		Fuels & lubricants	22.2
Total incl. others	**225.3**	Total incl. others	**185.9**

Main export destinations		**Main origins of imports**	
	% of total		*% of total*
China	28.2	China	20.1
United States	13.4	United States	17.3
Netherlands	4.5	Argentina	6.0
Argentina	4.3	Germany	4.1

Balance of payments, reserves and debt, $bn

Visible exports fob	225.8	Change in reserves	-17.8
Visible imports fob	-199.3	Level of reserves	
Trade balance	26.5	end Dec.	356.9
Invisibles inflows	59.4	No. months of import cover	12.7
Invisibles outflows	-152.2	Official gold holdings, m oz	2.2
Net transfers	1.2	Foreign debt	569.4
Current account balance	-65.0	– as % of GDP	30.3
– as % of GDP	-3.5	– as % of total exports	197.4
Capital balance	38.7	Debt service ratio	52.6
Overall balance	-26.1		

Health and education

Health spending, % of GDP	9.5	Education spending, % of GDP	6.3
Doctors per 1,000 pop.	2.2	Enrolment, %: primary	114
Hospital beds per 1,000 pop.	2.1	secondary	105
At least basic drinking water,		tertiary	...
% of pop.	98.2		

Society

No. of households, m	66.5	Cost of living, Dec. 2020	
Av. no. per household	3.2	New York = 100	43
Marriages per 1,000 pop.	...	Cars per 1,000 pop.	187
Divorces per 1,000 pop.	...	Telephone lines per 100 pop.	16.0
Religion, % of pop.		Mobile telephone subscribers	
Christian	88.9	per 100 pop.	95.7
Non-religious	7.9	Internet access, %	73.9
Other	3.1	Broadband subs per 100 pop.	15.6
Hindu	<0.1	Broadband speed, Mbps	4.8
Jewish	<0.1		
Muslim	<0.1		

BULGARIA

Area, sq km	111,000	Capital	Sofia
Arable as % of total land	32.0	Currency	Lev (BGL)

People

Population, m	7.0	Life expectancy: men	72.1 yrs
Pop. per sq km	63.1	women	79.1 yrs
Average annual rate of change		Adult literacy	98.4
in pop. 2020–25, %	-0.8	Fertility rate (per woman)	1.6
Pop. aged 0–19, 2025, %	19.5	Urban population, %	75.3
Pop. aged 65 and over, 2025, %	22.6		per 1,000 pop.
No. of men per 100 women	94.4	Crude birth rate	8.7
Human Development Index	81.6	Crude death rate	15.6

The economy

GDP	$69bn	GDP per head	$9,828
GDP	BG120bn	GDP per head in purchasing	
Av. ann. growth in real		power parity (USA=100)	38.8
GDP 2014–19	3.6%	Economic freedom index	70.4

Origins of GDP		**Components of GDP**	
	% of total		% of total
Agriculture	3.7	Private consumption	58.9
Industry, of which:	25.0	Public consumption	16.8
manufacturing	15.4	Investment	21.1
Services	71.2	Exports	64.2
		Imports	-61.0

Structure of employment

	% of total		% of labour force
Agriculture	6.6	Unemployed 2020	5.7
Industry	30.0	Av. ann. rate 2010–20	8.7
Services	63.4		

Energy

	m TOE		
Total output	11.8	Net energy imports as %	
Total consumption	19.1	of energy use	38
Consumption per head			
kg oil equivalent	2,732		

Inflation and finance

Consumer price			% change 2019–20
inflation 2020	1.2%	Narrow money (M1)	35.4
Av. ann. inflation 2015–20	1.2%	Broad money	10.9
Deposit rate, Dec. 2020	0.01%		

Exchange rates

	end 2020		December 2020
			2010 = 100
BGL per $	1.59	Effective rates	
BGL per SDR	2.30	– nominal	112.9
BGL per €	1.96	– real	104.7

Trade

Principal exports		**Principal imports**	
	$bn fob		*$bn cif*
Raw materials	13.1	Raw materials	13.1
Consumer goods	8.5	Capital goods	10.2
Capital goods	8.1	Consumer goods	8.6
Mineral fuels & lubricants	2.6	Mineral fuels & lubricants	4.6
Total incl. others	**33.4**	Total incl. others	**37.8**

Main export destinations		**Main origins of imports**	
	% of total		*% of total*
Germany	14.8	Germany	12.0
Romania	8.7	Russia	9.7
Italy	7.3	Italy	7.4
Turkey	7.2	Romania	7.1
EU28	66.5	EU28	62.5

Balance of payments, reserves and debt, $bn

Visible exports fob	32.6	Change in reserves	-0.8
Visible imports fob	-35.8	Level of reserves	
Trade balance	-3.3	end Dec.	27.9
Invisibles inflows	12.9	No. months of import cover	7.2
Invisibles outflows	-10.4	Official gold holdings, m oz	1.3
Net transfers	2.0	Foreign debt	40.5
Current account balance	1.2	– as % of GDP	59.1
– as % of GDP	1.8	– as % of total exports	84.8
Capital balance	-2.2	Debt service ratio	12.4
Overall balance	-0.6		

Health and education

Health spending, % of GDP	7.4	Education spending, % of GDP	4.1
Doctors per 1,000 pop.	4.0	Enrolment, %: primary	87
Hospital beds per 1,000 pop.	7.5	secondary	97
At least basic drinking water,		tertiary	72
% of pop.	99.1		

Society

No. of households, m	2.7	Cost of living, Dec. 2020	
Av. no. per household	2.6	New York = 100	53
Marriages per 1,000 pop.	4.1	Cars per 1,000 pop.	477
Divorces per 1,000 pop.	1.5	Telephone lines per 100 pop.	13.9
Religion, % of pop.		Mobile telephone subscribers	
Christian	82.1	per 100 pop.	116.2
Muslim	13.7	Internet access, %	67.9
Non-religious	4.2	Broadband subs per 100 pop.	28.8
Hindu	<0.1	Broadband speed, Mbps	17.0
Jewish	<0.1		
Other	<0.1		

CAMEROON

Area, sq km	475,440	Capital	Yaoundé
Arable as % of total land	13.1	Currency	CFA franc (CFAfr)

People

Population, m	25.9	Life expectancy: men	59.0 yrs
Pop. per sq km	54.5	women	61.7 yrs
Average annual rate of change		Adult literacy	77.1
in pop. 2020–25, %	2.5	Fertility rate (per woman)	4.3
Pop. aged 0–19, 2025, %	51.4	Urban population, %	57.0
Pop. aged 65 and over, 2025, %	2.8		per 1,000 pop.
No. of men per 100 women	100.1	Crude birth rate	33.4
Human Development Index	56.3	Crude death rate	8.5

The economy

GDP	$39bn	GDP per head	$1,507
GDP	CFA fr22,855bn	GDP per head in purchasing	
Av. ann. growth in real		power parity (USA=100)	5.8
GDP 2014–19	4.3%	Economic freedom index	53.4

Origins of GDP		**Components of GDP**	
	% of total		% of total
Agriculture	15.8	Private consumption	10.9
Industry, of which:	28.3	Public consumption	71.0
manufacturing	15.4	Investment	22.6
Services	55.9	Exports	20.2
		Imports	-24.7

Structure of employment

	% of total		% of labour force
Agriculture	43.5	Unemployed 2020	3.6
Industry	14.4	Av. ann. rate 2010–20	3.6
Services	42.1		

Energy

	m TOE		
Total output	6.7	Net energy imports as %	
Total consumption	4.0	of energy use	-68
Consumption per head			
kg oil equivalent	155		

Inflation and finance

Consumer price			% change 2019–20
inflation 2020	2.8%	Narrow money (M1)	13.0
Av. ann. inflation 2015–20	1.6%	Broad money	12.4
Monetary policy rate, Dec. 2020	3.25%		

Exchange rates

	end 2020		December 2020
CFAfr per $	534.56	Effective rates	2010 = 100
CFAfr per SDR	769.91	– nominal	...
CFAfr per €	657.51	– real	...

Trade

Principal exports

	$bn fob
Fuels & lubricants	2.2
Cocoa beans & products	0.6
Timber	0.5
Cotton	0.2
Total incl. others	**4.1**

Principal imports

	$bn cif
Fuels & lubricants	1.7
Food, drink & tobacco	1.4
Machinery & transport equip.	1.2
Chemicals	0.7
Total incl. others	**6.6**

Main export destinations

	% of total
Netherlands	18.4
China	14.4
Italy	11.2
India	9.8

Main origins of imports

	% of total
China	20.1
France	9.2
Thailand	5.0
Nigeria	4.7

Balance of payments, reserves and debt, $bn

Visible exports fob	5.5	Change in reserves	0.0
Visible imports fob	-6.3	Level of reserves	
Trade balance	-0.7	end Dec.	3.5
Invisibles inflows	2.4	No. months of import cover	4.1
Invisibles outflows	-3.9	Official gold holdings, m oz	0.0
Net transfers	0.5	Foreign debt	12.8
Current account balance	-1.7	– as % of GDP	32.9
– as % of GDP	-4.3	– as % of total exports	154.5
Capital balance	2.0	Debt service ratio	15.1
Overall balance	0.2		

Health and education

Health spending, % of GDP	3.5	Education spending, % of GDP	3.1
Doctors per 1,000 pop.	...	Enrolment, %: primary	106
Hospital beds per 1,000 pop.	1.3	secondary	60
At least basic drinking water,		tertiary	14
% of pop.	60.4		

Society

No. of households, m	5.3	Cost of living, Dec. 2020	
Av. no. per household	4.9	New York = 100	...
Marriages per 1,000 pop.	...	Cars per 1,000 pop.	11
Divorces per 1,000 pop.	...	Telephone lines per 100 pop.	3.3
Religion, % of pop.		Mobile telephone subscribers	
Christian	70.3	per 100 pop.	82.7
Muslim	18.3	Internet access, %	23.2
Other	6.0	Broadband subs per 100 pop.	1.5
Non-religious	5.3	Broadband speed, Mbps	1.0
Hindu	<0.1		
Jewish	<0.1		

CANADA

Area, sq kmª	9,984,670	Capital	Ottawa
Arable as % of total land	4.3	Currency	Canadian dollar (C$)

People

Population, m	37.4	Life expectancy: men	81.2 yrs
Pop. per sq km	3.7	women	84.7 yrs
Average annual rate of change		Adult literacy	...
in pop. 2020–25, %	0.8	Fertility rate (per woman)	1.5
Pop. aged 0–19, 2025, %	20.7	Urban population, %	81.5
Pop. aged 65 and over, 2025, %	20.5		per 1,000 pop.
No. of men per 100 women	98.5	Crude birth rate	10.1
Human Development Index	92.9	Crude death rate	7.9

The economy

GDP	$1,736bn	GDP per head	$46,195
GDP	C$2,304bn	GDP per head in purchasing	
Av. ann. growth in real		power parity (USA=100)	79.1
GDP 2014–19	1.7%	Economic freedom index	77.9

Origins of GDP		**Components of GDP**	
	% of total		% of total
Agriculture	2.2	Private consumption	57.8
Industry, of which:	27.2	Public consumption	21.2
manufacturing	10.0	Investment	22.7
Services	70.6	Exports	31.6
		Imports	-33.3

Structure of employment

	% of total		% of labour force
Agriculture	1.5	Unemployed 2020	9.5
Industry	19.3	Av. ann. rate 2010–20	7.1
Services	79.2		

Energy

	m TOE		
Total output	597.5	Net energy imports as %	
Total consumption	383.4	of energy use	-56
Consumption per head			
kg oil equivalent	10,249		

Inflation and finance

		% change 2019–20	
Consumer price			
inflation 2020	0.7%	Narrow money (M1)	29.5
Av. ann. inflation 2015–20	1.6%	Broad money	12.0
Monetary policy rate, Dec. 2020	0.25%		

Exchange rates

	end 2020		December 2020
			2010 = 100
C$ per $	1.29	Effective rates	83.0
C$ per SDR	1.85	– nominal	83.0
C$ per €	1.59	– real	80.6

Trade

Principal exports		**Principal imports**	
	$bn fob		*$bn cif*
Energy products	85.7	Consumer goods	94.5
Motor vehicles & parts	70.2	Motor vehicles & parts	86.5
Consumer goods	53.4	Electronic & electrical equip.	54.4
Metal & mineral products	49.1	Industrial machinery & equip.	52.3
Total incl. others	**450.8**	Total incl. others	**462.4**

Main export destinations		**Main origins of imports**	
	% of total		*% of total*
United States	75.7	United States	50.8
China	3.9	China	12.5
United Kingdom	3.3	Mexico	6.1
Japan	2.1	Germany	3.2
EU28	5.3	EU28	11.3

Balance of payments, reserves and aid, $bn

Visible exports fob	450.8	Overall balance	-1.2
Visible imports fob	-462.4	Change in reserves	1.4
Trade balance	-11.6	Level of reserves	
Invisibles inflows	217.5	end Dec.	85.3
Invisibles outflows	-239.8	No. months of import cover	1.5
Net transfers	-1.8	Official gold holdings, m oz	0.0
Current account balance	-35.7	Aid given	4.7
– as % of GDP	-2.1	– as % of GNI	0.3
Capital balance	37.1		

Health and education

Health spending, % of GDP	10.8	Education spending, % of GDP	...
Doctors per 1,000 pop.	2.6	Enrolment, %: primary	102
Hospital beds per 1,000 pop.	2.5	secondary	114
At least basic drinking water,		tertiary	70
% of pop.	99.4		

Society

No. of households, m	15.6	Cost of living, Dec. 2020	
Av. no. per household	2.4	New York = 100	74
Marriages per 1,000 pop.	...	Cars per 1,000 pop.	613
Divorces per 1,000 pop.	...	Telephone lines per 100 pop.	35.5
Religion, % of pop.		Mobile telephone subscribers	
Christian	69.0	per 100 pop.	91.9
Non-religious	23.7	Internet access, %	92.7
Other	2.8	Broadband subs per 100 pop.	40.8
Muslim	2.1	Broadband speed, Mbps	28.8
Hindu	1.4		
Jewish	1.0		

a Including freshwater.

CHILE

Area, sq km	756,700	Capital	Santiago
Arable as % of total land	1.6	Currency	Chilean peso (Ps)

People

Population, m	19.0	Life expectancy: men	78.5 yrs
Pop. per sq km	25.1	women	82.8 yrs
Average annual rate of change		Adult literacy	96.4
in pop. 2020–25, %	0.1	Fertility rate (per woman)	1.6
Pop. aged 0–19, 2025, %	24.7	Urban population, %	87.6
Pop. aged 65 and over, 2025, %	14.6		per 1,000 pop.
No. of men per 100 women	97.3	Crude birth rate	11.7
Human Development Index	85.1	Crude death rate	6.6

The economy

GDP	$282bn	GDP per head	$14,896
GDP	Peso198,441bn	GDP per head in purchasing	
Av. ann. growth in real		power parity (USA=100)	41.4
GDP 2014–19	2.0%	Economic freedom index	75.2

Origins of GDP		**Components of GDP**	
	% of total		% of total
Agriculture	3.6	Private consumption	63.0
Industry, of which:	33.7	Public consumption	14.6
manufacturing	10.4	Investment	22.8
Services	62.7	Exports	28.2
		Imports	-28.6

Structure of employment

	% of total		% of labour force
Agriculture	9.0	Unemployed 2020	11.5
Industry	22.3	Av. ann. rate 2010–20	7.4
Services	68.8		

Energy

	m TOE		
Total output	11.2	Net energy imports as %	
Total consumption	38.9	of energy use	71
Consumption per head			
kg oil equivalent	2,054		

Inflation and finance

			% change 2019–20
Consumer price			
inflation 2020	3.0%	Narrow money (M1)	145.3
Av. ann. inflation 2015–20	2.7%	Broad money	13.7
Deposit rate, Dec. 2020	0.43%		

Exchange rates

	end 2020		December 2020
Ps per $	728.96	Effective rates	2010 = 100
Ps per SDR	1,049.90	– nominal	84.3
Ps per €	894.51	– real	84.9

Trade

Principal exports		**Principal imports**	
	$bn fob		*$bn cif*
Copper	32.5	Intermediate goods	34.6
Fresh fruit	6.0	Consumer goods	20.1
Salmon & trout	5.1	Capital goods	15.2
Cellulose & paper products	3.2		
Total incl. others	**69.9**	Total incl. others	**69.8**

Main export destinations		**Main origins of imports**	
	% of total		*% of total*
China	32.4	China	23.6
United States	13.7	United States	19.7
Japan	9.2	Brazil	8.1
South Korea	6.6	Argentina	5.1

Balance of payments, reserves and debt, $bn

Visible exports fob	68.8	Change in reserves	0.8
Visible imports fob	-65.8	Level of reserves	
Trade balance	3.0	end Dec.	40.7
Invisibles inflows	20.2	No. months of import cover	4.8
Invisibles outflows	-35.5	Official gold holdings, m oz	0.0
Net transfers	1.8	Foreign debt	198.1
Current account balance	-10.5	– as % of GDP	70.2
– as % of GDP	-3.7	– as % of total exports	227.6
Capital balance	9.7	Debt service ratio	35.1
Overall balance	-0.1		

Health and education

Health spending, % of GDP	9.1	Education spending, % of GDP	5.4
Doctors per 1,000 pop.	2.6	Enrolment, %: primary	102
Hospital beds per 1,000 pop.	2.1	secondary	102
At least basic drinking water,		tertiary	91
% of pop.	99.8		

Society

No. of households, m	5.8	Cost of living, Dec. 2020	
Av. no. per household	3.3	New York = 100	60
Marriages per 1,000 pop.	3.4	Cars per 1,000 pop.	184
Divorces per 1,000 pop.	...	Telephone lines per 100 pop.	14.5
Religion, % of pop.		Mobile telephone subscribers	
Christian	89.4	per 100 pop.	132.2
Non-religious	8.6	Internet access, %	82.3
Other	1.9	Broadband subs per 100 pop.	18.1
Jewish	0.1	Broadband speed, Mbps	3.9
Hindu	<0.1		
Muslim	<0.1		

CHINA

Area, sq km	9,562,910	Capital	Beijing
Arable as % of total land	12.7	Currency	Yuan

People

Population, m	1,433.8	Life expectancy: men	75.4 yrs
Pop. per sq km	149.9	women	79.7 yrs
Average annual rate of change		Adult literacy	96.8
in pop. 2020–25, %	0.3	Fertility rate (per woman)	1.7
Pop. aged 0–19, 2025, %	22.7	Urban population, %	60.3
Pop. aged 65 and over, 2025, %	14.0		per 1,000 pop.
No. of men per 100 women	105.3	Crude birth rate	10.6
Human Development Index	76.1	Crude death rate	7.8

The economy

GDP	$14,343bn	GDP per head	$10,262
GDP	Yuan 98,652bn	GDP per head in purchasing	
Av. ann. growth in real		power parity (USA=100)	25.8
GDP 2014–19	6.7%	Economic freedom index	58.4

Origins of GDP

Components of GDP

	% of total		% of total
Agriculture	7.5	Private consumption	39.2
Industry, of which:	38.8	Public consumption	16.8
manufacturing	26.8	Investment	43.3
Services	53.8	Exports	18.5
		Imports	-17.3

Structure of employment

	% of total		% of labour force
Agriculture	25.3	Unemployed 2020	4.6
Industry	27.4	Av. ann. rate 2010–20	5.0
Services	47.3		

Energy

	m TOE		
Total output	2,970.7	Net energy imports as %	
Total consumption	3,721.6	of energy use	20
Consumption per head			
kg oil equivalent	2,596		

Inflation and finance

Consumer price			% change 2019–20
inflation 2020	2.4%	Narrow money (M1)	8.6
Av. ann. inflation 2015–20	2.2%	Broad money	10.1
Deposit rate, Dec. 2020	1.50%		

Exchange rates

	end 2020		December 2020
Yuan per $	6.53	Effective rates	2010 = 100
Yuan per SDR	9.41	– nominal	117.6
Yuan per €	8.02	– real	123.4

Trade

Principal exports		**Principal imports**	
	$bn fob		*$bn cif*
Electrical goods	327.1	Electrical machinery	477.1
Telecoms equipment	320.0	Petroleum products	280.1
Office machinery	210.2	Metal ores & scrap	153.8
Clothing & apparel	154.3	Professional instruments	83.8
Total incl. others	**2,499.5**	Total incl. others	**2,078.4**

Main export destinations		**Main origins of imports**	
	% of total		*% of total*
United States	16.8	South Korea	8.4
Hong Kong	11.2	Taiwan	8.4
Japan	5.7	Japan	8.3
South Korea	4.4	United States	6.0
EU28	14.6	EU28	12.2

Balance of payments, reserves and debt, $bn

Visible exports fob	2,386.6	Change in reserves	54.3
Visible imports fob	-1,993.6	Level of reserves	
Trade balance	393.0	end Dec.	3,222.4
Invisibles inflows	517.9	No. months of import cover	13.8
Invisibles outflows	-818.2	Official gold holdings, m oz	62.6
Net transfers	10.3	Foreign debt	2,114.2
Current account balance	102.9	– as % of GDP	14.7
– as % of GDP	0.7	– as % of total exports	73.0
Capital balance	7.0	Debt service ratio	9.5
Overall balance	-19.3		

Health and education

Health spending, % of GDP	5.4	Education spending, % of GDP	...
Doctors per 1,000 pop.	2.0	Enrolment, %: primary	102
Hospital beds per 1,000 pop.	4.3	secondary	...
At least basic drinking water,		tertiary	54
% of pop.	92.8		

Society

No. of households, m	480.2	Cost of living, Dec. 2020	
Av. no. per household	3.0	New York = 100	75
Marriages per 1,000 pop.	...	Cars per 1,000 pop.	112
Divorces per 1,000 pop.	...	Telephone lines per 100 pop.	13.3
Religion, % of pop.		Mobile telephone subscribers	
Non-religious	52.2	per 100 pop.	121.8
Other	22.7	Internet access, %	64.6
Buddhist	18.2	Broadband subs per 100 pop.	31.3
Christian	5.1	Broadband speed, Mbps	2.7
Muslim	1.8		
Jewish	<0.1		

Note: Data exclude Special Administrative Regions, ie, Hong Kong and Macau.

COLOMBIA

Area, sq km	1,141,748	Capital	Bogotá
Arable as % of total land	5.4	Currency	Colombian peso (peso)

People

Population, m	50.3	Life expectancy: men	75.2 yrs
Pop. per sq km	44.1	women	80.5 yrs
Average annual rate of change		Adult literacy	95.1
in pop. 2020–25, %	0.4	Fertility rate (per woman)	1.7
Pop. aged 0–19, 2025, %	28.1	Urban population, %	81.1
Pop. aged 65 and over, 2025, %	10.9		per 1,000 pop.
No. of men per 100 women	96.5	Crude birth rate	13.8
Human Development Index	76.7	Crude death rate	5.9

The economy

GDP	$324bn	GDP per head	$6,429
GDP	1,061trn peso	GDP per head in purchasing	
Av. ann. growth in real		power parity (USA=100)	24.5
GDP 2014–19	2.4%	Economic freedom index	68.1

Origins of GDP		**Components of GDP**	
	% of total		% of total
Agriculture	7.4	Private consumption	68.4
Industry, of which:	29.0	Public consumption	15.4
manufacturing	12.1	Investment	22.3
Services	63.6	Exports	15.8
		Imports	-21.9

Structure of employment

	% of total		% of labour force
Agriculture	15.8	Unemployed 2020	15.4
Industry	20.1	Av. ann. rate 2010–20	9.9
Services	64.1		

Energy

	m TOE		
Total output	127.7	Net energy imports as %	
Total consumption	42.7	of energy use	-199
Consumption per head			
kg oil equivalent	847		

Inflation and finance

			% change 2019–20
Consumer price			
inflation 2020	2.5%	Narrow money (M1)	18.0
Av. ann. inflation 2015–20	4.2%	Broad money	12.7
Deposit rate, Dec. 2020	1.93%		

Exchange rates

	end 2020		December 2020
Peso per $	3,444.90	Effective rates	2010 = 100
Peso per SDR	4,961.58	– nominal	67.1
Peso per €	4,227.24	– real	67.1

Trade

Principal exports

	$bn fob
Petroleum & products	16.0
Coal	5.7
Coffee	2.3
Gold	1.7
Total incl. others	**39.5**

Principal imports

	$bn cif
Intermediate goods & raw materials	23.7
Capital goods	16.5
Consumer goods	12.5
Total	**52.7**

Main export destinations

	% of total
United States	31.1
China	11.6
Panama	6.0
Ecuador	4.9

Main origins of imports

	% of total
United States	25.4
China	20.8
Mexico	7.4
Brazil	6.0

Balance of payments, reserves and debt, $bn

Visible exports fob	42.4	Change in reserves	4.8
Visible imports fob	-50.8	Level of reserves	
Trade balance	-8.5	end Dec.	52.6
Invisibles inflows	17.6	No. months of import cover	7.6
Invisibles outflows	-32.2	Official gold holdings, m oz	0.4
Net transfers	8.7	Foreign debt	138.7
Current account balance	-14.3	– as % of GDP	42.9
– as % of GDP	-4.4	– as % of total exports	207.7
Capital balance	16.6	Debt service ratio	28.8
Overall balance	3.3		

Health and education

Health spending, % of GDP	7.6	Education spending, % of GDP	4.5
Doctors per 1,000 pop.	2.2	Enrolment, %: primary	114
Hospital beds per 1,000 pop.	1.7	secondary	101
At least basic drinking water, % of pop.	97.3	tertiary	55

Society

No. of households, m	14.5	Cost of living, Dec. 2020	
Av. no. per household	3.5	New York = 100	50
Marriages per 1,000 pop.	...	Cars per 1,000 pop.	68
Divorces per 1,000 pop.	...	Telephone lines per 100 pop.	13.9
Religion, % of pop.		Mobile telephone subscribers	
Christian	92.5	per 100 pop.	131.7
Non-religious	6.6	Internet access, %	65.0
Other	0.8	Broadband subs per 100 pop.	13.8
Hindu	<0.1	Broadband speed, Mbps	3.5
Jewish	<0.1		
Muslim	<0.1		

CZECH REPUBLIC

Area, sq km	78,870	Capital	Prague
Arable as % of total land	32.3	Currency	Koruna (Kc)

People

Population, m	10.7	Life expectancy: men	77.3 yrs
Pop. per sq km	135.7	women	82.4 yrs
Average annual rate of change		Adult literacy	99.8
in pop. 2020–25, %	0.1	Fertility rate (per woman)	1.7
Pop. aged 0–19, 2025, %	20.7	Urban population, %	73.9
Pop. aged 65 and over, 2025, %	21.3		per 1,000 pop.
No. of men per 100 women	97.0	Crude birth rate	9.7
Human Development Index	90.0	Crude death rate	10.9

The economy

GDP	$251bn	GDP per head	$23,495
GDP	Kc5,749bn	GDP per head in purchasing	
Av. ann. growth in real		power parity (USA=100)	67.8
GDP 2014–19	3.7%	Economic freedom index	73.8

Origins of GDP		**Components of GDP**	
	% of total		% of total
Agriculture	2.1	Private consumption	47.3
Industry, of which:	34.8	Public consumption	19.7
manufacturing	24.8	Investment	26.9
Services	63.0	Exports	74.4
		Imports	-68.4

Structure of employment

	% of total		% of labour force
Agriculture	2.7	Unemployed 2020	2.9
Industry	37.3	Av. ann. rate 2010–20	4.8
Services	60.1		

Energy

	m TOE		
Total output	26.2	Net energy imports as %	
Total consumption	44.5	of energy use	41
Consumption per head			
kg oil equivalent	4,167		

Inflation and finance

Consumer price			% change 2019–20
inflation 2020	3.2%	Narrow money (M1)	-1.8
Av. ann. inflation 2015–20	2.3%	Broad money	10.0
Deposit rate, Dec. 2020	0.21%		

Exchange rates

	end 2020		December 2020
Kc per $	21.39	Effective rates	2010 = 100
Kc per SDR	30.80	– nominal	99.7
Kc per €	26.24	– real	100.0

Trade

Principal exports		**Principal imports**	
	$bn fob		*$bn cif*
Machinery & transport equip.	117.6	Machinery & transport equip.	86.5
Semi-manufactures	28.2	Semi-manufactures	27.9
Misc. manufactured goods	24.2	Misc. manufactured goods	21.2
Chemicals	13.0	Chemicals	20.1
Total incl. others	**199.7**	Total incl. others	**179.6**

Main export destinations		**Main origins of imports**	
	% of total		*% of total*
Germany	31.8	Germany	28.5
Slovakia	7.6	China	9.2
Poland	6.0	Poland	9.0
France	5.1	Netherlands	6.1
EU28	83.9	EU28	76.1

Balance of payments, reserves and debt, $bn

Visible exports fob	156.1	Change in reserves	7.3
Visible imports fob	-145.6	Level of reserves	
Trade balance	10.5	end Dec.	149.9
Invisibles inflows	43.7	No. months of import cover	9.1
Invisibles outflows	-51.8	Official gold holdings, m oz	0.3
Net transfers	-1.5	Foreign debt	194.1
Current account balance	0.9	– as % of GDP	77.4
– as % of GDP	0.4	– as % of total exports	95.9
Capital balance	5.4	Debt service ratio	8.4
Overall balance	4.8		

Health and education

Health spending, % of GDP	7.7	Education spending, % of GDP	...
Doctors per 1,000 pop.	4.1	Enrolment, %: primary	101
Hospital beds per 1,000 pop.	6.6	secondary	102
At least basic drinking water,		tertiary	64
% of pop.	99.9		

Society

No. of households, m	4.8	Cost of living, Dec. 2020	
Av. no. per household	2.2	New York = 100	59
Marriages per 1,000 pop.	5.1	Cars per 1,000 pop.	504
Divorces per 1,000 pop.	2.3	Telephone lines per 100 pop.	14.0
Religion, % of pop.		Mobile telephone subscribers	
Non-religious	76.4	per 100 pop.	122.6
Christian	23.3	Internet access, %	80.9
Other	0.2	Broadband subs per 100 pop.	35.0
Hindu	<0.1	Broadband speed, Mbps	23.3
Jewish	<0.1		
Muslim	<0.1		

DENMARK

Area, sq km	42,920	Capital	Copenhagen
Arable as % of total land	59.8	Currency	Danish krone (DKr)

People

Population, m	5.8	Life expectancy: men	79.5 yrs
Pop. per sq km	135.1	women	83.3 yrs
Average annual rate of change		Adult literacy	...
in pop. 2020–25, %	0.4	Fertility rate (per woman)	1.8
Pop. aged 0–19, 2025, %	21.8	Urban population, %	88.0
Pop. aged 65 and over, 2025, %	21.3		per 1,000 pop.
No. of men per 100 women	98.8	Crude birth rate	11.1
Human Development Index	94.0	Crude death rate	10.0

The economy

GDP	$350bn	GDP per head	$60,170
GDP	DKr2,335bn	GDP per head in purchasing	
Av. ann. growth in real		power parity (USA=100)	95.1
GDP 2014–19	2.7%	Economic freedom index	77.8

Origins of GDP		**Components of GDP**	
	% of total		% of total
Agriculture	1.5	Private consumption	46.1
Industry, of which:	24.2	Public consumption	23.8
manufacturing	15.2	Investment	22.7
Services	74.3	Exports	58.3
		Imports	-51.0

Structure of employment

	% of total		% of labour force
Agriculture	2.2	Unemployed 2020	5.7
Industry	18.5	Av. ann. rate 2010–20	6.5
Services	79.2		

Energy

	m TOE		
Total output	15.1	Net energy imports as %	
Total consumption	18.4	of energy use	18
Consumption per head			
kg oil equivalent	3,188		

Inflation and finance

			% change 2019–20
Consumer price			
inflation 2020	0.3%	Narrow money (M1)	1.6
Av. ann. inflation 2015–20	0.6%	Broad money	9.2
Money market rate, Dec. 2020	-0.15%		

Exchange rates

	end 2020		December 2020
DKr per $	6.06	Effective rates	2010 = 100
DKr per SDR	8.72	– nominal	104.2
DKr per €	7.43	– real	96.7

Trade

Principal exports		Principal imports	
	$bn fob		*$bn cif*
Machinery & transport equip.	29.7	Machinery & transport equip.	32.9
Chemicals & related products	26.3	Food, drink & tobacco	13.4
Food, drink & tobacco	19.4	Chemicals & related products	12.1
Mineral fuels & lubricants	4.6	Mineral fuels & lubricants	6.4
Total incl. others	**110.0**	Total incl. others	**97.2**

Main export destinations		Main origins of imports	
	% of total		*% of total*
Germany	15.0	Germany	21.7
Sweden	10.6	Sweden	12.0
United States	10.3	Netherlands	8.0
United Kingdom	6.2	China	7.2
EU28	58.8	EU28	70.3

Balance of payments, reserves and aid, $bn

Visible exports fob	120.6	Overall balance	-3.2
Visible imports fob	-102.5	Change in reserves	-4.1
Trade balance	18.2	Level of reserves	
Invisibles inflows	114.6	end Dec.	66.8
Invisibles outflows	-96.7	No. months of import cover	4.0
Net transfers	-5.1	Official gold holdings, m oz	2.1
Current account balance	30.9	Aid given	2.6
– as % of GDP	8.8	– as % of GNI	0.7
Capital balance	-25.0		

Health and education

Health spending, % of GDP	10.1	Education spending, % of GDP	7.8
Doctors per 1,000 pop.	4.0	Enrolment, %: primary	101
Hospital beds per 1,000 pop.	2.6	secondary	130
At least basic drinking water,		tertiary	81
% of pop.	100		

Society

No. of households, m	2.4	Cost of living, Dec. 2020	
Av. no. per household	2.4	New York = 100	96
Marriages per 1,000 pop.	5.3	Cars per 1,000 pop.	429
Divorces per 1,000 pop.	2.6	Telephone lines per 100 pop.	17.4
Religion, % of pop.		Mobile telephone subscribers	
Christian	83.5	per 100 pop.	125.5
Non-religious	11.8	Internet access, %	96.5
Muslim	4.1	Broadband subs per 100 pop.	43.9
Hindu	0.4	Broadband speed, Mbps	49.2
Other	0.2		
Jewish	<0.1		

EGYPT

Area, sq km	1,001,450	Capital	Cairo
Arable as % of total land	2.9	Currency	Egyptian pound (£E)

People

Population, m	100.4	Life expectancy: men	70.2 yrs
Pop. per sq km	100.3	women	75.0 yrs
Average annual rate of change		Adult literacy	...
in pop. 2020–25, %	1.8	Fertility rate (per woman)	3.1
Pop. aged 0–19, 2025, %	42.1	Urban population, %	42.7
Pop. aged 65 and over, 2025, %	5.8		per 1,000 pop.
No. of men per 100 women	102.1	Crude birth rate	23.6
Human Development Index	70.7	Crude death rate	5.7

The economy

GDP	$303bn	GDP per head	$3,019
GDP	E£5,322bn	GDP per head in purchasing	
Av. ann. growth in real		power parity (USA=100)	18.8
GDP 2014–19	4.8%	Economic freedom index	55.7

Origins of GDP		**Components of GDP**	
	% of total		% of total
Agriculture	11.2	Private consumption	82.9
Industry, of which:	34.8	Public consumption	7.7
manufacturing	16.2	Investment	17.7
Services	53.9	Exports	17.5
		Imports	-25.8

Structure of employment

	% of total		% of labour force
Agriculture	20.6	Unemployed 2020	10.4
Industry	26.9	Av. ann. rate 2010–20	11.5
Services	52.4		

Energy

	m TOE		
Total output	95.6	Net energy imports as %	
Total consumption	101.9	of energy use	6
Consumption per head			
kg oil equivalent	1,015		

Inflation and finance

			% change 2019–20
Consumer price			
inflation 2020	5.7%	Narrow money (M1)	-10.5
Av. ann. inflation 2015–20	14.6%	Broad money	19.7
Deposit rate, Dec. 2020	7.40%		

Exchange rates

	end 2020		December 2020
£E per $	15.68	Effective rates	2010 = 100
£E per SDR	22.59	– nominal	...
£E per €	19.25	– real	...

Trade

Principal exports		**Principal imports**	
	$bn fob		*$bn cif*
Petroleum & products	11.6	Petroleum & products	11.5
Food	3.4	Machinery & equip.	11.4
Chemicals	2.8	Chemicals	6.3
Finished goods incl. textiles	2.5	Vehicles	4.3
Total incl. others	**28.5**	Total incl. others	**66.0**

Main export destinations		**Main origins of imports**	
	% of total		*% of total*
United States	7.2	China	15.3
United Arab Emirates	6.8	Saudi Arabia	6.6
Turkey	5.7	United States	6.6
Saudi Arabia	5.6	Germany	5.5

Balance of payments, reserves and debt, $bn

Visible exports fob	28.5	Change in reserves	2.7
Visible imports fob	-57.8	Level of reserves	
Trade balance	-29.3	end Dec.	44.5
Invisibles inflows	26.1	No. months of import cover	5.8
Invisibles outflows	-33.8	Official gold holdings, m oz	2.5
Net transfers	26.8	Foreign debt	115.1
Current account balance	-10.2	– as % of GDP	33.6
– as % of GDP	-3.4	– as % of total exports	141.5
Capital balance	12.8	Debt service ratio	10.8
Overall balance	-2.0		

Health and education

Health spending, % of GDP	5.0	Education spending, % of GDP	...
Doctors per 1,000 pop.	0.5	Enrolment, %: primary	106
Hospital beds per 1,000 pop.	1.4	secondary	89
At least basic drinking water,		tertiary	...
% of pop.	99.1		

Society

No. of households, m	24.5	Cost of living, Dec. 2020	
Av. no. per household	4.1	New York = 100	54
Marriages per 1,000 pop.	9.6	Cars per 1,000 pop.	48
Divorces per 1,000 pop.	2.1	Telephone lines per 100 pop.	8.7
Religion, % of pop.		Mobile telephone subscribers	
Muslim	94.9	per 100 pop.	95.0
Christian	5.1	Internet access, %	57.3
Hindu	<0.1	Broadband subs per 100 pop.	7.6
Jewish	<0.1	Broadband speed, Mbps	1.6
Non-religious	<0.1		
Other	<0.1		

FINLAND

Area, sq km	338,450	Capital	Helsinki
Arable as % of total land	7.4	Currency	Euro (€)

People

Population, m	5.5	Life expectancy: men	79.8 yrs
Pop. per sq km	16.3	women	85.5 yrs
Average annual rate of change		Adult literacy	...
in pop. 2020–25, %	0.1	Fertility rate (per woman)	1.4
Pop. aged 0–19, 2025, %	20.4	Urban population, %	85.4
Pop. aged 65 and over, 2025, %	24.4		per 1,000 pop.
No. of men per 100 women	97.3	Crude birth rate	8.6
Human Development Index	93.8	Crude death rate	10.1

The economy

GDP	$269bn	GDP per head	$48,783
GDP	€241bn	GDP per head in purchasing	
Av. ann. growth in real		power parity (USA=100)	81.4
GDP 2014–19	1.9%	Economic freedom index	76.1

Origins of GDP		**Components of GDP**	
	% of total		% of total
Agriculture	2.8	Private consumption	52.4
Industry, of which:	27.7	Public consumption	23.0
manufacturing	16.7	Investment	24.2
Services	69.5	Exports	40.2
		Imports	-39.9

Structure of employment

	% of total		% of labour force
Agriculture	3.8	Unemployed 2020	7.8
Industry	21.6	Av. ann. rate 2010–20	8.1
Services	74.6		

Energy

	m TOE		
Total output	13.4	Net energy imports as %	
Total consumption	30.9	of energy use	56
Consumption per head			
kg oil equivalent	5,585		

Inflation and finance

			% change 2019–20
Consumer price			
inflation 2020	0.4%	Narrow money (M1)	13.5
Av. ann. inflation 2015–20	0.8%	Broad money	10.3
Deposit rate, Dec. 2020	0.04%		

Exchange rates

	end 2020		December 2020
€ per $	0.81	Effective rates	2010 = 100
€ per SDR	1.17	– nominal	106.8
		– real	98.2

Trade

Principal exports		**Principal imports**	
	$bn fob		*$bn cif*
Machinery & transport equip.	24.3	Machinery & transport equip.	26.4
Mineral fuels & lubricants	6.9	Mineral fuels & lubricants	11.4
Raw materials	6.9	Chemicals & related products	8.3
Chemicals & related products	6.7	Food, drink & tobacco	5.3
Total incl. others	**72.7**	Total incl. others	**70.1**

Main export destinations		**Main origins of imports**	
	% of total		*% of total*
Germany	14.6	Germany	18.5
Sweden	10.3	Sweden	17.1
United States	7.6	Russia	14.3
Netherlands	6.1	Netherlands	8.5
EU28	58.8	EU28	71.4

Balance of payments, reserves and aid, $bn

Visible exports fob	72.6	Overall balance	0.6
Visible imports fob	-70.1	Change in reserves	1.1
Trade balance	2.5	Level of reserves	
Invisibles inflows	59.2	end Dec.	11.4
Invisibles outflows	-59.5	No. months of import cover	1.1
Net transfers	-2.6	Official gold holdings, m oz	1.6
Current account balance	-0.5	Aid given	1.1
– as % of GDP	-0.2	– as % of GNI	0.4
Capital balance	10.5		

Health and education

Health spending, % of GDP	9.0	Education spending, % of GDP	6.4
Doctors per 1,000 pop.	3.8	Enrolment, %: primary	100
Hospital beds per 1,000 pop.	3.6	secondary	155
At least basic drinking water,		tertiary	90
% of pop.	100		

Society

No. of households, m	2.7	Cost of living, Dec. 2020	
Av. no. per household	2.0	New York = 100	86
Marriages per 1,000 pop.	4.0	Cars per 1,000 pop.	481
Divorces per 1,000 pop.	2.4	Telephone lines per 100 pop.	4.9
Religion, % of pop.		Mobile telephone subscribers	
Christian	81.6	per 100 pop.	129.2
Non-religious	17.6	Internet access, %	89.6
Muslim	0.8	Broadband subs per 100 pop.	32.5
Hindu	<0.1	Broadband speed, Mbps	29.3
Jewish	<0.1		
Other	<0.1		

FRANCE

Area, sq km	549,086	Capital	Paris
Arable as % of total land	33.1	Currency	Euro (€)

People

Population, m	65.1	Life expectancy: men	80.3 yrs
Pop. per sq km	118.6	women	85.8 yrs
Average annual rate of change		Adult literacy	...
in pop. 2020–25, %	0.2	Fertility rate (per woman)	1.9
Pop. aged 0–19, 2025, %	23.0	Urban population, %	80.7
Pop. aged 65 and over, 2025, %	22.4		per 1,000 pop.
No. of men per 100 women	93.8	Crude birth rate	10.9
Human Development Index	90.1	Crude death rate	9.5

The economy

GDP	$2,716bn	GDP per head	$40,494
GDP	€2,426bn	GDP per head in purchasing	
Av. ann. growth in real		power parity (USA=100)	78.1
GDP 2014–19	1.6%	Economic freedom index	65.7

Origins of GDP		**Components of GDP**	
	% of total		% of total
Agriculture	1.8	Private consumption	53.7
Industry, of which:	19.3	Public consumption	23.1
manufacturing	11.0	Investment	24.2
Services	78.9	Exports	31.8
		Imports	-32.8

Structure of employment

	% of total		% of labour force
Agriculture	2.5	Unemployed 2020	8.6
Industry	20.4	Av. ann. rate 2010–20	9.4
Services	77.0		

Energy

	m TOE		
Total output	133.5	Net energy imports as %	
Total consumption	259.7	of energy use	49
Consumption per head			
kg oil equivalent	3,988		

Inflation and finance

			% change 2019–20
Consumer price			
inflation 2020	0.5%	Narrow money (M1)	13.5
Av. ann. inflation 2015–20	1.1%	Broad money	10.3
Deposit rate, Dec. 2020	0.06%		

Exchange rates

	end 2020		December 2020
€ per $	0.81	Effective rates	2010 = 100
€ per SDR	1.17	– nominal	103.0
		– real	94.7

Trade

Principal exports

	$bn fob
Machinery & transport equip.	222.2
Chemicals & related products	107.6
Food, drink and tobacco	66.8
Mineral fuels & lubricants	17.6
Total incl. others	**570.0**

Principal imports

	$bn cif
Machinery & transport equip.	239.5
Chemicals & related products	85.7
Mineral fuels & lubricants	66.1
Food, drink and tobacco	57.4
Total incl. others	**635.0**

Main export destinations

	% of total
Germany	13.9
United States	8.3
Italy	7.5
Spain	7.4
EU28	58.2

Main origins of imports

	% of total
Germany	17.6
Belgium	9.8
Italy	8.1
Netherlands	8.0
EU28	68.0

Balance of payments, reserves and aid, $bn

Visible exports fob	597.1	Overall balance	3.2
Visible imports fob	-649.7	Change in reserves	22.1
Trade balance	-52.6	Level of reserves	
Invisibles inflows	506.1	end Dec.	188.4
Invisibles outflows	-421.6	No. months of import cover	2.1
Net transfers	-50.4	Official gold holdings, m oz	78.3
Current account balance	-18.4	Aid given	12.2
– as % of GDP	-0.7	– as % of GNI	0.4
Capital balance	37.8		

Health and education

Health spending, % of GDP	11.3	Education spending, % of GDP	5.5
Doctors per 1,000 pop.	3.3	Enrolment, %: primary	103
Hospital beds per 1,000 pop.	5.9	secondary	104
At least basic drinking water,		tertiary	68
% of pop.	100		

Society

No. of households, m	30.0	Cost of living, Dec. 2020	
Av. no. per household	2.2	New York = 100	103
Marriages per 1,000 pop.	3.5	Cars per 1,000 pop.	497
Divorces per 1,000 pop.	1.9	Telephone lines per 100 pop.	58.0
Religion, % of pop.		Mobile telephone subscribers	
Christian	63.0	per 100 pop.	110.6
Non-religious	28.0	Internet access, %	83.3
Muslim	7.5	Broadband subs per 100 pop.	45.7
Other	1.0	Broadband speed, Mbps	30.4
Jewish	0.5		
Hindu	<0.1		

GERMANY

Area, sq km	357,580	Capital	Berlin
Arable as % of total land	33.6	Currency	Euro (€)

People

Population, m	83.5	Life expectancy: men	79.6 yrs
Pop. per sq km	233.5	women	84.1 yrs
Average annual rate of change		Adult literacy	...
in pop. 2020–25, %	-0.1	Fertility rate (per woman)	1.6
Pop. aged 0–19, 2025, %	18.8	Urban population, %	77.4
Pop. aged 65 and over, 2025, %	23.5		per 1,000 pop.
No. of men per 100 women	97.8	Crude birth rate	9.4
Human Development Index	94.7	Crude death rate	11.7

The economy

GDP	$3,861bn	GDP per head	$46,445
GDP	€3,449bn	GDP per head in purchasing	
Av. ann. growth in real		power parity (USA=100)	88.1
GDP 2014–19	1.6%	Economic freedom index	72.5

Origins of GDP		**Components of GDP**	
	% of total		% of total
Agriculture	0.8	Private consumption	52.4
Industry, of which:	29.7	Public consumption	20.4
manufacturing	21.2	Investment	21.4
Services	69.5	Exports	46.9
		Imports	-41.1

Structure of employment

	% of total		% of labour force
Agriculture	1.2	Unemployed 2020	4.3
Industry	27.2	Av. ann. rate 2010–20	4.7
Services	71.6		

Energy

	m TOE		
Total output	121.3	Net energy imports as %	
Total consumption	349.4	of energy use	65
Consumption per head			
kg oil equivalent	4,183		

Inflation and finance

		% change 2019–20	
Consumer price			
inflation 2020	0.4%	Narrow money (M1)	13.5
Av. ann. inflation 2015–20	1.1%	Broad money	10.3
Deposit rate, Dec. 2020	-0.42%		

Exchange rates

	end 2020		December 2020
€ per $	0.81	Effective rates	2010 = 100
€ per SDR	1.17	– nominal	103.8
		– real	96.7

Trade

Principal exports		**Principal imports**	
	$bn fob		*$bn cif*
Machinery & transport equip.	732.9	Machinery & transport equip.	474.6
Chemicals & related products	242.3	Chemicals & related products	176.8
Food, drink and tobacco	77.6	Mineral fuels & lubricants	107.3
Mineral fuels & lubricants	37.7	Food, drink and tobacco	89.5
Total incl. others	**1,492.8**	Total incl. others	**1,239.4**

Main export destinations		**Main origins of imports**	
	% of total		*% of total*
United States	9.0	Netherlands	14.0
France	8.0	China	7.0
China	7.2	France	6.3
Netherlands	6.9	Belgium	5.9
EU28	58.4	EU28	66.8

Balance of payments, reserves and aid, $bn

Visible exports fob	1,460.9	Overall balance	-0.6
Visible imports fob	-1,218.4	Change in reserves	25.4
Trade balance	242.5	Level of reserves	
Invisibles inflows	612.4	end Dec.	223.1
Invisibles outflows	-511.0	No. months of import cover	1.5
Net transfers	-54.3	Official gold holdings, m oz	108.2
Current account balance	289.6	Aid given	24.2
– as % of GDP	7.5	– as % of GNI	0.6
Capital balance	-229.0		

Health and education

Health spending, % of GDP	11.4	Education spending, % of GDP	4.9
Doctors per 1,000 pop.	4.2	Enrolment, %: primary	104
Hospital beds per 1,000 pop.	8.0	secondary	98
At least basic drinking water,		tertiary	70
% of pop.	100		

Society

No. of households, m	40.9	Cost of living, Dec. 2020	
Av. no. per household	2.0	New York = 100	75
Marriages per 1,000 pop.	5.4	Cars per 1,000 pop.	540
Divorces per 1,000 pop.	1.8	Telephone lines per 100 pop.	48.4
Religion, % of pop.		Mobile telephone subscribers	
Christian	68.7	per 100 pop.	128.4
Non-religious	24.7	Internet access, %	88.1
Muslim	5.8	Broadband subs per 100 pop.	42.0
Other	0.5	Broadband speed, Mbps	24.6
Jewish	0.3		
Hindu	<0.1		

GREECE

Area, sq km	131,960	Capital	Athens
Arable as % of total land	16.6	Currency	Euro (€)

People

Population, m	10.5	Life expectancy: men	80.5 yrs
Pop. per sq km	79.6	women	85.1 yrs
Average annual rate of change		Adult literacy	97.9
in pop. 2020–25, %	-0.5	Fertility rate (per woman)	1.3
Pop. aged 0–19, 2025, %	17.4	Urban population, %	79.4
Pop. aged 65 and over, 2025, %	24.4		per 1,000 pop.
No. of men per 100 women	96.4	Crude birth rate	6.9
Human Development Index	88.8	Crude death rate	11.4

The economy

GDP	$210bn	GDP per head	$19,583
GDP	€187bn	GDP per head in purchasing	
Av. ann. growth in real		power parity (USA=100)	49.8
GDP 2014–19	0.9%	Economic freedom index	60.9

Origins of GDP		**Components of GDP**	
	% of total		% of total
Agriculture	4.4	Private consumption	68.0
Industry, of which:	14.9	Public consumption	19.5
manufacturing	8.9	Investment	12.5
Services	80.8	Exports	37.2
		Imports	-37.2

Structure of employment

	% of total		% of labour force
Agriculture	11.6	Unemployed 2020	16.9
Industry	15.3	Av. ann. rate 2010–20	21.1
Services	73.1		

Energy

	m TOE		
Total output	8.7	Net energy imports as %	
Total consumption	29.5	of energy use	71
Consumption per head			
kg oil equivalent	2,815		

Inflation and finance

			% change 2019–20
Consumer price			
inflation 2020	-1.3%	Narrow money (M1)	13.5
Av. ann. inflation 2015–20	0.2%	Broad money	10.3
Deposit rate, Dec. 2020	0.12%		

Exchange rates

	end 2020		December 2020
			2010 = 100
€ per $	0.81	Effective rates	107.1
€ per SDR	1.17	– nominal	107.1
		– real	87.7

Trade

Principal exports

	$bn fob
Mineral fuels & lubricants	11.9
Food, drink and tobacco	6.2
Chemicals & related products	4.6
Machinery & transport equip.	3.6
Total incl. others	**37.9**

Principal imports

	$bn cif
Mineral fuels & lubricants	16.8
Machinery & transport equip.	11.8
Chemicals & related products	9.7
Food, drink and tobacco	7.6
Total incl. others	**62.5**

Main export destinations

	% of total
Italy	10.9
Germany	6.8
Cyprus	6.1
Turkey	5.8
EU28	56.1

Main origins of imports

	% of total
Germany	11.1
Italy	8.7
Iraq	8.2
Russia	7.3
EU28	53.3

Balance of payments, reserves and debt, $bn

Visible exports fob	36.3	Overall balance	4.9
Visible imports fob	-61.9	Change in reserves	0.9
Trade balance	-25.6	Level of reserves	
Invisibles inflows	51.8	end Dec.	8.5
Invisibles outflows	-30.0	No. months of import cover	1.1
Net transfers	0.7	Official gold holdings, m oz	3.6
Current account balance	-3.1	Aid given	0.4
– as % of GDP	-1.5	– as % of GNI	0.2
Capital balance	6.4		

Health and education

Health spending, % of GDP	7.7	Education spending, % of GDP	...
Doctors per 1,000 pop.	5.5	Enrolment, %: primary	99
Hospital beds per 1,000 pop.	4.2	secondary	105
At least basic drinking water,		tertiary	143
% of pop.	100		

Society

No. of households, m	4.5	Cost of living, Dec. 2020	
Av. no. per household	2.3	New York = 100	61
Marriages per 1,000 pop.	4.4	Cars per 1,000 pop.	500
Divorces per 1,000 pop.	1.8	Telephone lines per 100 pop.	46.0
Religion, % of pop.		Mobile telephone subscribers	
Christian	88.1	per 100 pop.	113.4
Non-religious	6.1	Internet access, %	75.7
Muslim	5.3	Broadband subs per 100 pop.	39.6
Other	0.3	Broadband speed, Mbps	13.4
Hindu	0.1		
Jewish	<0.1		

HONG KONG

Area, sq km	1,110	Capital	Victoria
Arable as % of total land	2.9	Currency	Hong Kong dollar (HK$)

People

Population, m	7.4	Life expectancy: men	82.4 yrs
Pop. per sq km	6,666.7	women	88.2 yrs
Average annual rate of change		Adult literacy	...
in pop. 2020–25, %	0.7	Fertility rate (per woman)	1.4
Pop. aged 0–19, 2025, %	17.6	Urban population, %	100.0
Pop. aged 65 and over, 2025, %	22.1		per 1,000 pop.
No. of men per 100 women	84.8	Crude birth rate	10.8
Human Development Index	94.9	Crude death rate	7.2

The economy

GDP	$366bn	GDP per head	$48,713
GDP	HK$2,866bn	GDP per head in purchasing	
Av. ann. growth in real		power parity (USA=100)	95.7
GDP 2014–19	2.0%	Economic freedom index	...

Origins of GDP

Components of GDP

	% of total		% of total
Agriculture	0.1	Private consumption	68.7
Industry, of which:	6.5	Public consumption	10.8
manufacturing	1.1	Investment	18.9
Services	93.4	Exports	177.5
		Imports	-175.8

Structure of employment

	% of total		% of labour force
Agriculture	0.2	Unemployed 2020	5.8
Industry	11.1	Av. ann. rate 2010–20	3.6
Services	88.8		

Energy

	m TOE		
Total output	0.0	Net energy imports as %	
Total consumption	33.9	of energy use	100
Consumption per head			
kg oil equivalent	4,555		

Inflation and finance

			% change 2019–20
Consumer price			
inflation 2020	0.3%	Narrow money (M1)	19.8
Av. ann. inflation 2015–20	1.9%	Broad money	6.0
Deposit rate, Dec. 2020	0.02%		

Exchange rates

	end 2020		December 2020
HK$ per $	7.75	Effective rates	2010 = 100
HK$ per SDR	11.17	– nominal	105.5
HK$ per €	9.51	– real	...

Trade

Principal exports[a]		**Principal imports**[a]	
	$bn fob		*$bn cif*
Capital goods	200.2	Raw materials &	
Semi-finished goods	201.1	semi-manufactures	227.9
Consumer goods	91.6	Capital goods & raw materials	193.0
Foodstuffs	7.5	Consumer goods	110.0
		Foodstuffs	23.5
Total incl. others	**509.6**	Total incl. others	**563.8**

Main export destinations		**Main origins of imports**	
	% of total		*% of total*
China	55.3	China	45.7
United States	7.3	Taiwan	7.3
India	2.9	Singapore	6.5
Japan	2.9	South Korea	5.8

Balance of payments, reserves and debt, $bn

Visible exports fob	547.8	Change in reserves	16.7
Visible imports fob	-563.9	Level of reserves	
Trade balance	-16.1	end Dec.	441.3
Invisibles inflows	314.8	No. months of import cover	6.3
Invisibles outflows	-274.2	Official gold holdings, m oz	0.1
Net transfers	-2.8	Foreign debt	710.0
Current account balance	21.8	– as % of GDP	194.1
– as % of GDP	6.0	– as % of total exports	82.1
Capital balance	-31.5	Debt service ratio	9.5
Overall balance	-1.1		

Health and education

Health spending, % of GDP	...	Education spending, % of GDP	3.8
Doctors per 1,000 pop.	...	Enrolment, %: primary	109
Hospital beds per 1,000 pop.	...	secondary	108
At least basic drinking water,		tertiary	81
% of pop.	100		

Society

No. of households, m	2.6	Cost of living, Dec. 2020	
Av. no. per household	2.8	New York = 100	103
Marriages per 1,000 pop.	5.9	Cars per 1,000 pop.	...
Divorces per 1,000 pop.	...	Telephone lines per 100 pop.	54.2
Religion, % of pop.		Mobile telephone subscribers	
Non-religious	56.1	per 100 pop.	288.5
Christian	14.3	Internet access, %	91.7
Other	14.2	Broadband subs per 100 pop.	37.7
Buddhist	13.2	Broadband speed, Mbps	31.4
Muslim	1.8		
Hindu	0.4		

a Including re-exports.
Note: Hong Kong became a Special Administrative Region of China on July 1 1997.

HUNGARY

Area, sq km	93,030	Capital	Budapest
Arable as % of total land	47.4	Currency	Forint (Ft)

People

Population, m	9.7	Life expectancy: men	73.8 yrs
Pop. per sq km	104.3	women	80.7 yrs
Average annual rate of change		Adult literacy	...
in pop. 2020–25, %	-0.3	Fertility rate (per woman)	1.5
Pop. aged 0–19, 2025, %	19.3	Urban population, %	71.6
Pop. aged 65 and over, 2025, %	21.7		per 1,000 pop.
No. of men per 100 women	90.8	Crude birth rate	9.3
Human Development Index	85.4	Crude death rate	13.0

The economy

GDP	$163bn	GDP per head	$16,732
GDP	Ft47,514bn	GDP per head in purchasing	
Av. ann. growth in real		power parity (USA=100)	53.5
GDP 2014–19	4.0%	Economic freedom index	67.2

Origins of GDP		**Components of GDP**	
	% of total		% of total
Agriculture	3.9	Private consumption	49.1
Industry, of which:	29.5	Public consumption	19.6
manufacturing	20.9	Investment	28.2
Services	66.6	Exports	82.2
		Imports	-79.1

Structure of employment

	% of total		% of labour force
Agriculture	4.7	Unemployed 2020	4.3
Industry	32.1	Av. ann. rate 2010–20	7.2
Services	63.2		

Energy

	m TOE		
Total output	9.3	Net energy imports as %	
Total consumption	26.7	of energy use	65
Consumption per head			
kg oil equivalent	2,759		

Inflation and finance

Consumer price		% change 2019–20	
inflation 2020	3.3%	Narrow money (M1)	40.0
Av. ann. inflation 2015–20	2.5%	Broad money	20.9
Deposit rate, Dec. 2020	0.47%		

Exchange rates

	end 2020		December 2020
Ft per $	297.36	Effective rates	2010 = 100
Ft per SDR	428.28	– nominal	82.3
Ft per €	364.89	– real	85.5

Trade

Principal exports		**Principal imports**	
	$bn fob		*$bn cif*
Machinery & equipment	70.1	Machinery & equipment	56.5
Manufactured goods	37.4	Manufactured goods	42.0
Food, drink & tobacco	8.5	Fuels & energy	9.4
Raw materials	2.8	Food, drink & tobacco	6.2
Total incl. others	**122.0**	Total incl. others	**117.2**

Main export destinations		**Main origins of imports**	
	% of total		*% of total*
Germany	28.1	Germany	25.6
Slovakia	5.4	China	7.2
Romania	5.3	Austria	6.5
Italy	5.2	Poland	5.8
EU28	81.8	EU28	73.6

Balance of payments, reserves and debt, $bn

Visible exports fob	104.2	Change in reserves	0.5
Visible imports fob	-107.6	Level of reserves	
Trade balance	-3.4	end Dec.	31.8
Invisibles inflows	46.5	No. months of import cover	2.5
Invisibles outflows	-42.7	Official gold holdings, m oz	1.0
Net transfers	-1.0	Foreign debt	147.3
Current account balance	-0.6	– as % of GDP	90.3
– as % of GDP	-0.4	– as % of total exports	98.6
Capital balance	2.8	Debt service ratio	49.0
Overall balance	0.3		

Health and education

Health spending, % of GDP	6.7	Education spending, % of GDP	4.7
Doctors per 1,000 pop.	3.4	Enrolment, %: primary	97
Hospital beds per 1,000 pop.	7.0	secondary	104
At least basic drinking water,		tertiary	50
% of pop.	100		

Society

No. of households, m	4.1	Cost of living, Dec. 2020	
Av. no. per household	2.4	New York = 100	50
Marriages per 1,000 pop.	5.2	Cars per 1,000 pop.	335
Divorces per 1,000 pop.	1.7	Telephone lines per 100 pop.	31.5
Religion, % of pop.		Mobile telephone subscribers	
Christian	81.0	per 100 pop.	106.1
Non-religious	18.6	Internet access, %	80.4
Other	0.2	Broadband subs per 100 pop.	32.9
Jewish	0.1	Broadband speed, Mbps	31.1
Hindu	<0.1		
Muslim	<0.1		

INDIA

Area, sq km	3,287,259	Capital	New Delhi
Arable as % of total land	52.6	Currency	Indian rupee (Rs)

People

Population, m	1,366.4	Life expectancy: men	69.2 yrs
Pop. per sq km	415.7	women	71.8 yrs
Average annual rate of change		Adult literacy	74.4
in pop. 2020–25, %	0.9	Fertility rate (per woman)	2.1
Pop. aged 0–19, 2025, %	32.9	Urban population, %	34.5
Pop. aged 65 and over, 2025, %	7.6		per 1,000 pop.
No. of men per 100 women	108.2	Crude birth rate	16.9
Human Development Index	64.5	Crude death rate	7.4

The economy

GDP	$2,869bn	GDP per head	$2,100
GDP	Rs203,398bn	GDP per head in purchasing	
Av. ann. growth in real		power parity (USA=100)	10.7
GDP 2014–19	6.7%	Economic freedom index	56.5

Origins of GDP		**Components of GDP**	
	% of total		% of total
Agriculture	17.6	Private consumption	60.3
Industry, of which:	29.0	Public consumption	12.0
manufacturing	16.3	Investment	29.7
Services	53.4	Exports	18.4
		Imports	-21.1

Structure of employment

	% of total		% of labour force
Agriculture	42.6	Unemployed 2020	7.1
Industry	25.1	Av. ann. rate 2010–20	5.7
Services	32.3		

Energy

	m TOE		
Total output	433.5	Net energy imports as %	
Total consumption	790.1	of energy use	45
Consumption per head			
kg oil equivalent	578		

Inflation and finance

			% change 2019–20
Consumer price			
inflation 2020	6.2%	Narrow money (M1)	14.8
Av. ann. inflation 2015–20	4.5%	Broad money	12.5
Money market rate, Dec. 2020	3.87%		

Exchange rates

	end 2020		December 2020
			2010 = 100
Rs per $	73.05	Effective rates	
Rs per SDR	105.22	– nominal	...
Rs per €	89.64	– real	...

Trade

Principal exports		**Principal imports**	
	$bn fob		*$bn cif*
Engineering products	78.7	Petroleum & products	130.5
Petroleum & products	41.2	Electronic goods	52.5
Gems & jewellery	35.9	Machinery	39.6
Agricultural products	34.4	Gold & silver	31.0
Total incl. others	**313.1**	Total incl. others	**474.0**

Main export destinations		**Main origins of imports**	
	% of total		*% of total*
United States	16.4	China	13.6
United Arab Emirates	9.1	United States	6.9
China	5.2	United Arab Emirates	6.0
Hong Kong	3.6	Saudi Arabia	5.4

Balance of payments, reserves and debt, $bn

Visible exports fob	331.3	Change in reserves	64.2
Visible imports fob	-488.9	Level of reserves	
Trade balance	-157.7	end Dec.	463.3
Invisibles inflows	238.1	No. months of import cover	8.3
Invisibles outflows	-183.3	Official gold holdings, m oz	20.4
Net transfers	73.1	Foreign debt	560.0
Current account balance	-29.8	– as % of GDP	19.5
– as % of GDP	-1.0	– as % of total exports	85.8
Capital balance	85.0	Debt service ratio	7.9
Overall balance	55.8		

Health and education

Health spending, % of GDP	3.5	Education spending, % of GDP	...
Doctors per 1,000 pop.	0.9	Enrolment, %: primary	97
Hospital beds per 1,000 pop.	0.5	secondary	74
At least basic drinking water,		tertiary	29
% of pop.	92.7		

Society

No. of households, m	299.6	Cost of living, Dec. 2020	
Av. no. per household	4.6	New York = 100	42
Marriages per 1,000 pop.	...	Cars per 1,000 pop.	19
Divorces per 1,000 pop.	...	Telephone lines per 100 pop.	1.5
Religion, % of pop.		Mobile telephone subscribers	
Hindu	79.5	per 100 pop.	84.3
Muslim	14.4	Internet access, %	20.1
Other	3.6	Broadband subs per 100 pop.	1.4
Christian	2.5	Broadband speed, Mbps	8.7
Jewish	<0.1		
Non-religious	<0.1		

INDONESIA

Area, sq km	1,913,580	Capital	Jakarta
Arable as % of total land	14.0	Currency	Rupiah (Rp)

People

Population, m	270.6	Life expectancy: men	70.1 yrs
Pop. per sq km	141.4	women	74.6 yrs
Average annual rate of change		Adult literacy	95.7
in pop. 2020–25, %	1.0	Fertility rate (per woman)	2.2
Pop. aged 0–19, 2025, %	32.7	Urban population, %	56.0
Pop. aged 65 and over, 2025, %	7.6		per 1,000 pop.
No. of men per 100 women	101.4	Crude birth rate	16.8
Human Development Index	71.8	Crude death rate	6.8

The economy

GDP	$1,119bn	GDP per head	$4,136
GDP	Rs15,833,943bn	GDP per head in purchasing	
Av. ann. growth in real		power parity (USA=100)	18.9
GDP 2014–19	5.0%	Economic freedom index	66.9

Origins of GDP		**Components of GDP**	
	% of total		% of total
Agriculture	13.3	Private consumption	57.9
Industry, of which:	40.6	Public consumption	8.8
manufacturing	20.5	Investment	33.8
Services	46.1	Exports	18.4
		Imports	-18.9

Structure of employment

	% of total		% of labour force
Agriculture	28.5	Unemployed 2020	4.1
Industry	22.4	Av. ann. rate 2010–20	4.4
Services	49.1		

Energy

	m TOE		
Total output	399.4	Net energy imports as %	
Total consumption	201.6	of energy use	-98
Consumption per head			
kg oil equivalent	745		

Inflation and finance

			% change 2019–20
Consumer price			
inflation 2020	2.0%	Narrow money (M1)	0.4
Av. ann. inflation 2015–20	3.1%	Broad money	12.4
Deposit rate, Dec. 2020	4.38%		

Exchange rates

	end 2020		December 2020
Rp per $	14,105.01	Effective rates	2010 = 100
Rp per SDR	20,314.99	– nominal	...
Rp per €	17,308.25	– real	...

Trade

Principal exports		**Principal imports**	
	$bn fob		*$bn cif*
Manufactured goods	123.0	Raw materials & auxiliary	
Mining & other sector products	34.2	materials	118.4
Agricultural goods	5.8	Capital goods	29.1
Unclassified exports	1.9	Consumer goods	23.6
Total incl. others	**167.7**	Total incl. others	**171.3**

Main export destinations		**Main origins of imports**	
	% of total		*% of total*
China	16.7	China	25.8
United States	10.6	Singapore	10.1
Japan	9.5	Japan	9.0
Singapore	7.7	Thailand	5.4

Balance of payments, reserves and debt, $bn

Visible exports fob	168.5	Change in reserves	8.5
Visible imports fob	-164.9	Level of reserves	
Trade balance	3.5	end Dec.	129.2
Invisibles inflows	39.0	No. months of import cover	6.3
Invisibles outflows	-80.4	Official gold holdings, m oz	2.5
Net transfers	7.6	Foreign debt	402.1
Current account balance	-30.3	– as % of GDP	35.9
– as % of GDP	-2.7	– as % of total exports	183.5
Capital balance	36.6	Debt service ratio	37.3
Overall balance	4.7		

Health and education

Health spending, % of GDP	2.9	Education spending, % of GDP	3.6
Doctors per 1,000 pop.	0.4	Enrolment, %: primary	106
Hospital beds per 1,000 pop.	1.0	secondary	89
At least basic drinking water,		tertiary	36
% of pop.	89.3		

Society

No. of households, m	69.9	Cost of living, Dec. 2020	
Av. no. per household	3.9	New York = 100	56
Marriages per 1,000 pop.	...	Cars per 1,000 pop.	57
Divorces per 1,000 pop.	...	Telephone lines per 100 pop.	3.6
Religion, % of pop.		Mobile telephone subscribers	
Muslim	87.2	per 100 pop.	126.1
Christian	9.9	Internet access, %	47.7
Hindu	1.7	Broadband subs per 100 pop.	3.8
Other	1.1	Broadband speed, Mbps	6.6
Jewish	<0.1		
Non-religious	<0.1		

IRAN

Area, sq km	1,745,150	Capital	Tehran
Arable as % of total land	9.0	Currency	Rial (IR)

People

Population, m	82.9	Life expectancy: men	76.2 yrs
Pop. per sq km	47.5	women	78.5 yrs
Average annual rate of change		Adult literacy	...
in pop. 2020–25, %	1.1	Fertility rate (per woman)	2.1
Pop. aged 0–19, 2025, %	31.2	Urban population, %	75.4
Pop. aged 65 and over, 2025, %	8.0		per 1,000 pop.
No. of men per 100 women	102.0	Crude birth rate	16.3
Human Development Index	78.3	Crude death rate	4.8

The economy

GDP	$765bn	GDP per head	$8,648
GDP	IR24,412,569bn	GDP per head in purchasing	
Av. ann. growth in real		power parity (USA=100)	19.8
GDP 2014–19	0.3%	Economic freedom index	47.2

Origins of GDP[a]		**Components of GDP**[a]	
	% of total		% of total
Agriculture	12.2	Private consumption	49.7
Industry, of which:	31.8	Public consumption	11.6
manufacturing	14.8	Investment	40.7
Services	56.0	Exports	25.3
		Imports	-30.9

Structure of employment

	% of total		% of labour force
Agriculture	17.4	Unemployed 2020	11.0
Industry	31.4	Av. ann. rate 2010–20	11.8
Services	51.2		

Energy

	m TOE		
Total output	455.5	Net energy imports as %	
Total consumption	294.7	of energy use	-55
Consumption per head			
kg oil equivalent	3,554		

Inflation and finance

			% change 2019–20
Consumer price			
inflation 2020	36.5%	Narrow money (M1)	65.0
Av. ann. inflation 2015–20	23.4%	Broad money	39.0
Deposit rate, Feb. 2017	12.70%		

Exchange rates

	end 2020		December 2020
IR per $	42,000.00	Effective rates	2010 = 100
IR per SDR	60,491.28	– nominal	29.7
IR per €	51,538.20	– real	152.7

Trade

Principal exports[b]

	$bn fob
Oil & gas	60.7
Petrochemicals	9.2
Rubber & plastic products	5.6
Basic metals & articles	4.6
Total incl. others	**93.1**

Principal imports[b]

	$bn fob
Machinery & transport equip.	16.2
Foodstuffs	8.0
Chemicals	6.4
Intermediate goods	4.8
Total incl. others	**60.8**

Main export destinations

	% of total
China	41.5
Turkey	11.2
India	10.5
South Korea	6.3

Main origins of imports

	% of total
China	25.9
India	13.4
United Arab Emirates	11.1
Turkey	8.7

Balance of payments[a], reserves and debt, $bn

Visible exports fob	59.4	Change in reserves	-100.1
Visible imports fob	-52.2	Level of reserves	
Trade balance	7.2	end Dec.	12.4
Invisibles inflows	12.6	No. months of import cover	2.2
Invisibles outflows	-16.7	Official gold holdings, m oz	...
Net transfers	0.6	Foreign debt	4.8
Current account balance	3.8	– as % of GDP	0.8
– as % of GDP	0.6	– as % of total exports	6.6
Capital balance	-5.4	Debt service ratio	0.7
Overall balance	2.6		

Health and education

Health spending, % of GDP	8.7	Education spending, % of GDP	4.0
Doctors per 1,000 pop.	1.6	Enrolment, %: primary	111
Hospital beds per 1,000 pop.	1.6	secondary	86
At least basic drinking water,		tertiary	63
% of pop.	95.2		

Society

No. of households, m	25.8	Cost of living, Dec. 2020	
Av. no. per household	3.2	New York = 100	62
Marriages per 1,000 pop.	6.7	Cars per 1,000 pop.	171
Divorces per 1,000 pop.	2.1	Telephone lines per 100 pop.	34.9
Religion, % of pop.		Mobile telephone subscribers	
Muslim	99.5	per 100 pop.	142.4
Christian	0.2	Internet access, %	70.0
Other	0.2	Broadband subs per 100 pop.	10.6
Non-religious	0.1	Broadband speed, Mbps	4.4
Hindu	<0.1		
Jewish	<0.1		

a Iranian year ending March 19 2020.
b Iranian year ending March 20 2019.

IRELAND

Area, sq km	70,280	Capital	Dublin
Arable as % of total land	6.5	Currency	Euro (€)

People

Population, m	4.9	Life expectancy: men	81.3 yrs
Pop. per sq km	69.7	women	84.3 yrs
Average annual rate of change		Adult literacy	...
in pop. 2020–25, %	0.7	Fertility rate (per woman)	1.8
Pop. aged 0–19, 2025, %	25.8	Urban population, %	63.4
Pop. aged 65 and over, 2025, %	16.2		per 1,000 pop.
No. of men per 100 women	98.6	Crude birth rate	11.3
Human Development Index	95.5	Crude death rate	6.5

The economy

GDP	$389bn	GDP per head	$78,661
GDP	€347bn	GDP per head in purchasing	
Av. ann. growth in real		power parity (USA=100)	137.3
GDP 2014–19	9.9%	Economic freedom index	81.4

Origins of GDP		Components of GDP	
	% of total		% of total
Agriculture	1.0	Private consumption	30.4
Industry, of which:	37.6	Public consumption	12.0
manufacturing	33.5	Investment	43.8
Services	61.4	Exports	126.8
		Imports	-112.4

Structure of employment

	% of total		% of labour force
Agriculture	4.4	Unemployed 2020	5.9
Industry	18.8	Av. ann. rate 2010–20	10.2
Services	76.8		

Energy

	m TOE		
Total output	5.5	Net energy imports as %	
Total consumption	16.6	of energy use	67
Consumption per head			
kg oil equivalent	3,404		

Inflation and finance

Consumer price			% change 2019–20
inflation 2020	-0.5%	Narrow money (M1)	13.5
Av. ann. inflation 2015–20	0.2%	Broad money	10.3
Deposit rate, Dec. 2020	-0.10%		

Exchange rates

	end 2020		December 2020
€ per $	0.81	Effective rates	2010 = 100
€ per SDR	1.17	– nominal	98.6
		– real	88.4

Trade

Principal exports		**Principal imports**	
	$bn fob		*$bn cif*
Chemicals & related products	104.0	Machinery & transport equip.	44.5
Machinery & transport equip.	26.0	Chemicals & related products	19.7
Food, drink and tobacco	15.0	Food, drink and tobacco	9.8
Raw materials	1.9	Mineral fuels & lubricants	6.1
Total incl. others	**170.8**	Total incl. others	**101.7**

Main export destinations		**Main origins of imports**	
	% of total		*% of total*
United States	30.6	United Kingdom	27.3
Belgium	10.2	United States	13.7
United Kingdom	10.2	France	13.4
Germany	8.8	Germany	8.6
EU28	47.4	EU28	65.8

Balance of payments, reserves and aid, $bn

Visible exports fob	254.7	Overall balance	0.5
Visible imports fob	-121.3	Change in reserves	0.5
Trade balance	133.4	Level of reserves	
Invisibles inflows	369.5	end Dec.	5.7
Invisibles outflows	-543.8	No. months of import cover	0.1
Net transfers	-4.0	Official gold holdings, m oz	0.2
Current account balance	-44.9	Aid given	1.0
– as % of GDP	-11.6	– as % of GNI	0.3
Capital balance	35.1		

Health and education

Health spending, % of GDP	6.9	Education spending, % of GDP	3.5
Doctors per 1,000 pop.	3.3	Enrolment, %: primary	101
Hospital beds per 1,000 pop.	3.0	secondary	155
At least basic drinking water,		tertiary	77
% of pop.	97.4		

Society

No. of households, m	1.9	Cost of living, Dec. 2020	
Av. no. per household	2.6	New York = 100	85
Marriages per 1,000 pop.	4.3	Cars per 1,000 pop.	417
Divorces per 1,000 pop.	0.7	Telephone lines per 100 pop.	36.2
Religion, % of pop.		Mobile telephone subscribers	
Christian	92.0	per 100 pop.	105.7
Non-religious	6.2	Internet access, %	84.5
Muslim	1.1	Broadband subs per 100 pop.	30.0
Other	0.4	Broadband speed, Mbps	23.9
Hindu	0.2		
Jewish	<0.1		

ISRAEL

Area, sq km	22,070	Capital	Jerusalem[a]
Arable as % of total land	17.7	Currency	New Shekel (NIS)

People

Population, m	8.5	Life expectancy: men	82.0 yrs
Pop. per sq km	385.1	women	84.9 yrs
Average annual rate of change		Adult literacy	...
in pop. 2020–25, %	1.5	Fertility rate (per woman)	2.9
Pop. aged 0–19, 2025, %	35.0	Urban population, %	92.5
Pop. aged 65 and over, 2025, %	13.1		per 1,000 pop.
No. of men per 100 women	99.1	Crude birth rate	19.0
Human Development Index	91.9	Crude death rate	5.3

The economy

GDP	$395bn	GDP per head	$43,592
GDP	NIS1,407bn	GDP per head in purchasing	
Av. ann. growth in real		power parity (USA=100)	65.7
GDP 2014–19	3.3%	Economic freedom index	73.8

Origins of GDP		Components of GDP	
	% of total		% of total
Agriculture	1.2	Private consumption	54.2
Industry, of which:	20.4	Public consumption	22.6
manufacturing	12.0	Investment	21.4
Services	78.4	Exports	29.3
		Imports	-27.4

Structure of employment

	% of total		% of labour force
Agriculture	0.9	Unemployed 2020	4.6
Industry	17.2	Av. ann. rate 2010–20	5.6
Services	81.9		

Energy

	m TOE		
Total output	9.9	Net energy imports as %	
Total consumption	25.1	of energy use	60
Consumption per head			
kg oil equivalent	2,941		

Inflation and finance

			% change 2019–20
Consumer price			
inflation 2020	-0.6%	Narrow money (M1)	29.4
Av. ann. inflation 2015–20	0.1%	Broad money	26.0
Deposit rate, May 2020	0.54%		

Exchange rates

	end 2020		December 2020
NIS per $	3.22	Effective rates	2010 = 100
NIS per SDR	4.63	– nominal	128.8
NIS per €	3.95	– real	111.2

Trade

Principal exports		**Principal imports**	
	$bn fob		*$bn cif*
Chemicals & chemical products	14.0	Machinery & equipment	17.6
Machinery & equipment	13.0	Fuels	9.3
Optical, photographic &		Chemicals & chemical products	7.3
medical instruments	5.5	Diamonds	3.9
Polished diamonds	4.8		
Total incl. others	**51.9**	Total incl. others	**75.7**

Main export destinations		**Main origins of imports**	
	% of total		*% of total*
United States	30.8	United States	16.2
United Kingdom	9.7	Switzerland	10.7
China	8.9	China	8.9
Hong Kong	5.7	Germany	7.3

Balance of payments, reserves and debt, $bn

Visible exports fob	60.2	Change in reserves	10.7
Visible imports fob	-76.1	Level of reserves	
Trade balance	-15.9	end Dec.	126.0
Invisibles inflows	69.8	No. months of import cover	12.1
Invisibles outflows	-48.7	Official gold holdings, m oz	0.0
Net transfers	7.9	Foreign debt	105.0
Current account balance	13.1	– as % of GDP	26.6
– as % of GDP	3.3	– as % of total exports	79.9
Capital balance	3.7	Debt service ratio	11.6
Overall balance	6.5		

Health and education

Health spending, % of GDP	7.5	Education spending, % of GDP	6.1
Doctors per 1,000 pop.	4.6	Enrolment, %: primary	105
Hospital beds per 1,000 pop.	3.0	secondary	106
At least basic drinking water,		tertiary	61
% of pop.	100		

Society

No. of households, m	2.6	Cost of living, Dec. 2020	
Av. no. per household	3.3	New York = 100	101
Marriages per 1,000 pop.	5.7	Cars per 1,000 pop.	330
Divorces per 1,000 pop.	1.7	Telephone lines per 100 pop.	36.9
Religion, % of pop.		Mobile telephone subscribers	
Jewish	75.6	per 100 pop.	137.3
Muslim	18.6	Internet access, %	86.8
Non-religious	3.1	Broadband subs per 100 pop.	29.1
Christian	2.0	Broadband speed, Mbps	8.8
Other	0.6		
Hindu	<0.1		

a Sovereignty over the city is disputed.

ITALY

Area, sq km	301,340	Capital	Rome
Arable as % of total land	22.6	Currency	Euro (€)

People

Population, m	60.6	Life expectancy: men	81.9 yrs
Pop. per sq km	201.1	women	86.0 yrs
Average annual rate of change		Adult literacy	99.2
in pop. 2020–25, %	-0.2	Fertility rate (per woman)	1.3
Pop. aged 0–19, 2025, %	16.8	Urban population, %	70.7
Pop. aged 65 and over, 2025, %	25.1		per 1,000 pop.
No. of men per 100 women	94.9	Crude birth rate	7.0
Human Development Index	89.2	Crude death rate	10.9

The economy

GDP	$2,004bn	GDP per head	$33,228
GDP	€1,790bn	GDP per head in purchasing	
Av. ann. growth in real		power parity (USA=100)	70.0
GDP 2014–19	1.0%	Economic freedom index	64.9

Origins of GDP		Components of GDP	
	% of total		% of total
Agriculture	2.1	Private consumption	60.1
Industry, of which:	23.8	Public consumption	18.7
manufacturing	16.6	Investment	18.1
Services	74.0	Exports	31.5
		Imports	-28.5

Structure of employment

	% of total		% of labour force
Agriculture	3.9	Unemployed 2020	9.3
Industry	25.9	Av. ann. rate 2010–20	10.6
Services	70.2		

Energy

	m TOE		
Total output	37.4	Net energy imports as %	
Total consumption	172.1	of energy use	78
Consumption per head			
kg oil equivalent	2,842		

Inflation and finance

Consumer price			% change 2019–20
inflation 2020	-0.1%	Narrow money (M1)	13.5
Av. ann. inflation 2015–20	0.6%	Broad money	10.3
Deposit rate, Dec. 2020	-0.04%		

Exchange rates

	end 2020		December 2020
			2010 = 100
€ per $	0.81	Effective rates	
€ per SDR	1.17	– nominal	105.1
		– real	95.0

Trade

Principal exports

	$bn fob
Machinery & transport equip.	182.5
Chemicals & related products	75.9
Food, drink and tobacco	46.2
Mineral fuels & lubricants	18.1
Total incl. others	**539.7**

Principal imports

	$bn cif
Machinery & transport equip.	137.1
Chemicals & related products	77.0
Mineral fuels & lubricants	58.5
Food, drink and tobacco	42.6
Total incl. others	**476.0**

Main export destinations

	% of total
Germany	12.2
France	10.5
United States	9.5
Switzerland	5.4
EU28	56.4

Main origins of imports

	% of total
Germany	16.2
France	8.2
China	7.5
Spain	5.4
EU28	59.4

Balance of payments, reserves and aid, $bn

Visible exports fob	513.8	Overall balance	3.6
Visible imports fob	-446.5	Change in reserves	22.6
Trade balance	67.3	Level of reserves	
Invisibles inflows	208.4	end Dec.	174.8
Invisibles outflows	-192.5	No. months of import cover	3.3
Net transfers	-19.2	Official gold holdings, m oz	78.8
Current account balance	64.0	Aid given	4.4
– as % of GDP	3.2	– as % of GNI	0.2
Capital balance	-50.2		

Health and education

Health spending, % of GDP	8.7	Education spending, % of GDP	4.0
Doctors per 1,000 pop.	4.0	Enrolment, %: primary	101
Hospital beds per 1,000 pop.	3.1	secondary	101
At least basic drinking water,		tertiary	64
% of pop.	99.4		

Society

No. of households, m	26.0	Cost of living, Dec. 2020	
Av. no. per household	2.3	New York = 100	77
Marriages per 1,000 pop.	3.2	Cars per 1,000 pop.	625
Divorces per 1,000 pop.	1.5	Telephone lines per 100 pop.	32.2
Religion, % of pop.		Mobile telephone subscribers	
Christian	83.3	per 100 pop.	131.3
Non-religious	12.4	Internet access, %	74.4
Muslim	3.7	Broadband subs per 100 pop.	28.9
Other	0.4	Broadband speed, Mbps	17.3
Hindu	0.1		
Jewish	<0.1		

IVORY COAST

Area, sq km	322,460	Capital	Yamoussoukro
Arable as % of total land	11.0	Currency	CFA franc (CFAfr)

People

Population, m	25.7	Life expectancy: men	57.5 yrs
Pop. per sq km	79.7	women	60.1 yrs
Average annual rate of change		Adult literacy	47.2
in pop. 2020–25, %	2.5	Fertility rate (per woman)	4.4
Pop. aged 0–19, 2025, %	51.3	Urban population, %	51.2
Pop. aged 65 and over, 2025, %	3.0		per 1,000 pop.
No. of men per 100 women	101.7	Crude birth rate	34.3
Human Development Index	53.8	Crude death rate	9.4

The economy

GDP	$59bn	GDP per head	$2,276
GDP	CFAfr34,299bn	GDP per head in purchasing	
Av. ann. growth in real		power parity (USA=100)	8.3
GDP 2014–19	7.3%	Economic freedom index	61.7

Origins of GDP

	% of total
Agriculture	22.1
Industry, of which:	22.7
manufacturing	12.6
Services	55.2

Components of GDP

	% of total
Private consumption	68.7
Public consumption	10.1
Investment	20.1
Exports	23.8
Imports	-22.6

Structure of employment

	% of total		% of labour force
Agriculture	40.2	Unemployed 2020	3.5
Industry	12.9	Av. ann. rate 2010–20	4.3
Services	47.0		

Energy

	m TOE		
Total output	4.6	Net energy imports as %	
Total consumption	4.9	of energy use	7
Consumption per head			
kg oil equivalent	191		

Inflation and finance

			% change 2019–20
Consumer price			
inflation 2020	2.5%	Narrow money (M1)	22.1
Av. ann. inflation 2015–20	1.0%	Broad money	21.1
Benchmark interest rate, Dec. 2020	4.5%		

Exchange rates

	end 2020		December 2020
CFAfr per $	534.56	Effective rates	2010 = 100
CFAfr per SDR	769.91	– nominal	117.5
CFAfr per €	655.96	– real	98.5

Trade

Principal exports		**Principal imports**	
	$bn fob		*$bn cif*
Cocoa beans & butter	4.9	Machinery & equipment	2.7
Petroleum products	2.1	Fuels & lubricants	2.2
Rubber	0.9	Food, dink & tobacco	1.2
Cotton	0.2	Pharmaceuticals	0.4
Total incl. others	**12.7**	Total incl. others	**10.5**

Main export destinations		**Main origins of imports**	
	% of total		*% of total*
Netherlands	10.7	China	17.1
United States	6.0	Nigeria	13.4
France	5.9	France	10.7
Malaysia	5.0	United States	5.0

Balance of payments, reserves and debt, $bn

Visible exports fob	12.6	Change in reserves	0.8
Visible imports fob	-9.5	Level of reserves	
Trade balance	3.2	end Dec.	7.4
Invisibles inflows	1.5	No. months of import cover	5.9
Invisibles outflows	-5.5	Official gold holdings, m oz	0.0
Net transfers	-0.6	Foreign debt	19.2
Current account balance	-1.3	– as % of GDP	32.8
– as % of GDP	-2.3	– as % of total exports	135.3
Capital balance	2.4	Debt service ratio	21.2
Overall balance	1.1		

Health and education

Health spending, % of GDP	4.2	Education spending, % of GDP	3.3
Doctors per 1,000 pop.	...	Enrolment, %: primary	100
Hospital beds per 1,000 pop.	...	secondary	55
At least basic drinking water,		tertiary	...
% of pop.	72.9		

Society

No. of households, m	5.2	Cost of living, Dec. 2020	
Av. no. per household	4.9	New York = 100	56
Marriages per 1,000 pop.	...	Cars per 1,000 pop.	18
Divorces per 1,000 pop.	...	Telephone lines per 100 pop.	1.1
Religion, % of pop.	...	Mobile telephone subscribers	
		per 100 pop.	145.3
		Internet access, %	36.3
		Broadband subs per 100 pop.	0.8
		Broadband speed, Mbps	1.8

JAPAN

Area, sq km	377,970	Capital	Tokyo
Arable as % of total land	11.4	Currency	Yen (¥)

People

Population, m	126.9	Life expectancy: men	81.9 yrs
Pop. per sq km	335.7	women	88.1 yrs
Average annual rate of change		Adult literacy	...
in pop. 2020–25, %	-0.4	Fertility rate (per woman)	1.4
Pop. aged 0–19, 2025, %	16.3	Urban population, %	91.7
Pop. aged 65 and over, 2025, %	29.6		per 1,000 pop.
No. of men per 100 women	95.4	Crude birth rate	7.0
Human Development Index	91.9	Crude death rate	11.5

The economy

GDP	$5,082bn	GDP per head	$40,247
GDP	Yen553,962bn	GDP per head in purchasing	
Av. ann. growth in real		power parity (USA=100)	66.8
GDP 2014–19	1.0%	Economic freedom index	74.1

Origins of GDP

	% of total
Agriculture	1.0
Industry, of which:	29.2
manufacturing	20.8
Services	69.8

Components of GDP

	% of total
Private consumption	54.5
Public consumption	19.8
Investment	25.8
Exports	17.4
Imports	-17.4

Structure of employment

	% of total		% of labour force
Agriculture	3.4	Unemployed 2020	3.0
Industry	24.2	Av. ann. rate 2010–20	3.5
Services	72.4		

Energy

	m TOE		
Total output	65.8	Net energy imports as %	
Total consumption	485.4	of energy use	86
Consumption per head			
kg oil equivalent	3,826		

Inflation and finance

			% change 2019–20
Consumer price			
inflation 2020	0.0%	Narrow money (M1)	19.2
Av. ann. inflation 2015–20	0.4%	Broad money	7.5
Central bank policy rate, Dec. 2020	-0.10%		

Exchange rates

	end 2020		December 2020
¥ per $	103.63	Effective rates	2010 = 100
¥ per SDR	149.26	– nominal	90.6
¥ per €	127.16	– real	77.3

Trade

Principal exports

	$bn fob
Capital equipment	350.4
Industrial supplies	167.1
Consumer durable goods	118.7
Consumer non-durable goods	8.9
Total incl. others	**705.7**

Principal imports

	$bn cif
Industrial supplies	321.3
Capital equipment	203.7
Food & direct consumer goods	64.5
Consumer durable goods	58.8
Total incl. others	**721.0**

Main export destinations

	% of total
United States	19.9
China	19.1
South Korea	6.6
Taiwan	6.1

Main origins of imports

	% of total
China	23.5
United States	11.3
Australia	6.3
South Korea	4.1

Balance of payments, reserves and aid, $bn

Visible exports fob	695.2	Overall balance	24.7
Visible imports fob	-693.8	Change in reserves	51.8
Trade balance	1.4	Level of reserves	
Invisibles inflows	523.1	end Dec.	1,322.2
Invisibles outflows	-335.1	No. months of import cover	15.4
Net transfers	-12.6	Official gold holdings, m oz	24.6
Current account balance	176.8	Aid given	15.6
– as % of GDP	3.5	– as % of GNI	0.3
Capital balance	-206.4		

Health and education

Health spending, % of GDP	11.0	Education spending, % of GDP	3.2
Doctors per 1,000 pop.	2.4	Enrolment, %: primary	...
Hospital beds per 1,000 pop.	13.0	secondary	...
At least basic drinking water,		tertiary	...
% of pop.	99.0		

Society

No. of households, m	54.4	Cost of living, Dec. 2020	
Av. no. per household	2.3	New York = 100	95
Marriages per 1,000 pop.	4.6	Cars per 1,000 pop.	488
Divorces per 1,000 pop.	1.6	Telephone lines per 100 pop.	49.5
Religion, % of pop.		Mobile telephone subscribers	
Non-religious	57.0	per 100 pop.	147.0
Buddhist	36.2	Internet access, %	92.7
Other	5.0	Broadband subs per 100 pop.	33.5
Christian	1.6	Broadband speed, Mbps	42.8
Muslim	0.2		
Jewish	<0.1		

KENYA

Area, sq km	580,370	Capital	Nairobi
Arable as % of total land	10.2	Currency	Kenyan shilling (KSh)

People

Population, m	52.6	Life expectancy: men	65.0 yrs
Pop. per sq km	90.6	women	69.9 yrs
Average annual rate of change		Adult literacy	81.5
in pop. 2020–25, %	2.2	Fertility rate (per woman)	3.3
Pop. aged 0–19, 2025, %	46.9	Urban population, %	27.5
Pop. aged 65 and over, 2025, %	2.9		per 1,000 pop.
No. of men per 100 women	98.8	Crude birth rate	27.4
Human Development Index	60.1	Crude death rate	5.3

The economy

GDP	$96bn	GDP per head	$1,817
GDP	KSh9,740bn	GDP per head in purchasing	
Av. ann. growth in real		power parity (USA=100)	6.9
GDP 2014–19	5.6%	Economic freedom index	54.9

Origins of GDP		**Components of GDP**	
	% of total		% of total
Agriculture	37.9	Private consumption	82.5
Industry, of which:	17.6	Public consumption	13.1
manufacturing	8.2	Investment	17.4
Services	45.0	Exports	12.0
		Imports	-21.4

Structure of employment

	% of total		% of labour force
Agriculture	54.3	Unemployed 2020	3.0
Industry	6.2	Av. ann. rate 2010–20	2.8
Services	39.4		

Energy

	m TOE		
Total output	2.2	Net energy imports as %	
Total consumption	8.8	of energy use	75
Consumption per head			
kg oil equivalent	167		

Inflation and finance

		% change 2019–20	
Consumer price			
inflation 2020	5.3%	Narrow money (M1)	8.7
Av. ann. inflation 2015–20	5.9%	Broad money	6.3
Deposit rate, Dec. 2020	6.66%		

Exchange rates

	end 2020		December 2020
KSh per $	109.17	Effective rates	2010 = 100
KSh per SDR	157.24	– nominal	...
KSh per €	133.96	– real	...

Trade

Principal exports		**Principal imports**	
	$bn fob		*$bn cif*
Tea	1.4	Industrial supplies	6.0
Horticultural products	0.8	Machinery & other capital equip.	2.8
Coffee	0.2	Transport equipment	1.9
		Food & beverages	1.7
Total incl. others	**5.9**	Total incl. others	**16.6**

Main export destinations		**Main origins of imports**	
	% of total		*% of total*
Uganda	10.7	China	20.7
United States	8.7	India	9.8
Netherlands	8.1	United Arab Emirates	9.4
Pakistan	7.6	Saudi Arabia	7.2

Balance of payments, reserves and debt, $bn

Visible exports fob	5.9	Change in reserves	1.0
Visible imports fob	-16.6	Level of reserves	
Trade balance	-10.7	end Dec.	9.1
Invisibles inflows	5.8	No. months of import cover	4.9
Invisibles outflows	-6.0	Official gold holdings, m oz	0.0
Net transfers	5.3	Foreign debt	34.2
Current account balance	-5.6	– as % of GDP	35.8
– as % of GDP	-5.8	– as % of total exports	235.2
Capital balance	6.4	Debt service ratio	29.5
Overall balance	1.1		

Health and education

Health spending, % of GDP	5.2	Education spending, % of GDP	5.3
Doctors per 1,000 pop.	0.2	Enrolment, %: primary	103
Hospital beds per 1,000 pop.	...	secondary	...
At least basic drinking water,		tertiary	11
% of pop.	58.9		

Society

No. of households, m	13.1	Cost of living, Dec. 2020	
Av. no. per household	4.0	New York = 100	63
Marriages per 1,000 pop.	...	Cars per 1,000 pop.	18
Divorces per 1,000 pop.	...	Telephone lines per 100 pop.	0.1
Religion, % of pop.		Mobile telephone subscribers	
Christian	84.8	per 100 pop.	103.8
Muslim	9.7	Internet access, %	22.6
Other	3.0	Broadband subs per 100 pop.	0.9
Non-religious	2.5	Broadband speed, Mbps	7.6
Hindu	0.1		
Jewish	<0.1		

MALAYSIA

Area, sq km	330,345	Capital	Kuala Lumpur
Arable as % of total land	2.5	Currency	Malaysian dollar/ringgit (M$)

People

Population, m	32.0	Life expectancy: men	74.7 yrs
Pop. per sq km	96.9	women	78.8 yrs
Average annual rate of change		Adult literacy	94.9
in pop. 2020–25, %	1.2	Fertility rate (per woman)	1.9
Pop. aged 0–19, 2025, %	29.9	Urban population, %	76.6
Pop. aged 65 and over, 2025, %	8.6		per 1,000 pop.
No. of men per 100 women	105.7	Crude birth rate	15.9
Human Development Index	81.0	Crude death rate	5.5

The economy

GDP	$365bn	GDP per head	$11,414
GDP	M$1,511bn	GDP per head in purchasing	
Av. ann. growth in real		power parity (USA=100)	45.4
GDP 2014–19	4.9%	Economic freedom index	74.4

Origins of GDP		**Components of GDP**	
	% of total		% of total
Agriculture	7.3	Private consumption	59.8
Industry, of which:	37.4	Public consumption	11.7
manufacturing	21.4	Investment	21.0
Services	55.3	Exports	65.2
		Imports	-57.8

Structure of employment

	% of total		% of labour force
Agriculture	10.3	Unemployed 2020	4.6
Industry	27.0	Av. ann. rate 2010–20	3.3
Services	62.7		

Energy

	m TOE		
Total output	114.0	Net energy imports as %	
Total consumption	95.7	of energy use	-19
Consumption per head			
kg oil equivalent	2,995		

Inflation and finance

			% change 2019–20
Consumer price			
inflation 2020	-1.1%	Narrow money (M1)	-16.1
Av. ann. inflation 2015–20	1.3%	Broad money	4.9
Deposit rate, Dec. 2020	1.58%		

Exchange rates

	end 2020		December 2020
M$ per $	4.01	Effective rates	2010 = 100
M$ per SDR	5.78	– nominal	85.9
M$ per €	4.92	– real	84.3

Trade

Principal exports		Principal imports	
	$bn fob		*$bn cif*
Machinery & transport equip.	104.6	Machinery & transport equip.	85.9
Mineral fuels	34.5	Mineral fuels	29.8
Manufactured goods	22.6	Manufactured goods	23.9
Chemicals	20.0	Chemicals	22.5
Total incl. others	**238.2**	Total incl. others	**205.0**

Main export destinations		Main origins of imports	
	% of total		*% of total*
China	14.1	China	20.7
Singapore	13.9	Singapore	10.5
United States	9.7	United States	8.1
Hong Kong	6.7	Japan	7.5

Balance of payments, reserves and debt, $bn

Visible exports fob	196.8	Change in reserves	2.2
Visible imports fob	-167.1	Level of reserves	
Trade balance	29.8	end Dec.	103.6
Invisibles inflows	56.6	No. months of import cover	5.3
Invisibles outflows	-69.0	Official gold holdings, m oz	1.3
Net transfers	-5.1	Foreign debt	231.0
Current account balance	12.3	– as % of GDP	63.3
– as % of GDP	3.4	– as % of total exports	90.5
Capital balance	-8.1	Debt service ratio	5.2
Overall balance	-1.7		

Health and education

Health spending, % of GDP	3.8	Education spending, % of GDP	4.2
Doctors per 1,000 pop.	1.5	Enrolment, %: primary	105
Hospital beds per 1,000 pop.	1.9	secondary	84
At least basic drinking water,		tertiary	43
% of pop.	96.7		

Society

No. of households, m	7.9	Cost of living, Dec. 2020	
Av. no. per household	4.1	New York = 100	57
Marriages per 1,000 pop.	6.4	Cars per 1,000 pop.	413
Divorces per 1,000 pop.	1.6	Telephone lines per 100 pop.	23.3
Religion, % of pop.		Mobile telephone subscribers	
Muslim	63.7	per 100 pop.	139.6
Buddhist	17.7	Internet access, %	84.2
Christian	9.4	Broadband subs per 100 pop.	9.3
Hindu	6.0	Broadband speed, Mbps	23.9
Other	2.5		
Non-religious	0.7		

MEXICO

Area, sq km	1,964,375	Capital	Mexico City
Arable as % of total land	12.3	Currency	Mexican peso (PS)

People

Population, m	127.6	Life expectancy: men	72.6 yrs
Pop. per sq km	65.0	women	78.2 yrs
Average annual rate of change		Adult literacy	95.4
in pop. 2020–25, %	1.0	Fertility rate (per woman)	2.0
Pop. aged 0–19, 2025, %	32.4	Urban population, %	80.4
Pop. aged 65 and over, 2025, %	8.8		per 1,000 pop.
No. of men per 100 women	95.8	Crude birth rate	16.3
Human Development Index	77.9	Crude death rate	6.3

The economy

GDP	$1,269bn	GDP per head	$9,946
GDP	PS24,443bn	GDP per head in purchasing	
Av. ann. growth in real		power parity (USA=100)	32.1
GDP 2014–19	2.0%	Economic freedom index	65.5

Origins of GDP		**Components of GDP**	
	% of total		% of total
Agriculture	3.4	Private consumption	64.9
Industry, of which:	33.3	Public consumption	11.4
manufacturing	18.7	Investment	21.1
Services	63.3	Exports	38.8
		Imports	-39.1

Structure of employment

	% of total		% of labour force
Agriculture	12.5	Unemployed 2020	4.7
Industry	25.5	Av. ann. rate 2010–20	4.4
Services	62.0		

Energy

	m TOE		
Total output	158.5	Net energy imports as %	
Total consumption	201.7	of energy use	21
Consumption per head			
kg oil equivalent	1,581		

Inflation and finance

			% change 2019–20
Consumer price			
inflation 2020	3.4%	Narrow money (M1)	21.6
Av. ann. inflation 2015–20	4.2%	Broad money	10.4
Deposit rate, Dec. 2020	0.55%		

Exchange rates

	end 2020		December 2020
PS per $	19.95	Effective rates	2010 = 100
PS per SDR	28.73	– nominal	64.3
PS per €	24.48	– real	77.4

Trade

Principal exports		**Principal imports**	
	$bn fob		*$bn cif*
Manufactured goods	410.8	Intermediate goods	352.3
Crude oil & products	25.1	Consumer goods	61.2
Agricultural products	17.8	Capital goods	41.8
Mining products	6.2		
Total incl. others	**460.7**	Total	**455.3**

Main export destinations		**Main origins of imports**	
	% of total		*% of total*
United States	80.5	United States	47.9
Canada	3.1	China	19.3
China	1.5	Japan	4.2
Germany	1.5	Germany	4.1

Balance of payments, reserves and debt, $bn

Visible exports fob	461.0	Change in reserves	6.6
Visible imports fob	-455.8	Level of reserves	
Trade balance	5.2	end Dec.	183.0
Invisibles inflows	46.3	No. months of import cover	4.0
Invisibles outflows	-91.4	Official gold holdings, m oz	3.9
Net transfers	35.7	Foreign debt	469.7
Current account balance	-4.2	– as % of GDP	37.0
– as % of GDP	-0.3	– as % of total exports	86.5
Capital balance	17.5	Debt service ratio	11.5
Overall balance	2.6		

Health and education

Health spending, % of GDP	5.4	Education spending, % of GDP	4.5
Doctors per 1,000 pop.	2.4	Enrolment, %: primary	105
Hospital beds per 1,000 pop.	1.0	secondary	105
At least basic drinking water,		tertiary	42
% of pop.	99.3		

Society

No. of households, m	35.2	Cost of living, Dec. 2020	
Av. no. per household	3.6	New York = 100	64
Marriages per 1,000 pop.	4.0	Cars per 1,000 pop.	232
Divorces per 1,000 pop.	1.2	Telephone lines per 100 pop.	17.8
Religion, % of pop.		Mobile telephone subscribers	
Christian	95.1	per 100 pop.	95.7
Non-religious	4.7	Internet access, %	70.1
Hindu	<0.1	Broadband subs per 100 pop.	15.2
Jewish	<0.1	Broadband speed, Mbps	6.0
Muslim	<0.1		
Other	<0.1		

MOROCCO

Area, sq km	446,550	Capital	Rabat
Arable as % of total land	16.8	Currency	Dirham (Dh)

People

Population, m	36.5	Life expectancy: men	76.2 yrs
Pop. per sq km	81.7	women	78.7 yrs
Average annual rate of change		Adult literacy	73.8
in pop. 2020–25, %	1.1	Fertility rate (per woman)	2.3
Pop. aged 0–19, 2025, %	33.4	Urban population, %	63.0
Pop. aged 65 and over, 2025, %	9.3		per 1,000 pop.
No. of men per 100 women	98.5	Crude birth rate	17.2
Human Development Index	68.6	Crude death rate	5.1

The economy

GDP	$120bn	GDP per head	$3,204
GDP	Dh1,151bn	GDP per head in purchasing	
Av. ann. growth in real		power parity (USA=100)	12.0
GDP 2014–19	3.1%	Economic freedom index	63.3

Origins of GDP		**Components of GDP**	
	% of total		% of total
Agriculture	13.8	Private consumption	57.4
Industry, of which:	28.7	Public consumption	19.4
manufacturing	16.9	Investment	32.2
Services	57.6	Exports	39.1
		Imports	-48.0

Structure of employment

	% of total		% of labour force
Agriculture	33.3	Unemployed 2020	10.1
Industry	23.1	Av. ann. rate 2010–20	9.3
Services	43.7		

Energy

	m TOE		
Total output	1.6	Net energy imports as %	
Total consumption	21.4	of energy use	93
Consumption per head			
kg oil equivalent	588		

Inflation and finance

Consumer price		% change 2019–20	
inflation 2020	0.6%	Narrow money (M1)	18.0
Av. ann. inflation 2015–20	0.9%	Broad money	9.4
Deposit rate, Dec. 2020	2.80%		

Exchange rates

	end 2020		December 2020
Dh per $	8.90	Effective rates	2010 = 100
Dh per SDR	12.83	– nominal	111.4
Dh per €	10.93	– real	100.7

Trade

Principal exports		**Principal imports**	
	$bn fob		*$bn cif*
Consumer goods	8.9	Capital goods	13.2
Capital goods	6.3	Consumer goods	11.8
Semi-finished goods	6.0	Semi-finished goods	10.9
Food, drink & tobacco	5.9	Fuel & lubricants	7.9
Total incl. others	**29.6**	Total incl. others	**51.1**

Main export destinations		**Main origins of imports**	
	% of total		*% of total*
Spain	23.7	Spain	15.2
France	21.0	France	12.2
Italy	4.7	China	10.2
Brazil	4.1	United States	7.5

Balance of payments, reserves and debt, $bn

Visible exports fob	24.7	Change in reserves	1.9
Visible imports fob	-44.5	Level of reserves	
Trade balance	-19.8	end Dec.	26.4
Invisibles inflows	20.0	No. months of import cover	5.6
Invisibles outflows	-12.3	Official gold holdings, m oz	0.7
Net transfers	7.7	Foreign debt	55.0
Current account balance	-4.4	– as % of GDP	45.9
– as % of GDP	-3.7	– as % of total exports	106.7
Capital balance	5.3	Debt service ratio	8.0
Overall balance	1.9		

Health and education

Health spending, % of GDP	5.3	Education spending, % of GDP	...
Doctors per 1,000 pop.	0.7	Enrolment, %: primary	115
Hospital beds per 1,000 pop.	1.0	secondary	81
At least basic drinking water,		tertiary	39
% of pop.	86.8		

Society

No. of households, m	8.2	Cost of living, Dec. 2020	
Av. no. per household	4.5	New York = 100	52
Marriages per 1,000 pop.	...	Cars per 1,000 pop.	77
Divorces per 1,000 pop.	...	Telephone lines per 100 pop.	5.6
Religion, % of pop.		Mobile telephone subscribers	
Muslim	99.9	per 100 pop.	128.0
Christian	<0.1	Internet access, %	74.4
Hindu	<0.1	Broadband subs per 100 pop.	4.8
Jewish	<0.1	Broadband speed, Mbps	5.5
Non-religious	<0.1		
Other	<0.1		

NETHERLANDS

Area, sq km[a]	41,540	Capital	Amsterdam
Arable as % of total land	30.3	Currency	Euro (€)

People

Population, m	17.1	Life expectancy: men	81.2 yrs
Pop. per sq km	411.7	women	84.4 yrs
Average annual rate of change		Adult literacy	...
in pop. 2020–25, %	0.2	Fertility rate (per woman)	1.7
Pop. aged 0–19, 2025, %	20.7	Urban population, %	91.9
Pop. aged 65 and over, 2025, %	22.2		per 1,000 pop.
No. of men per 100 women	99.3	Crude birth rate	10.2
Human Development Index	94.4	Crude death rate	9.2

The economy

GDP	$907bn	GDP per head	$52,331
GDP	€810bn	GDP per head in purchasing	
Av. ann. growth in real		power parity (USA=100)	93.9
GDP 2014–19	2.2%	Economic freedom index	76.8

Origins of GDP		**Components of GDP**	
	% of total		% of total
Agriculture	1.8	Private consumption	43.8
Industry, of which:	19.9	Public consumption	24.5
manufacturing	12.3	Investment	21.3
Services	78.3	Exports	83.3
		Imports	-72.9

Structure of employment

	% of total		% of labour force
Agriculture	2.1	Unemployed 2020	4.1
Industry	16.1	Av. ann. rate 2010–20	5.4
Services	81.8		

Energy

	m TOE		
Total output	38.8	Net energy imports as %	
Total consumption	96.6	of energy use	60
Consumption per head			
kg oil equivalent	5,651		

Inflation and finance

			% change 2019–20
Consumer price			
inflation 2020	1.1%	Narrow money (M1)	13.5
Av. ann. inflation 2015–20	1.4%	Broad money	10.3
Deposit rate, Dec. 2020	-0.43%		

Exchange rates

	end 2020		December 2020
€ per $	0.81	Effective rates	2010 = 100
€ per SDR	1.17	– nominal	103.2
		– real	101.3

Trade

Principal exports		**Principal imports**	
	$bn fob		*$bn cif*
Machinery & transport equip.	231.3	Machinery & transport equip.	222.7
Chemicals & related products	121.3	Mineral fuels & lubricants	99.4
Mineral fuels & lubricants	90.9	Chemicals & related products	85.1
Food, drink & tobacco	86.3	Food, drink & tobacco	58.2
Total incl. others	**576.8**	Total incl. others	**514.9**

Main export destinations		**Main origins of imports**	
	% of total		*% of total*
Germany	29.0	China	19.3
Belgium	13.4	Germany	18.0
France	10.3	Belgium	9.9
United Kingdom	10.0	United States	9.5
EU28	74.2	EU28	45.2

Balance of payments, reserves and aid, $bn

Visible exports fob	553.0	Overall balance	0.9
Visible imports fob	-476.6	Change in reserves	4.8
Trade balance	76.4	Level of reserves	
Invisibles inflows	542.4	end Dec.	43.2
Invisibles outflows	-520.7	No. months of import cover	0.5
Net transfers	-7.9	Official gold holdings, m oz	19.7
Current account balance	90.2	Aid given	5.3
– as % of GDP	9.9	– as % of GNI	0.6
Capital balance	-92.5		

Health and education

Health spending, % of GDP	10.0	Education spending, % of GDP	5.2
Doctors per 1,000 pop.	3.6	Enrolment, %: primary	105
Hospital beds per 1,000 pop.	3.2	secondary	134
At least basic drinking water,		tertiary	87
% of pop.	100		

Society

No. of households, m	7.9	Cost of living, Dec. 2020	
Av. no. per household	2.2	New York = 100	77
Marriages per 1,000 pop.	3.7	Cars per 1,000 pop.	503
Divorces per 1,000 pop.	1.8	Telephone lines per 100 pop.	32.5
Religion, % of pop.		Mobile telephone subscribers	
Christian	50.6	per 100 pop.	127.3
Non-religious	42.1	Internet access, %	93.9
Muslim	6.0	Broadband subs per 100 pop.	43.6
Other	0.6	Broadband speed, Mbps	40.2
Hindu	0.5		
Jewish	0.2		

a Includes water.

NEW ZEALAND

Area, sq km	267,710	Capital	Wellington
Arable as % of total land	1.9	Currency	New Zealand dollar (NZ$)

People

Population, m	4.8	Life expectancy: men	81.2 yrs
Pop. per sq km	17.9	women	84.4 yrs
Average annual rate of change		Adult literacy	...
in pop. 2020–25, %	0.8	Fertility rate (per woman)	1.9
Pop. aged 0–19, 2025, %	25.0	Urban population, %	86.6
Pop. aged 65 and over, 2025, %	18.4		per 1,000 pop.
No. of men per 100 women	96.7	Crude birth rate	12.2
Human Development Index	93.1	Crude death rate	7.2

The economy

GDP	$207bn	GDP per head	$42,084
GDP	NZ$314bn	GDP per head in purchasing	
Av. ann. growth in real		power parity (USA=100)	69.5
GDP 2014–19	3.3%	Economic freedom index	83.9

Origins of GDP		**Components of GDP**	
	% of total		% of total
Agriculture	6.2	Private consumption	57.7
Industry, of which:	22.3	Public consumption	18.6
manufacturing	10.9	Investment	24.0
Services	71.5	Exports	27.2
		Imports	-27.5

Structure of employment

	% of total		% of labour force
Agriculture	5.8	Unemployed 2020	4.6
Industry	19.3	Av. ann. rate 2010–20	5.4
Services	74.9		

Energy

	m TOE		
Total output	15.8	Net energy imports as %	
Total consumption	23.0	of energy use	31
Consumption per head			
kg oil equivalent	4,800		

Inflation and finance

Consumer price			% change 2019–20
inflation 2020	1.7%	Narrow money (M1)	154.0
Av. ann. inflation 2015–20	1.5%	Broad money	12.2
Deposit rate, Dec. 2020	0.83%		

Exchange rates

	end 2020		December 2020
NZ$ per $	1.38	Effective rates	2010 = 100
NZ$ per SDR	1.99	– nominal	103.8
NZ$ per €	1.69	– real	100.6

Trade

Principal exports		**Principal imports**	
	$bn fob		*$bn cif*
Dairy produce	10.4	Machinery & electrical equip.	9.7
Meat	5.3	Transport equipment	6.7
Forestry products	3.3	Mineral fuels	4.7
Fruit	2.2	Textiles	1.9
Total incl. others	**39.5**	Total incl. others	**42.4**

Main export destinations		**Main origins of imports**	
	% of total		*% of total*
China	28.3	China	20.2
Australia	14.7	Australia	11.5
United States	9.6	United States	10.0
Japan	5.9	Japan	6.5

Balance of payments, reserves and aid, $bn

Visible exports fob	39.7	Overall balance	-0.3
Visible imports fob	-42.1	Change in reserves	0.2
Trade balance	-2.4	Level of reserves	
Invisibles inflows	23.5	end Dec.	17.8
Invisibles outflows	-27.6	No. months of import cover	3.1
Net transfers	-0.4	Official gold holdings, m oz	0.0
Current account balance	-6.8	Aid given	0.6
– as % of GDP	-3.3	– as % of GNI	0.3
Capital balance	4.1		

Health and education

Health spending, % of GDP	9.2	Education spending, % of GDP	6.3
Doctors per 1,000 pop.	3.6	Enrolment, %: primary	101
Hospital beds per 1,000 pop.	2.6	secondary	115
At least basic drinking water,		tertiary	83
% of pop.	100		

Society

No. of households, m	1.9	Cost of living, Dec. 2020	
Av. no. per household	2.5	New York = 100	77
Marriages per 1,000 pop.	3.9	Cars per 1,000 pop.	693
Divorces per 1,000 pop.	1.7	Telephone lines per 100 pop.	37.1
Religion, % of pop.		Mobile telephone subscribers	
Christian	57.0	per 100 pop.	134.9
Non-religious	36.6	Internet access, %	90.8
Other	2.8	Broadband subs per 100 pop.	34.7
Hindu	2.1	Broadband speed, Mbps	32.7
Muslim	1.2		
Jewish	0.2		

NIGERIA

Area, sq km	923,770	Capital	Abuja
Arable as % of total land	37.3	Currency	Naira (N)

People

Population, m	201.0	Life expectancy: men	54.8 yrs
Pop. per sq km	217.6	women	56.8 yrs
Average annual rate of change		Adult literacy	62.0
in pop. 2020–25, %	2.5	Fertility rate (per woman)	5.1
Pop. aged 0–19, 2025, %	53.2	Urban population, %	51.2
Pop. aged 65 and over, 2025, %	2.8		per 1,000 pop.
No. of men per 100 women	102.8	Crude birth rate	36.0
Human Development Index	53.9	Crude death rate	11.0

The economy

GDP	$448bn	GDP per head	$2,230
GDP	N146trn	GDP per head in purchasing	
Av. ann. growth in real		power parity (USA=100)	8.2
GDP 2014–19	1.2%	Economic freedom index	58.7

Origins of GDP

	% of total
Agriculture	22.1
Industry, of which:	27.7
manufacturing	11.6
Services	50.2

Components of GDP

	% of total
Private consumption	73.5
Public consumption	5.9
Investment	26.2
Exports	14.2
Imports	-19.8

Structure of employment

	% of total		% of labour force
Agriculture	35.0	Unemployed 2020	9.0
Industry	12.0	Av. ann. rate 2010–20	5.9
Services	53.0		

Energy

	m TOE		
Total output	149.5	Net energy imports as %	
Total consumption	41.8	of energy use	-258
Consumption per head			
kg oil equivalent	208		

Inflation and finance

			% change 2019–20
Consumer price			
inflation 2020	13.2%	Narrow money (M1)	50.9
Av. ann. inflation 2015–20	13.8%	Broad money	10.8
Deposit rate, Dec. 2020	2.74%		

Exchange rates

	end 2020		December 2020
N per $	381.00	Effective rates	2010 = 100
N per SDR	548.74	– nominal	50.2
N per €	468.63	– real	117.5

Trade

Principal exports	$bn fob	Principal imports	$bn cif
Crude oil	47.9	Machinery & transport equip.	25.3
Gas	6.5	Mineral fuels	8.6
Prepared foods, drink & tobacco	0.6	Chemicals	6.4
Vegetable products	0.5	Food & live animals	4.9
Total incl. others	**62.5**	Total incl. others	**55.3**

Main export destinations	% of total	Main origins of imports	% of total
India	28.1	China	21.4
Indonesia	9.0	United States	9.6
China	6.8	Belgium	6.6
France	6.3	India	5.0

Balance of payments, reserves and debt, $bn

Visible exports fob	65.0	Change in reserves	-4.5
Visible imports fob	-62.1	Level of reserves	
Trade balance	2.9	end Dec.	38.3
Invisibles inflows	7.3	No. months of import cover	4.1
Invisibles outflows	-51.1	Official gold holdings, m oz	0.0
Net transfers	26.4	Foreign debt	54.8
Current account balance	-14.6	– as % of GDP	11.5
– as % of GDP	-3.3	– as % of total exports	58.4
Capital balance	16.9	Debt service ratio	5.5
Overall balance	-4.5		

Health and education

Health spending, % of GDP	3.9	Education spending, % of GDP	...
Doctors per 1,000 pop.	0.4	Enrolment, %: primary	85
Hospital beds per 1,000 pop.	...	secondary	42
At least basic drinking water,		tertiary	...
% of pop.	71.4		

Society

No. of households, m	42.9	Cost of living, Dec. 2020	
Av. no. per household	4.7	New York = 100	42
Marriages per 1,000 pop.	...	Cars per 1,000 pop.	16
Divorces per 1,000 pop.	...	Telephone lines per 100 pop.	0.1
Religion, % of pop.		Mobile telephone subscribers	
Christian	49.3	per 100 pop.	91.9
Muslim	48.8	Internet access, %	25.7
Other	1.4	Broadband subs per 100 pop.	0.1
Non-religious	0.4	Broadband speed, Mbps	1.6
Hindu	<0.1		
Jewish	<0.1		

NORWAY

Area, sq km	385,207	Capital	Oslo
Arable as % of total land	2.2	Currency	Norwegian krone (Nkr)

People

Population, m	5.4	Life expectancy: men	81.1 yrs
Pop. per sq km	14.0	women	84.8 yrs
Average annual rate of change		Adult literacy	...
in pop. 2020–25, %	0.8	Fertility rate (per woman)	1.7
Pop. aged 0–19, 2025, %	22.5	Urban population, %	82.6
Pop. aged 65 and over, 2025, %	18.9		per 1,000 pop.
No. of men per 100 women	102.2	Crude birth rate	11.2
Human Development Index	95.7	Crude death rate	7.9

The economy

GDP	$403bn	GDP per head	$75,420
GDP	NKr3,549bn	GDP per head in purchasing	
Av. ann. growth in real		power parity (USA=100)	107.2
GDP 2014–19	1.6%	Economic freedom index	73.4

Origins of GDP		**Components of GDP**	
	% of total		% of total
Agriculture	2.2	Private consumption	44.8
Industry, of which:	32.5	Public consumption	24.4
manufacturing	7.1	Investment	29.0
Services	65.4	Exports	36.9
		Imports	-35.2

Structure of employment

	% of total		% of labour force
Agriculture	2.1	Unemployed 2020	4.6
Industry	19.4	Av. ann. rate 2010–20	3.8
Services	78.5		

Energy

	m TOE		
Total output	238.8	Net energy imports as %	
Total consumption	47.8	of energy use	-399
Consumption per head			
kg oil equivalent	8,894		

Inflation and finance

			% change 2019–20
Consumer price			
inflation 2020	1.3%	Narrow money (M1)	-6.2
Av. ann. inflation 2015–20	2.3%	Broad money	12.1
Deposit rate, Dec. 2020	0.35%		

Exchange rates

	end 2020		December 2020
Nkr per $	8.53	Effective rates	2010 = 100
Nkr per SDR	12.29	– nominal	76.2
Nkr per €	10.00	– real	78.2

Trade

Principal exports

	$bn fob
Mineral fuels & lubricants	58.2
Food & beverages	12.7
Machinery & transport equip.	10.6
Manufactured goods	9.9
Total incl. others	**104.0**

Principal imports

	$bn cif
Machinery & transport equip.	34.3
Misc. manufactured goods	12.3
Manufactured goods	12.1
Chemicals & mineral products	8.4
Total incl. others	**86.2**

Main export destinations

	% of total
United Kingdom	19.9
Germany	14.2
Netherlands	10.9
Sweden	7.6
EU28	58.7

Main origins of imports

	% of total
Sweden	11.7
Germany	10.8
China	10.1
United States	7.9
EU28	55.9

Balance of payments, reserves and aid, $bn

Visible exports fob	103.3	Overall balance	0.1
Visible imports fob	-87.6	Change in reserves	3.8
Trade balance	15.7	Level of reserves	
Invisibles inflows	87.1	end Dec.	66.9
Invisibles outflows	-85.6	No. months of import cover	4.6
Net transfers	-6.7	Official gold holdings, m oz	0.0
Current account balance	10.4	Aid given	4.3
– as % of GDP	2.6	– as % of GNI	1.0
Capital balance	-0.7		

Health and education

Health spending, % of GDP	10.1	Education spending, % of GDP	7.9
Doctors per 1,000 pop.	2.9	Enrolment, %: primary	100
Hospital beds per 1,000 pop.	3.5	secondary	117
At least basic drinking water,		tertiary	73
% of pop.	100		

Society

No. of households, m	2.4	Cost of living, Dec. 2020	
Av. no. per household	2.3	New York = 100	90
Marriages per 1,000 pop.	4.3	Cars per 1,000 pop.	505
Divorces per 1,000 pop.	1.9	Telephone lines per 100 pop.	8.3
Religion, % of pop.		Mobile telephone subscribers	
Christian	84.7	per 100 pop.	107.4
Non-religious	10.1	Internet access, %	98.0
Muslim	3.7	Broadband subs per 100 pop.	42.0
Other	0.9	Broadband speed, Mbps	38.5
Hindu	0.5		
Jewish	<0.1		

PAKISTAN

Area, sq km	796,100	Capital	Islamabad
Arable as % of total land	39.6	Currency	Pakistan rupee (PRs)

People

Population, m	216.6	Life expectancy: men	66.8 yrs
Pop. per sq km	272.1	women	68.9 yrs
Average annual rate of change		Adult literacy	59.1
in pop. 2020–25, %	1.8	Fertility rate (per woman)	3.2
Pop. aged 0–19, 2025, %	43.2	Urban population, %	36.9
Pop. aged 65 and over, 2025, %	4.7		per 1,000 pop.
No. of men per 100 women	106.0	Crude birth rate	26.0
Human Development Index	55.7	Crude death rate	6.7

The economy

GDP	$278bn	GDP per head	$1,285
GDP	PRs37,972bn	GDP per head in purchasing	
Av. ann. growth in real		power parity (USA=100)	7.5
GDP 2014–19	4.5%	Economic freedom index	51.7

Origins of GDP		**Components of GDP**	
	% of total		% of total
Agriculture	23.4	Private consumption	82.9
Industry, of which:	19.5	Public consumption	11.7
manufacturing	13.2	Investment	15.6
Services	57.1	Exports	10.1
		Imports	-20.3

Structure of employment

	% of total		% of labour force
Agriculture	36.9	Unemployed 2020	4.7
Industry	25.0	Av. ann. rate 2010–20	2.9
Services	38.1		

Energy

	m TOE		
Total output	49.3	Net energy imports as %	
Total consumption	92.7	of energy use	47
Consumption per head			
kg oil equivalent	428		

Inflation and finance

			% change 2019–20
Consumer price			
inflation 2020	10.7%	Narrow money (M1)	14.1
Av. ann. inflation 2015–20	5.6%	Broad money	17.7
Deposit rate, Dec. 2020	5.67%		

Exchange rates

	end 2020		December 2020
PRs per $	159.59	Effective rates	2010 = 100
PRs per SDR	229.85	– nominal	61.7
PRs per €	196.08	– real	97.6

Trade

Principal exports		**Principal imports**	
	$bn fob		*$bn cif*
Knitwear	2.8	Petroleum products	5.3
Rice	2.3	Crude oil	4.1
Cotton fabrics	2.0	Palm oil	1.7
Cotton yarn & thread	1.1	Telecoms equipment	1.6
Total incl. others	**23.5**	Total incl. others	**49.7**

Main export destinations		**Main origins of imports**	
	% of total		*% of total*
United States	17.1	China	24.9
China	8.5	United Arab Emirates	12.7
United Kingdom	7.1	United States	4.9
Germany	5.6	Saudi Arabia	5.2

Balance of payments, reserves and debt, $bn

Visible exports fob	24.8	Change in reserves	4.7
Visible imports fob	-47.7	Level of reserves	
Trade balance	-22.9	end Dec.	16.6
Invisibles inflows	6.4	No. months of import cover	3.2
Invisibles outflows	-16.9	Official gold holdings, m oz	2.1
Net transfers	24.9	Foreign debt	100.8
Current account balance	-8.6	– as % of GDP	36.2
– as % of GDP	-3.1	– as % of total exports	189.0
Capital balance	11.8	Debt service ratio	20.6
Overall balance	3.4		

Health and education

Health spending, % of GDP	3.2	Education spending, % of GDP	2.9
Doctors per 1,000 pop.	1.0	Enrolment, %: primary	95
Hospital beds per 1,000 pop.	0.6	secondary	44
At least basic drinking water,		tertiary	9
% of pop.	91.5		

Society

No. of households, m	32.5	Cost of living, Dec. 2020	
Av. no. per household	6.7	New York = 100	35
Marriages per 1,000 pop.	...	Cars per 1,000 pop.	14
Divorces per 1,000 pop.	...	Telephone lines per 100 pop.	1.1
Religion, % of pop.		Mobile telephone subscribers	
Muslim	96.4	per 100 pop.	76.4
Hindu	1.9	Internet access, %	17.1
Christian	1.6	Broadband subs per 100 pop.	0.8
Jewish	<0.1	Broadband speed, Mbps	1.4
Non-religious	<0.1		
Other	<0.1		

PERU

Area, sq km	1,285,220	Capital	Lima
Arable as % of total land	2.7	Currency	Nuevo Sol (new Sol)

People

Population, m	32.5	Life expectancy: men	74.9 yrs
Pop. per sq km	25.3	women	80.2 yrs
Average annual rate of change		Adult literacy	94.4
in pop. 2020–25, %	0.9	Fertility rate (per woman)	2.2
Pop. aged 0–19, 2025, %	31.5	Urban population, %	78.1
Pop. aged 65 and over, 2025, %	10.0		per 1,000 pop.
No. of men per 100 women	98.7	Crude birth rate	16.9
Human Development Index	77.7	Crude death rate	5.9

The economy

GDP	$227bn	GDP per head	$6,978
GDP	New soles 757bn	GDP per head in purchasing	
Av. ann. growth in real		power parity (USA=100)	20.5
GDP 2014–19	3.2%	Economic freedom index	67.7

Origins of GDP

Components of GDP

	% of total		% of total
Agriculture	6.7	Private consumption	64.6
Industry, of which:	30.6	Public consumption	13.3
manufacturing	13.0	Investment	20.9
Services	62.7	Exports	24.2
		Imports	-22.9

Structure of employment

	% of total		% of labour force
Agriculture	27.4	Unemployed 2020	6.2
Industry	15.2	Av. ann. rate 2010–20	3.4
Services	57.4		

Energy

	m TOE		
Total output	28.0	Net energy imports as %	
Total consumption	28.7	of energy use	3
Consumption per head			
kg oil equivalent	883		

Inflation and finance

			% change 2019–20
Consumer price			
inflation 2020	1.8%	Narrow money (M1)	33.2
Av. ann. inflation 2015–20	2.3%	Broad money	11.8
Deposit rate, Dec. 2020	0.50%		

Exchange rates

	end 2020		December 2020
New Soles per $	3.44	Effective rates	2010 = 100
New Soles per SDR	4.69	– nominal	...
New Soles per €	3.70	– real	...

Trade

Principal exports		**Principal imports**	
	$bn fob		*$bn cif*
Copper	13.9	Intermediate goods	19.1
Gold	8.5	Capital goods	12.3
Zinc	2.1	Consumer goods	9.6
Fishmeal	1.9		
Total incl. others	**47.7**	Total incl. others	**41.1**

Main export destinations		**Main origins of imports**	
	% of total		*% of total*
China	27.1	China	27.0
United States	11.9	United States	22.1
Canada	5.2	Brazil	6.2
Switzerland	4.7	Mexico	4.7

Balance of payments, reserves and debt, $bn

Visible exports fob	47.7	Change in reserves	7.4
Visible imports fob	-40.7	Level of reserves	
Trade balance	7.0	end Dec.	67.7
Invisibles inflows	9.6	No. months of import cover	12.6
Invisibles outflows	-23.9	Official gold holdings, m oz	1.1
Net transfers	3.7	Foreign debt	64.2
Current account balance	-3.5	– as % of GDP	27.8
– as % of GDP	-1.6	– as % of total exports	105.9
Capital balance	10.4	Debt service ratio	10.9
Overall balance	8.1		

Health and education

Health spending, % of GDP	5.2	Education spending, % of GDP	3.8
Doctors per 1,000 pop.	1.3	Enrolment, %: primary	113
Hospital beds per 1,000 pop.	1.6	secondary	109
At least basic drinking water,		tertiary	71
% of pop.	91.1		

Society

No. of households, m	8.7	Cost of living, Dec. 2020	
Av. no. per household	3.7	New York = 100	63
Marriages per 1,000 pop.	2.9	Cars per 1,000 pop.	50
Divorces per 1,000 pop.	0.5	Telephone lines per 100 pop.	8.5
Religion, % of pop.		Mobile telephone subscribers	
Christian	95.5	per 100 pop.	131.8
Non-religious	3.0	Internet access, %	60.0
Other	1.5	Broadband subs per 100 pop.	7.9
Hindu	<0.1	Broadband speed, Mbps	2.9
Jewish	<0.1		
Muslim	<0.1		

PHILIPPINES

Area, sq km	300,000	Capital	Manila
Arable as % of total land	18.7	Currency	Philippine peso (P)

People

Population, m	108.1	Life expectancy: men	67.7 yrs
Pop. per sq km	360.3	women	75.9 yrs
Average annual rate of change		Adult literacy	98.2
in pop. 2020–25, %	1.3	Fertility rate (per woman)	2.5
Pop. aged 0–19, 2025, %	37.3	Urban population, %	47.1
Pop. aged 65 and over, 2025, %	6.5		per 1,000 pop.
No. of men per 100 women	100.9	Crude birth rate	19.6
Human Development Index	71.8	Crude death rate	6.2

The economy

GDP	$377bn	GDP per head	$3,485
GDP	P19,516bn	GDP per head in purchasing	
Av. ann. growth in real		power parity (USA=100)	14.2
GDP 2014–19	6.6%	Economic freedom index	64.1

Origins of GDP		**Components of GDP**	
	% of total		% of total
Agriculture	8.8	Private consumption	73.2
Industry, of which:	30.3	Public consumption	12.5
manufacturing	18.5	Investment	26.2
Services	60.9	Exports	28.3
		Imports	-40.3

Structure of employment

	% of total		% of labour force
Agriculture	22.9	Unemployed 2020	3.4
Industry	19.1	Av. ann. rate 2010–20	3.1
Services	58.0		

Energy

	m TOE		
Total output	16.9	Net energy imports as %	
Total consumption	48.4	of energy use	65
Consumption per head			
kg oil equivalent	448		

Inflation and finance

			% change 2019–20
Consumer price			
inflation 2020	2.6%	Narrow money (M1)	5.1
Av. ann. inflation 2015–20	2.9%	Broad money	8.6
Savings rate, Dec. 2020	1.28%		

Exchange rates

	end 2020		December 2020
P per $	48.04	Effective rates	2010 = 100
P per SDR	69.18	– nominal	100.2
P per €	50.00	– real	111.5

Trade

Principal exports		**Principal imports**	
	$bn fob		*$bn cif*
Electrical & electronic equip.	40.0	Raw materials & intermediate	
Mineral products	4.7	goods	40.6
Agricultural products	4.2	Capital goods	37.4
Machinery & transport equip.	4.1	Consumer goods	19.3
		Mineral fuels & lubricants	13.4
Total incl. others	**70.9**	Total incl. others	**117.4**

Main export destinations		**Main origins of imports**	
	% of total		*% of total*
United States	16.3	China	22.8
Japan	15.1	Japan	9.6
China	13.8	South Korea	7.5
Hong Kong	13.6	United States	7.3

Balance of payments, reserves and debt, $bn

Visible exports fob	53.5	Change in reserves	10.3
Visible imports fob	-102.8	Level of reserves	
Trade balance	-49.3	end Dec.	89.5
Invisibles inflows	54.7	No. months of import cover	7.7
Invisibles outflows	-36.4	Official gold holdings, m oz	6.4
Net transfers	27.9	Foreign debt	83.7
Current account balance	-3.0	– as % of GDP	22.2
– as % of GDP	-0.8	– as % of total exports	58.5
Capital balance	8.2	Debt service ratio	7.3
Overall balance	7.8		

Health and education

Health spending, % of GDP	4.4	Education spending, % of GDP	...
Doctors per 1,000 pop.	0.6	Enrolment, %: primary	99
Hospital beds per 1,000 pop.	...	secondary	90
At least basic drinking water,		tertiary	35
% of pop.	93.6		

Society

No. of households, m	25.9	Cost of living, Dec. 2020	
Av. no. per household	4.2	New York = 100	60
Marriages per 1,000 pop.	...	Cars per 1,000 pop.	32
Divorces per 1,000 pop.	...	Telephone lines per 100 pop.	3.9
Religion, % of pop.		Mobile telephone subscribers	
Christian	92.6	per 100 pop.	154.8
Muslim	5.5	Internet access, %	43.0
Other	1.7	Broadband subs per 100 pop.	5.5
Non-religious	0.1	Broadband speed, Mbps	6.0
Hindu	<0.1		
Jewish	<0.1		

POLAND

Area, sq km	312,680	Capital	Warsaw
Arable as % of total land	36.0	Currency	Zloty (Zl)

People

Population, m	37.9	Life expectancy: men	75.5 yrs
Pop. per sq km	121.2	women	83.0 yrs
Average annual rate of change		Adult literacy	...
in pop. 2020–25, %	-0.2	Fertility rate (per woman)	1.5
Pop. aged 0–19, 2025, %	19.9	Urban population, %	60.0
Pop. aged 65 and over, 2025, %	21.7		per 1,000 pop.
No. of men per 100 women	94.0	Crude birth rate	9.2
Human Development Index	88.0	Crude death rate	10.7

The economy

GDP	$596bn	GDP per head	$15,693
GDP	Zl2,288bn	GDP per head in purchasing	
Av. ann. growth in real		power parity (USA=100)	53.9
GDP 2014–19	4.4%	Economic freedom index	69.7

Origins of GDP		**Components of GDP**	
	% of total		% of total
Agriculture	2.7	Private consumption	57.5
Industry, of which:	31.8	Public consumption	18.0
manufacturing	18.9	Investment	19.7
Services	65.5	Exports	55.5
		Imports	-50.8

Structure of employment

	% of total		% of labour force
Agriculture	9.1	Unemployed 2020	3.5
Industry	32.1	Av. ann. rate 2010–20	7.1
Services	58.7		

Energy

	m TOE		
Total output	61.2	Net energy imports as %	
Total consumption	110.6	of energy use	45
Consumption per head			
kg oil equivalent	2,919		

Inflation and finance

		% change 2019–20	
Consumer price			
inflation 2020	3.4%	Narrow money (M1)	32.6
Av. ann. inflation 2015–20	1.7%	Broad money	16.9
Deposit rate, Dec. 2020	0.07%		

Exchange rates

	end 2020		December 2020
Zl per $	3.76	Effective rates	2010 = 100
Zl per SDR	5.41	– nominal	96.4
Zl per €	4.61	– real	92.8

Trade

Principal exports		**Principal imports**	
	$bn fob		*$bn cif*
Machinery & transport equip.	100.7	Machinery & transport equip.	95.4
Manufactured goods	48.0	Manufactured goods	43.1
Foodstuffs & live animals	28.3	Chemicals & mineral products	35.6
Total incl. others	**264.5**	Total incl. others	**262.5**

Main export destinations		**Main origins of imports**	
	% of total		*% of total*
Germany	28.0	Germany	27.3
Czech Republic	6.2	China	8.8
United Kingdom	6.0	Russia	6.1
France	5.9	Netherlands	5.7
EU28	79.0	EU28	69.0

Balance of payments, reserves and debt, $bn

Visible exports fob	260.8	Change in reserves	11.4
Visible imports fob	-259.4	Level of reserves	
Trade balance	1.3	end Dec.	128.3
Invisibles inflows	84.1	No. months of import cover	4.5
Invisibles outflows	-80.5	Official gold holdings, m oz	7.4
Net transfers	-2.0	Foreign debt	354.0
Current account balance	2.9	– as % of GDP	59.4
– as % of GDP	0.5	– as % of total exports	100.6
Capital balance	13.2	Debt service ratio	25.3
Overall balance	10.2		

Health and education

Health spending, % of GDP	6.3	Education spending, % of GDP	4.6
Doctors per 1,000 pop.	2.4	Enrolment, %: primary	97
Hospital beds per 1,000 pop.	6.5	secondary	112
At least basic drinking water,		tertiary	69
% of pop.	99.7		

Society

No. of households, m	14.9	Cost of living, Dec. 2020	
Av. no. per household	2.5	New York = 100	56
Marriages per 1,000 pop.	5.1	Cars per 1,000 pop.	593
Divorces per 1,000 pop.	1.7	Telephone lines per 100 pop.	18.0
Religion, % of pop.		Mobile telephone subscribers	
Christian	94.3	per 100 pop.	127.7
Non-religious	5.6	Internet access, %	80.4
Hindu	<0.1	Broadband subs per 100 pop.	20.5
Jewish	<0.1	Broadband speed, Mbps	24.4
Muslim	<0.1		
Other	<0.1		

PORTUGAL

Area, sq km	92,225	Capital	Lisbon
Arable as % of total land	10.0	Currency	Euro (€)

People

Population, m	10.2	Life expectancy: men	79.8 yrs
Pop. per sq km	110.6	women	85.3 yrs
Average annual rate of change		Adult literacy	96.1
in pop. 2020–25, %	-0.3	Fertility rate (per woman)	1.4
Pop. aged 0–19, 2025, %	17.2	Urban population, %	65.8
Pop. aged 65 and over, 2025, %	24.8		*per 1,000 pop.*
No. of men per 100 women	89.8	Crude birth rate	7.7
Human Development Index	86.4	Crude death rate	11.1

The economy

GDP	$239bn	GDP per head	$23,252
GDP	€213bn	GDP per head in purchasing	
Av. ann. growth in real		power parity (USA=100)	58.1
GDP 2014–19	2.5%	Economic freedom index	67.5

Origins of GDP   **Components of GDP**

	% of total		*% of total*
Agriculture	2.4	Private consumption	63.9
Industry, of which:	21.8	Public consumption	16.9
manufacturing	13.8	Investment	19.0
Services	75.8	Exports	43.5
		Imports	-43.3

Structure of employment

	% of total		*% of labour force*
Agriculture	5.5	Unemployed 2020	7.2
Industry	24.7	Av. ann. rate 2010–20	11.1
Services	69.8		

Energy

	m TOE		
Total output	7.1	Net energy imports as %	
Total consumption	26.9	of energy use	74
Consumption per head			
kg oil equivalent	2,627		

Inflation and finance

			% change 2019–20
Consumer price			
inflation 2020	-0.1%	Narrow money (M1)	13.5
Av. ann. inflation 2015–20	0.7%	Broad money	10.3
Deposit rate, Dec. 2020	0.02%		

Exchange rates

	end 2020		*December 2020*
€ per $	0.81	Effective rates	*2010 = 100*
€ per SDR	1.17	– nominal	105.2
		– real	97.1

Trade

Principal exports		**Principal imports**	
	$bn fob		*$bn cif*
Machinery & transport equip.	20.3	Machinery & transport equip.	30.2
Food, drink & tobacco	7.1	Chemicals & related products	12.0
Chemicals & related products	6.1	Food, drink & tobacco	10.9
Mineral fuels & lubricants	4.2	Mineral fuels & lubricants	10.2
Total incl. others	**67.1**	Total incl. others	**89.5**

Main export destinations		**Main origins of imports**	
	% of total		*% of total*
Spain	24.7	Spain	30.5
France	12.9	Germany	13.3
Germany	12.0	France	9.8
United Kingdom	6.1	Italy	5.1
EU28	76.8	EU28	76.4

Balance of payments, reserves and debt, $bn

Visible exports fob	64.9	Overall balance	-2.5
Visible imports fob	-83.1	Change in reserves	0.0
Trade balance	-18.2	Level of reserves	
Invisibles inflows	48.9	end Dec.	24.9
Invisibles outflows	-34.7	No. months of import cover	2.5
Net transfers	4.9	Official gold holdings, m oz	12.3
Current account balance	0.9	Aid given	0.4
– as % of GDP	0.4	– as % of GNI	0.2
Capital balance	-3.8		

Health and education

Health spending, % of GDP	9.4	Education spending, % of GDP	5.0
Doctors per 1,000 pop.	5.1	Enrolment, %: primary	107
Hospital beds per 1,000 pop.	3.5	secondary	121
At least basic drinking water,		tertiary	66
% of pop.	99.9		

Society

No. of households, m	4.1	Cost of living, Dec. 2020	
Av. no. per household	2.5	New York = 100	61
Marriages per 1,000 pop.	3.4	Cars per 1,000 pop.	454
Divorces per 1,000 pop.	2.0	Telephone lines per 100 pop.	49.8
Religion, % of pop.		Mobile telephone subscribers	
Christian	93.8	per 100 pop.	116.5
Non-religious	4.4	Internet access, %	75.3
Other	1.0	Broadband subs per 100 pop.	38.8
Muslim	0.6	Broadband speed, Mbps	22.7
Hindu	0.1		
Jewish	<0.1		

ROMANIA

Area, sq km	238,400	Capital	Bucharest
Arable as % of total land	37.8	Currency	Leu (RON)

People

Population, m	19.4	Life expectancy: men	73.1 yrs
Pop. per sq km	81.4	women	79.9 yrs
Average annual rate of change		Adult literacy	98.8
in pop. 2020–25, %	-0.5	Fertility rate (per woman)	1.7
Pop. aged 0–19, 2025, %	20.5	Urban population, %	54.1
Pop. aged 65 and over, 2025, %	20.9		per 1,000 pop.
No. of men per 100 women	94.6	Crude birth rate	9.3
Human Development Index	82.8	Crude death rate	13.4

The economy

GDP	$250bn	GDP per head	$12,920
GDP	RON1,060bn	GDP per head in purchasing	
Av. ann. growth in real		power parity (USA=100)	51.1
GDP 2014–19	4.7%	Economic freedom index	69.5

Origins of GDP		**Components of GDP**	
	% of total		% of total
Agriculture	4.6	Private consumption	63.6
Industry, of which:	30.1	Public consumption	17.3
manufacturing	18.9	Investment	22.9
Services	65.3	Exports	40.4
		Imports	-44.2

Structure of employment

	% of total		% of labour force
Agriculture	21.2	Unemployed 2020	4.8
Industry	30.1	Av. ann. rate 2010–20	5.9
Services	48.7		

Energy

	m TOE		
Total output	27.1	Net energy imports as %	
Total consumption	35.6	of energy use	24
Consumption per head			
kg oil equivalent	1,838		

Inflation and finance

			% change 2019–20
Consumer price			
inflation 2020	2.6%	Narrow money (M1)	22.5
Av. ann. inflation 2015–20	2.2%	Broad money	15.3
Deposit rate, Dec. 2020	1.75%		

Exchange rates

	end 2020		December 2020
Lei per $	3.97	Effective rates	2010 = 100
Lei per SDR	5.71	– nominal	95.1
Lei per €	4.87	– real	98.8

Trade

Principal exports

	$bn fob
Machinery & transport equip.	36.6
Manufactured goods	24.4
Food, drink & tobacco	6.8
Chemicals & related products	3.5
Total incl. others	**77.3**

Principal imports

	$bn cif
Machinery & transport equip.	35.9
Manufactured goods	29.3
Chemicals & related products	12.7
Food, drink & tobacco	8.4
Total incl. others	**96.7**

Main export destinations

	% of total
Germany	22.6
Italy	11.3
France	6.9
Hungary	4.8
EU28	76.9

Main origins of imports

	% of total
Germany	20.2
Italy	9.1
Hungary	7.1
Poland	6.0
EU28	74.7

Balance of payments, reserves and debt, $bn

Visible exports fob	70.6	Change in reserves	-0.1
Visible imports fob	-90.6	Level of reserves	
Trade balance	-20.0	end Dec.	42.0
Invisibles inflows	37.3	No. months of import cover	4.1
Invisibles outflows	-31.2	Official gold holdings, m oz	3.3
Net transfers	1.7	Foreign debt	117.2
Current account balance	-12.2	– as % of GDP	46.9
– as % of GDP	-4.9	– as % of total exports	104.5
Capital balance	8.6	Debt service ratio	15.9
Overall balance	-0.3		

Health and education

Health spending, % of GDP	5.6	Education spending, % of GDP	3.1
Doctors per 1,000 pop.	3.0	Enrolment, %: primary	87
Hospital beds per 1,000 pop.	6.9	secondary	89
At least basic drinking water,		tertiary	51
% of pop.	100.0		

Society

No. of households, m	7.5	Cost of living, Dec. 2020	
Av. no. per household	2.6	New York = 100	45
Marriages per 1,000 pop.	7.4	Cars per 1,000 pop.	285
Divorces per 1,000 pop.	1.6	Telephone lines per 100 pop.	17.5
Religion, % of pop.		Mobile telephone subscribers	
Christian	99.5	per 100 pop.	117.1
Muslim	0.3	Internet access, %	73.7
Non-religious	0.1	Broadband subs per 100 pop.	27.3
Hindu	<0.1	Broadband speed, Mbps	21.8
Jewish	<0.1		
Other	<0.1		

RUSSIA

Area, sq km	17,098,250	Capital	Moscow
Arable as % of total land	7.4	Currency	Rouble (Rb)

People

Population, m	145.9	Life expectancy: men	67.6 yrs
Pop. per sq km	8.5	women	78.2 yrs
Average annual rate of change		Adult literacy	...
in pop. 2020–25, %	-0.1	Fertility rate (per woman)	1.8
Pop. aged 0–19, 2025, %	24.2	Urban population, %	74.6
Pop. aged 65 and over, 2025, %	17.8		per 1,000 pop.
No. of men per 100 women	86.4	Crude birth rate	11.3
Human Development Index	82.4	Crude death rate	13.1

The economy

GDP	$1,700bn	GDP per head	$11,585
GDP	Rb110,046bn	GDP per head in purchasing	
Av. ann. growth in real		power parity (USA=100)	44.7
GDP 2014–19	0.8%	Economic freedom index	61.5

Origins of GDP

	% of total
Agriculture	3.9
Industry, of which:	36.0
manufacturing	14.5
Services	60.1

Components of GDP

	% of total
Private consumption	50.4
Public consumption	18.3
Investment	23.1
Exports	28.3
Imports	-20.8

Structure of employment

	% of total		% of labour force
Agriculture	5.8	Unemployed 2020	5.7
Industry	26.8	Av. ann. rate 2010–20	5.6
Services	67.4		

Energy

	m TOE		
Total output	1,600.5	Net energy imports as %	
Total consumption	839.9	of energy use	-91
Consumption per head			
kg oil equivalent	5,758		

Inflation and finance

		% change 2019–20	
Consumer price			
inflation 2020	3.4%	Narrow money (M1)	9.8
Av. ann. inflation 2015–20	4.3%	Broad money	16.7
Deposit rate, Dec. 2020	3.38%		

Exchange rates

	end 2020		December 2020
Rb per $	73.88	Effective rates	2010 = 100
Rb per SDR	106.40	– nominal	59.2
Rb per €	90.65	– real	80.3

Trade

Principal exports

	$bn fob
Fuels	264.5
Ores & metals	51.4
Machinery & equipment	29.0
Chemicals	25.2
Total incl.others	**424.5**

Principal imports

	$bn cif
Machinery & equipment	110.5
Chemicals	41.9
Food & agricultural products	29.0
Metals	16.9
Total incl.others	**244.3**

Main export destinations

	% of total
China	12.9
Netherlands	10.6
Germany	6.6
Turkey	5.0
EU28	41.3

Main origins of imports

	% of total
China	22.1
Germany	10.3
United States	5.5
Belarus	5.0
EU28	34.5

Balance of payments, reserves and debt, $bn

Visible exports fob	419.9	Change in reserves	86.1
Visible imports fob	-254.6	Level of reserves	
Trade balance	165.3	end Dec.	554.6
Invisibles inflows	115.8	No. months of import cover	14.4
Invisibles outflows	-206.1	Official gold holdings, m oz	73.0
Net transfers	-10.2	Foreign debt	490.7
Current account balance	64.8	– as % of GDP	28.9
– as % of GDP	3.8	– as % of total exports	89.9
Capital balance	3.2	Debt service ratio	17.3
Overall balance	66.5		

Health and education

Health spending, % of GDP	5.3	Education spending, % of GDP	4.7
Doctors per 1,000 pop.	4.0	Enrolment, %: primary	105
Hospital beds per 1,000 pop.	7.1	secondary	104
At least basic drinking water,		tertiary	85
% of pop.	97.1		

Society

No. of households, m	57.7	Cost of living, Dec. 2020	
Av. no. per household	2.5	New York = 100	52
Marriages per 1,000 pop.	...	Cars per 1,000 pop.	334
Divorces per 1,000 pop.	...	Telephone lines per 100 pop.	19.0
Religion, % of pop.		Mobile telephone subscribers	
Christian	73.3	per 100 pop.	164.4
Non-religious	16.2	Internet access, %	82.6
Muslim	10.0	Broadband subs per 100 pop.	22.5
Jewish	0.2	Broadband speed, Mbps	14.9
Hindu	<0.1		
Other	<0.1		

SAUDI ARABIA

Area, sq km	2,149,690	Capital	Riyadh
Arable as % of total land	1.6	Currency	Riyal (SR)

People

Population, m	34.3	Life expectancy: men	74.5 yrs
Pop. per sq km	16.0	women	77.4 yrs
Average annual rate of change		Adult literacy	95.3
in pop. 2020–25, %	1.4	Fertility rate (per woman)	2.2
Pop. aged 0–19, 2025, %	30.5	Urban population, %	84.1
Pop. aged 65 and over, 2025, %	4.4		per 1,000 pop.
No. of men per 100 women	137.1	Crude birth rate	15.7
Human Development Index	85.4	Crude death rate	3.7

The economy

GDP	$793bn	GDP per head	$23,140
GDP	Sr2,974bn	GDP per head in purchasing	
Av. ann. growth in real		power parity (USA=100)	75.1
GDP 2014–19	1.5%	Economic freedom index	66.0

Origins of GDP		**Components of GDP**	
	% of total		% of total
Agriculture	2.2	Private consumption	38.9
Industry, of which:	47.4	Public consumption	23.8
manufacturing	12.5	Investment	28.8
Services	50.3	Exports	36.0
		Imports	-27.6

Structure of employment

	% of total		% of labour force
Agriculture	2.4	Unemployed 2020	8.2
Industry	24.8	Av. ann. rate 2010–20	6.0
Services	72.8		

Energy

	m TOE		
Total output	745.1	Net energy imports as %	
Total consumption	256.6	of energy use	-190
Consumption per head			
kg oil equivalent	7,488		

Inflation and finance

			% change 2019–20
Consumer price			
inflation 2020	3.4%	Narrow money (M1)	15.6
Av. ann. inflation 2015–20	1.0%	Broad money	15.6
Policy rate, Dec. 2020	1.00%		

Exchange rates

	end 2020		December 2020
			2010 = 100
SR per $	3.75	Effective rates	
SR per SDR	5.40	– nominal	118.8
SR per €	4.60	– real	115.2

Trade

Principal exports		Principal imports	
	$bn fob		*$bn cif*
Crude oil	134.6	Machinery & transport equip.	63.6
Refined petroleum products	43.5	Foodstuffs	21.7
		Chemical & metal products	14.4
Total incl. others	**261.6**	Total incl. others	**153.8**

Main export destinations		Main origins of imports	
	% of total		*% of total*
China	18.3	China	19.1
India	10.5	United States	11.7
Japan	10.3	United Arab Emirates	7.6
South Korea	8.0	Germany	4.9

Balance of payments, reserves and aid, $bn

Visible exports fob	261.6	Change in reserves	5.4
Visible imports fob	-140.3	Level of reserves	
Trade balance	121.3	end Dec.	514.9
Invisibles inflows	44.9	No. months of import cover	26.7
Invisibles outflows	-91.4	Official gold holdings, m oz	10.4
Net transfers	-36.6	Foreign debt	254.1
Current account balance	38.2	– as % of GDP	32.0
– as % of GDP	4.8	– as % of total exports	82.9
Capital balance	-34.9	Debt service ratio	9.2
Overall balance	3.0		

Health and education

Health spending, % of GDP	6.4	Education spending, % of GDP	...
Doctors per 1,000 pop.	2.6	Enrolment, %: primary	101
Hospital beds per 1,000 pop.	2.2	secondary	112
At least basic drinking water,		tertiary	71
% of pop.	100.0		

Society

No. of households, m	6.1	Cost of living, Dec. 2020	
Av. no. per household	5.6	New York = 100	54
Marriages per 1,000 pop.	...	Cars per 1,000 pop.	143
Divorces per 1,000 pop.	...	Telephone lines per 100 pop.	15.7
Religion, % of pop.		Mobile telephone subscribers	
Muslim	93.0	per 100 pop.	120.5
Christian	4.4	Internet access, %	95.7
Hindu	1.1	Broadband subs per 100 pop.	19.8
Other	0.9	Broadband speed, Mbps	5.3
Non-religious	0.7		
Jewish	<0.1		

SINGAPORE

Area, sq km	719	Capital	Singapore
Arable as % of total land	0.8	Currency	Singapore dollar (S$)

People

Population, m	5.8	Life expectancy: men	82.1 yrs
Pop. per sq km	8,066.8	women	86.2 yrs
Average annual rate of change		Adult literacy	97.3
in pop. 2020–25, %	0.8	Fertility rate (per woman)	1.2
Pop. aged 0–19, 2025, %	16.4	Urban population, %	100.0
Pop. aged 65 and over, 2025, %	18.1		per 1,000 pop.
No. of men per 100 women	109.8	Crude birth rate	8.3
Human Development Index	93.8	Crude death rate	5.2

The economy

GDP	$372bn	GDP per head	$65,233
GDP	S$508bn	GDP per head in purchasing	
Av. ann. growth in real		power parity (USA=100)	155.7
GDP 2014–19	2.9%	Economic freedom index	89.7

Origins of GDP

	% of total
Agriculture	0.0
Industry, of which:	25.5
manufacturing	20.5
Services	74.9

Components of GDP

	% of total
Private consumption	36.0
Public consumption	10.3
Investment	24.9
Exports	173.5
Imports	-145.6

Structure of employment

	% of total		% of labour force
Agriculture	0.0	Unemployed 2020	5.2
Industry	15.6	Av. ann. rate 2010–20	3.9
Services	84.4		

Energy

	m TOE		
Total output	1.1	Net energy imports as %	
Total consumption	94.4	of energy use	99
Consumption per head			
kg oil equivalent	16,258		

Inflation and finance

		% change 2019–20	
Consumer price			
inflation 2020	-0.2%	Narrow money (M1)	15.6
Av. ann. inflation 2015–20	0.2%	Broad money	13.2
Deposit rate, Dec. 2020	0.13%		

Exchange rates

	end 2020		December 2020
S$ per $	1.32	Effective rates	2010 = 100
S$ per SDR	1.90	– nominal	111.3
S$ per €	1.62	– real	103.7

Trade

Principal exports		**Principal imports**	
	$bn fob		*$bn cif*
Machinery & transport equip.	189.4	Machinery & transport equip.	173.6
Construction materials & metals	64.9	Mineral fuels	75.3
Mineral fuels	54.9	Misc. manufactured articles	29.9
Chemicals & chemical products	43.2	Chemicals & chemical products	29.7
Total incl.others	**390.5**	Total incl.others	**359.1**

Main export destinations		**Main origins of imports**	
	% of total		*% of total*
China	13.2	China	13.7
Hong Kong	11.4	United States	12.2
Malaysia	10.6	Malaysia	11.6
United States	8.8	Taiwan	9.0

Balance of payments, reserves and debt, $bn

Visible exports fob	441.3	Change in reserves	-7.3
Visible imports fob	-344.5	Level of reserves	
Trade balance	96.8	end Dec.	285.4
Invisibles inflows	326.2	No. months of import cover	4.8
Invisibles outflows	-361.9	Official gold holdings, m oz	4.1
Net transfers	-7.7	Foreign debt	674.1
Current account balance	53.4	– as % of GDP	180.0
– as % of GDP	14.4	– as % of total exports	87.8
Capital balance	-61.8	Debt service ratio	7.9
Overall balance	-8.4		

Health and education

Health spending, % of GDP	4.5	Education spending, % of GDP	...
Doctors per 1,000 pop.	2.3	Enrolment, %: primary	100
Hospital beds per 1,000 pop.	2.5	secondary	106
At least basic drinking water,		tertiary	89
% of pop.	100		

Society

No. of households, m	1.8	Cost of living, Dec. 2020	
Av. no. per household	3.2	New York = 100	102
Marriages per 1,000 pop.	6.3	Cars per 1,000 pop.	116
Divorces per 1,000 pop.	1.8	Telephone lines per 100 pop.	32.9
Religion, % of pop.		Mobile telephone subscribers	
Buddhist	33.9	per 100 pop.	115.6
Christian	18.2	Internet access, %	88.9
Non-religious	16.4	Broadband subs per 100 pop.	25.9
Muslim	14.3	Broadband speed, Mbps	70.9
Other	12.0		
Hindu	5.2		

SLOVAKIA

Area, sq km	49,030	Capital	Bratislava
Arable as % of total land	28.0	Currency	Euro (€)

People

Population, m	5.5	Life expectancy: men	74.6 yrs
Pop. per sq km	112.2	women	81.4 yrs
Average annual rate of change		Adult literacy	...
in pop. 2020–25, %	0.0	Fertility rate (per woman)	1.6
Pop. aged 0–19, 2025, %	20.5	Urban population, %	53.7
Pop. aged 65 and over, 2025, %	19.1		per 1,000 pop.
No. of men per 100 women	94.9	Crude birth rate	9.8
Human Development Index	86.0	Crude death rate	10.4

The economy

GDP	$105bn	GDP per head	$19,266
GDP	€94bn	GDP per head in purchasing	
Av. ann. growth in real		power parity (USA=100)	51.3
GDP 2014–19	3.2%	Economic freedom index	66.3

Origins of GDP		**Components of GDP**	
	% of total		% of total
Agriculture	2.8	Private consumption	56.4
Industry, of which:	31.7	Public consumption	19.7
manufacturing	20.3	Investment	23.6
Services	65.5	Exports	92.4
		Imports	-92.0

Structure of employment

	% of total		% of labour force
Agriculture	2.8	Unemployed 2020	6.7
Industry	36.1	Av. ann. rate 2010–20	10.7
Services	61.1		

Energy

	m TOE		
Total output	6.1	Net energy imports as %	
Total consumption	18.4	of energy use	67
Consumption per head			
kg oil equivalent	3,368		

Inflation and finance

Consumer price			% change 2019–20
inflation 2020	2.0%	Narrow money (M1)	13.5
Av. ann. inflation 2015–20	1.6%	Broad money	10.3
Deposit rate, Dec. 2020	0.01%		

Exchange rates

	end 2020		December 2020
€ per $	0.81	Effective rates	2010 = 100
€ per SDR	1.17	– nominal	105.6
		– real	102.6

Trade

Principal exports		**Principal imports**	
	$bn fob		*$bn cif*
Machinery & transport equip.	55.7	Machinery & transport equip.	46.0
Chemicals & related products	3.7	Chemicals & related products	7.3
Food, drink & tobacco	2.9	Mineral fuels & lubricants	5.8
Mineral fuels & lubricants	2.6	Food, drink & tobacco	5.0
Total incl. others	**89.5**	Total incl. others	**88.7**

Main export destinations		**Main origins of imports**	
	% of total		*% of total*
Germany	22.1	Germany	19.7
Czech Republic	11.1	Czech Republic	16.3
Poland	7.6	Austria	9.0
France	7.0	Poland	7.5
EU28	84.9	EU28	80.8

Balance of payments, reserves and debt, $bn

Visible exports fob	84.7	Overall balance	1.6
Visible imports fob	-85.8	Change in reserves	1.9
Trade balance	-1.1	Level of reserves	
Invisibles inflows	16.5	end Dec.	7.2
Invisibles outflows	-17.3	No. months of import cover	0.8
Net transfers	-1.0	Official gold holdings, m oz	1.0
Current account balance	-2.8	Aid given	0.1
– as % of GDP	-2.7	– as % of GNI	0.1
Capital balance	3.5		

Health and education

Health spending, % of GDP	6.7	Education spending, % of GDP	3.9
Doctors per 1,000 pop.	3.4	Enrolment, %: primary	100
Hospital beds per 1,000 pop.	5.7	secondary	91
At least basic drinking water,		tertiary	45
% of pop.	99.8		

Society

No. of households, m	1.9	Cost of living, Dec. 2020	
Av. no. per household	2.9	New York = 100	...
Marriages per 1,000 pop.	5.7	Cars per 1,000 pop.	402
Divorces per 1,000 pop.	1.8	Telephone lines per 100 pop.	12.4
Religion, % of pop.		Mobile telephone subscribers	
Christian	85.3	per 100 pop.	135.6
Non-religious	14.3	Internet access, %	82.9
Muslim	0.2	Broadband subs per 100 pop.	29.0
Other	0.1	Broadband speed, Mbps	29.5
Hindu	<0.1		
Jewish	<0.1		

SLOVENIA

Area, sq km	20,675	Capital	Ljubljana
Arable as % of total land	9.0	Currency	Euro (€)

People

Population, m	2.1	Life expectancy: men	79.3 yrs
Pop. per sq km	101.6	women	84.4 yrs
Average annual rate of change		Adult literacy	...
in pop. 2020–25, %	-0.1	Fertility rate (per woman)	1.6
Pop. aged 0–19, 2025, %	19.7	Urban population, %	54.8
Pop. aged 65 and over, 2025, %	23.2		per 1,000 pop.
No. of men per 100 women	99.2	Crude birth rate	8.9
Human Development Index	91.7	Crude death rate	10.5

The economy

GDP	$54bn	GDP per head	$25,946
GDP	€48bn	GDP per head in purchasing	
Av. ann. growth in real		power parity (USA=100)	65.0
GDP 2014–19	3.5%	Economic freedom index	68.3

Origins of GDP		Components of GDP	
	% of total		% of total
Agriculture	2.3	Private consumption	52.4
Industry, of which:	33.0	Public consumption	18.4
manufacturing	23.6	Investment	20.7
Services	64.7	Exports	83.7
		Imports	-75.3

Structure of employment

	% of total		% of labour force
Agriculture	4.3	Unemployed 2020	5.2
Industry	34.1	Av. ann. rate 2010–20	7.5
Services	61.6		

Energy

	m TOE		
Total output	3.5	Net energy imports as %	
Total consumption	7.4	of energy use	52
Consumption per head			
kg oil equivalent	3,569		

Inflation and finance

Consumer price			% change 2019–20
inflation 2020	-0.1%	Narrow money (M1)	13.5
Av. ann. inflation 2015–20	0.9%	Broad money	10.3
Deposit rate, Nov. 2020	0.01%		

Exchange rates

	end 2020		December 2020
			2010 = 100
€ per $	0.81	Effective rates	
€ per SDR	1.17	– nominal	...
		– real	...

Trade

Principal exports		**Principal imports**	
	$bn fob		*$bn cif*
Machinery & transport equip.	17.6	Machinery & transport equip.	15.1
Manufactures	12.7	Manufactures	11.3
Chemicals	8.4	Chemicals	8.4
Miscellaneous manufactures	6.2	Mineral fuels & lubricants	4.2
Total incl. others	**44.9**	Total incl. others	**44.0**

Main export destinations		**Main origins of imports**	
	% of total		*% of total*
Germany	17.5	Germany	14.0
Italy	11.2	Italy	12.1
Croatia	7.6	Austria	8.7
Austria	6.6	Switzerland	7.6
EU28	73.5	EU28	63.3

Balance of payments, reserves and debt, $bn

Visible exports fob	35.8	Overall balance	0.0
Visible imports fob	-34.4	Change in reserves	0.1
Trade balance	1.5	Level of reserves	
Invisibles inflows	11.5	end Dec.	1.0
Invisibles outflows	-9.3	No. months of import cover	0.3
Net transfers	-0.6	Official gold holdings, m oz	0.1
Current account balance	3.0	Aid given	0.1
– as % of GDP	5.6	– as % of GNI	0.2
Capital balance	-2.9		

Health and education

Health spending, % of GDP	8.3	Education spending, % of GDP	3.9
Doctors per 1,000 pop.	3.1	Enrolment, %: primary	100
Hospital beds per 1,000 pop.	4.4	secondary	91
At least basic drinking water,		tertiary	45
% of pop.	99.5		

Society

No. of households, m	0.9	Cost of living, Dec. 2020	
Av. no. per household	2.3	New York = 100	...
Marriages per 1,000 pop.	3.5	Cars per 1,000 pop.	533
Divorces per 1,000 pop.	1.1	Telephone lines per 100 pop.	34.0
Religion, % of pop.		Mobile telephone subscribers	
Christian	78.4	per 100 pop.	120.8
Non-religious	18.0	Internet access, %	83.1
Muslim	3.6	Broadband subs per 100 pop.	30.2
Hindu	<0.1	Broadband speed, Mbps	27.8
Jewish	<0.1		
Other	<0.1		

SOUTH AFRICA

Area, sq km	1,219,090	Capital	Pretoria
Arable as % of total land	9.9	Currency	Rand (R)

People

Population, m	58.6	Life expectancy: men	61.5 yrs
Pop. per sq km	48.1	women	68.4 yrs
Average annual rate of change		Adult literacy	87.0
in pop. 2020–25, %	1.1	Fertility rate (per woman)	2.3
Pop. aged 0–19, 2025, %	36.2	Urban population, %	66.9
Pop. aged 65 and over, 2025, %	6.1		per 1,000 pop.
No. of men per 100 women	97.1	Crude birth rate	19.0
Human Development Index	70.9	Crude death rate	9.4

The economy

GDP	$351bn	GDP per head	$6,001
GDP	R5,078bn	GDP per head in purchasing	
Av. ann. growth in real		power parity (USA=100)	20.0
GDP 2014–19	0.8%	Economic freedom index	59.7

Origins of GDP		**Components of GDP**	
	% of total		% of total
Agriculture	2.1	Private consumption	60.2
Industry, of which:	29.2	Public consumption	21.3
manufacturing	13.2	Investment	17.6
Services	68.7	Exports	29.9
		Imports	-29.4

Structure of employment

	% of total		% of labour force
Agriculture	5.3	Unemployed 2020	28.7
Industry	22.3	Av. ann. rate 2010–20	26.0
Services	72.4		

Energy

	m TOE		
Total output	148.8	Net energy imports as %	
Total consumption	142.0	of energy use	-5
Consumption per head			
kg oil equivalent	2,426		

Inflation and finance

			% change 2019–20
Consumer price			
inflation 2020	3.3%	Narrow money (M1)	6.1
Av. ann. inflation 2015–20	4.7%	Broad money	9.4
Deposit rate, Dec. 2020	3.92%		

Exchange rates

	end 2020		December 2020
R per $	14.69	Effective rates	2010 = 100
R per SDR	21.15	– nominal	55.1
R per €	18.02	– real	70.9

Trade

Principal exports

	$bn fob
Mineral products	22.4
Precious metals	15.4
Vehicles, aircraft & vessels	12.2
Iron & steel products	9.9
Total incl. others	**89.7**

Principal imports

	$bn cif
Machinery & equipment	19.8
Mineral products	15.2
Chemicals	9.4
Vehicles, aircraft & vessels	8.0
Total incl. others	**88.1**

Main export destinations

	% of total
China	10.7
Germany	8.3
United States	7.0
United Kingdom	5.2

Main origins of imports

	% of total
China	18.5
Germany	9.9
United States	6.6
India	4.9

Balance of payments, reserves and debt, $bn

Visible exports fob	90.1	Change in reserves	3.4
Visible imports fob	-87.4	Level of reserves	
Trade balance	2.7	end Dec.	55.0
Invisibles inflows	22.8	No. months of import cover	5.5
Invisibles outflows	-33.7	Official gold holdings, m oz	4.0
Net transfers	-2.5	Foreign debt	187.7
Current account balance	-10.7	– as % of GDP	53.4
– as % of GDP	-3.0	– as % of total exports	159.4
Capital balance	8.8	Debt service ratio	15.0
Overall balance	1.6		

Health and education

Health spending, % of GDP	8.3	Education spending, % of GDP	6.5
Doctors per 1,000 pop.	0.9	Enrolment, %: primary	99
Hospital beds per 1,000 pop.	...	secondary	101
At least basic drinking water,		tertiary	24
% of pop.	92.7		

Society

No. of households, m	18.5	Cost of living, Dec. 2020	
Av. no. per household	3.2	New York = 100	46
Marriages per 1,000 pop.	...	Cars per 1,000 pop.	116
Divorces per 1,000 pop.	...	Telephone lines per 100 pop.	3.5
Religion, % of pop.		Mobile telephone subscribers	
Christian	81.2	per 100 pop.	165.6
Non-religious	14.9	Internet access, %	56.2
Muslim	1.7	Broadband subs per 100 pop.	2.1
Hindu	1.1	Broadband speed, Mbps	8.4
Other	0.9		
Jewish	0.1		

SOUTH KOREA

Area, sq km	100,339	Capital	Seoul
Arable as % of total land	15.4	Currency	Won (W)

People

Population, m	51.2	Life expectancy: men	80.5 yrs
Pop. per sq km	510.3	women	86.4 yrs
Average annual rate of change		Adult literacy	...
in pop. 2020–25, %	0.0	Fertility rate (per woman)	1.1
Pop. aged 0–19, 2025, %	15.9	Urban population, %	81.4
Pop. aged 65 and over, 2025, %	20.2		per 1,000 pop.
No. of men per 100 women	100.2	Crude birth rate	6.8
Human Development Index	91.6	Crude death rate	6.9

The economy

GDP	$1,647bn	GDP per head	$31,846
GDP	W1,919trn	GDP per head in purchasing	
Av. ann. growth in real		power parity (USA=100)	67.4
GDP 2014–19	2.8%	Economic freedom index	74.0

Origins of GDP		**Components of GDP**	
	% of total		% of total
Agriculture	1.8	Private consumption	48.5
Industry, of which:	35.9	Public consumption	17.2
manufacturing	27.7	Investment	31.3
Services	62.4	Exports	39.9
		Imports	-37.0

Structure of employment

	% of total		% of labour force
Agriculture	5.1	Unemployed 2020	4.1
Industry	24.6	Av. ann. rate 2010–20	3.6
Services	70.3		

Energy

	m TOE		
Total output	38.8	Net energy imports as %	
Total consumption	312.5	of energy use	88
Consumption per head			
kg oil equivalent	6,100		

Inflation and finance

			% change 2019–20
Consumer price			
inflation 2020	3.3%	Narrow money (M1)	15.5
Av. ann. inflation 2015–20	4.7%	Broad money	9.8
Deposit rate, Dec. 2020	3.92%		

Exchange rates

	end 2020		December 2020
W per $	1,088.00	Effective rates	2010 = 100
W per SDR	1,567.01	– nominal	...
W per €	1,335.08	– real	...

Trade

Principal exports		**Principal imports**	
	$bn fob		*$bn cif*
Machinery & transport equip.	308.6	Machinery & transport equip.	171.1
Chemicals & related products	65.1	Mineral fuels & lubricants	127.3
Manufactured goods	67.8	Chemicals & related products	50.3
Mineral fuels & lubricants	42.2	Manufactured goods	44.8
Total incl. others	**542.4**	Total incl. others	**503.2**

Main export destinations		**Main origins of imports**	
	% of total		*% of total*
China	25.1	China	21.3
United States	13.6	United States	12.3
Vietnam	8.9	Japan	9.4
Hong Kong	5.9	Saudi Arabia	4.3

Balance of payments, reserves and debt, $bn

Visible exports fob	556.7	Change in reserves	5.7
Visible imports fob	-476.9	Level of reserves	
Trade balance	79.8	end Dec.	408.8
Invisibles inflows	145.2	No. months of import cover	7.7
Invisibles outflows	-159.2	Official gold holdings, m oz	3.4
Net transfers	-6.1	Foreign debt	430.9
Current account balance	59.7	– as % of GDP	26.2
– as % of GDP	3.6	– as % of total exports	60.5
Capital balance	-57.7	Debt service ratio	6.7
Overall balance	1.5		

Health and education

Health spending, % of GDP	7.6	Education spending, % of GDP	4.6
Doctors per 1,000 pop.	2.4	Enrolment, %: primary	100
Hospital beds per 1,000 pop.	12.4	secondary	99
At least basic drinking water,		tertiary	96
% of pop.	99.8		

Society

No. of households, m	20.5	Cost of living, Dec. 2020	
Av. no. per household	2.5	New York = 100	90
Marriages per 1,000 pop.	4.7	Cars per 1,000 pop.	345
Divorces per 1,000 pop.	2.2	Telephone lines per 100 pop.	48.3
Religion, % of pop.		Mobile telephone subscribers	
Non-religious	46.4	per 100 pop.	134.5
Christian	29.4	Internet access, %	96.2
Buddhist	22.9	Broadband subs per 100 pop.	42.8
Other	1.0	Broadband speed, Mbps	19.2
Muslim	0.2		
Jewish	<0.1		

SPAIN

Area, sq km	505,935	Capital	Madrid
Arable as % of total land	23.8	Currency	Euro (€)

People

Population, m	46.7	Life expectancy: men	81.3 yrs
Pop. per sq km	92.3	women	86.7 yrs
Average annual rate of change		Adult literacy	98.4
in pop. 2020–25, %	-0.1	Fertility rate (per woman)	1.4
Pop. aged 0–19, 2025, %	18.5	Urban population, %	80.6
Pop. aged 65 and over, 2025, %	22.1		per 1,000 pop.
No. of men per 100 women	96.6	Crude birth rate	7.9
Human Development Index	90.4	Crude death rate	9.5

The economy

GDP	$1,393bn	GDP per head	$29,600
GDP	€1,245bn	GDP per head in purchasing	
Av. ann. growth in real		power parity (USA=100)	66.6
GDP 2014–19	2.8%	Economic freedom index	69.9

Origins of GDP		Components of GDP	
	% of total		% of total
Agriculture	2.9	Private consumption	57.3
Industry, of which:	22.6	Public consumption	18.9
manufacturing	12.3	Investment	20.8
Services	74.5	Exports	34.9
		Imports	-31.9

Structure of employment

	% of total		% of labour force
Agriculture	4.0	Unemployed 2020	15.7
Industry	20.4	Av. ann. rate 2010–20	20.0
Services	75.5		

Energy

	m TOE		
Total output	39.9	Net energy imports as %	
Total consumption	148.2	of energy use	73
Consumption per head			
kg oil equivalent	3,172		

Inflation and finance

			% change 2019–20
Consumer price			
inflation 2020	-0.3%	Narrow money (M1)	13.5
Av. ann. inflation 2015–20	0.8%	Broad money	10.3
Deposit rate, Dec. 2020	0.01%		

Exchange rates

	end 2020		December 2020
€ per $	0.81	Effective rates	2010 = 100
€ per SDR	1.17	– nominal	106.5
		– real	96.1

Trade

Principal exports		**Principal imports**	
	$bn fob		*$bn cif*
Machinery & transport equip.	107.7	Machinery & transport equip.	117.1
Food, drink & tobacco	52.4	Chemicals & related products	55.3
Chemicals & related products	45.3	Mineral fuels & lubricants	50.0
Mineral fuels & lubricants	23.5	Food, drink & tobacco	37.3
Total incl. others	**325.7**	Total incl. others	**361.0**

Main export destinations		**Main origins of imports**	
	% of total		*% of total*
France	15.3	Germany	13.6
Germany	11.0	France	11.2
Italy	7.9	China	7.5
Portugal	7.5	Italy	6.5
EU28	66.6	EU28	58.4

Balance of payments, reserves and aid, $bn

Visible exports fob	329.0	Overall balance	0.8
Visible imports fob	-358.7	Change in reserves	4.0
Trade balance	-29.6	Level of reserves	
Invisibles inflows	226.1	end Dec.	74.7
Invisibles outflows	-152.5	No. months of import cover	1.8
Net transfers	-14.3	Official gold holdings, m oz	9.1
Current account balance	29.6	Aid given	2.9
– as % of GDP	2.1	– as % of GNI	0.2
Capital balance	-22.3		

Health and education

Health spending, % of GDP	9.0	Education spending, % of GDP	4.2
Doctors per 1,000 pop.	3.9	Enrolment, %: primary	102
Hospital beds per 1,000 pop.	3.0	secondary	126
At least basic drinking water,		tertiary	91
% of pop.	99.9		

Society

No. of households, m	18.7	Cost of living, Dec. 2020	
Av. no. per household	2.5	New York = 100	78
Marriages per 1,000 pop.	3.5	Cars per 1,000 pop.	484
Divorces per 1,000 pop.	2.0	Telephone lines per 100 pop.	42.0
Religion, % of pop.		Mobile telephone subscribers	
Christian	78.6	per 100 pop.	118.4
Non-religious	19.0	Internet access, %	90.7
Muslim	2.1	Broadband subs per 100 pop.	33.4
Jewish	0.1	Broadband speed, Mbps	36.1
Other	0.1		
Hindu	<0.1		

SWEDEN

Area, sq km	447,430	Capital	Stockholm
Arable as % of total land	6.3	Currency	Swedish krona (Skr)

People

Population, m	10.0	Life expectancy: men	81.7 yrs
Pop. per sq km	22.3	women	85.0 yrs
Average annual rate of change		Adult literacy	...
in pop. 2020–25, %	0.6	Fertility rate (per woman)	1.8
Pop. aged 0–19, 2025, %	23.2	Urban population, %	87.7
Pop. aged 65 and over, 2025, %	21.2		per 1,000 pop.
No. of men per 100 women	100.4	Crude birth rate	11.9
Human Development Index	94.5	Crude death rate	9.1

The economy

GDP	$531bn	GDP per head	$51,615
GDP	SKr5,021bn	GDP per head in purchasing	
Av. ann. growth in real		power parity (USA=100)	86.7
GDP 2014–19	2.5%	Economic freedom index	74.7

Origins of GDP		**Components of GDP**	
	% of total		% of total
Agriculture	1.6	Private consumption	45.4
Industry, of which:	25.0	Public consumption	25.9
manufacturing	14.7	Investment	25.2
Services	73.4	Exports	47.0
		Imports	-43.5

Structure of employment

	% of total		% of labour force
Agriculture	1.7	Unemployed 2020	8.4
Industry	18.4	Av. ann. rate 2010–20	7.6
Services	79.9		

Energy

	m TOE		
Total output	37.9	Net energy imports as %	
Total consumption	53.7	of energy use	29
Consumption per head			
kg oil equivalent	5,347		

Inflation and finance

			% change 2019–20
Consumer price			
inflation 2020	0.7%	Narrow money (M1)	207.2
Av. ann. inflation 2015–20	1.5%	Broad money	18.1
Repo rate, Dec. 2020	0.00%		

Exchange rates

	end 2020		December 2020
Skr per $	8.18	Effective rates	2010 = 100
Skr per SDR	11.78	– nominal	95.2
Skr per €	10.03	– real	87.7

Trade

Principal exports

	$bn fob
Machinery & transport equip.	63.9
Chemicals & related products	21.2
Raw materials	10.9
Food, drink & tobacco	9.9
Total incl. others	**161.1**

Principal imports

	$bn cif
Machinery & transport equip.	61.1
Chemicals & related products	17.9
Mineral fuels & lubricants	16.8
Food, drink & tobacco	16.5
Total incl. others	**158.8**

Main export destinations

	% of total
Norway	10.7
Germany	10.5
United States	8.0
Finland	7.2
EU28	57.9

Main origins of imports

	% of total
Germany	17.8
Netherlands	9.4
Norway	8.4
Denmark	6.6
EU28	70.1

Balance of payments, reserves and aid, $bn

Visible exports fob	176.3	Overall balance	-6.3
Visible imports fob	-158.1	Change in reserves	-5.1
Trade balance	18.2	Level of reserves	
Invisibles inflows	137.5	end Dec.	55.5
Invisibles outflows	-118.5	No. months of import cover	2.4
Net transfers	-10.1	Official gold holdings, m oz	4.0
Current account balance	27.2	Aid given	5.2
– as % of GDP	5.1	– as % of GNI	1.0
Capital balance	-28.0		

Health and education

Health spending, % of GDP	10.9	Education spending, % of GDP	7.6
Doctors per 1,000 pop.	4.0	Enrolment, %: primary	129
Hospital beds per 1,000 pop.	2.1	secondary	152
At least basic drinking water,		tertiary	72
% of pop.	100		

Society

No. of households, m	5.3	Cost of living, Dec. 2020	
Av. no. per household	1.9	New York = 100	72
Marriages per 1,000 pop.	5.0	Cars per 1,000 pop.	476
Divorces per 1,000 pop.	2.5	Telephone lines per 100 pop.	17.4
Religion, % of pop.		Mobile telephone subscribers	
Christian	67.2	per 100 pop.	128.5
Non-religious	27.0	Internet access, %	94.5
Muslim	4.6	Broadband subs per 100 pop.	40.2
Other	0.8	Broadband speed, Mbps	55.2
Hindu	0.2		
Jewish	0.1		

SWITZERLAND

Area, sq km	41,290	Capital	Berne
Arable as % of total land	10.1	Currency	Swiss franc (SFr)

People

Population, m	8.6	Life expectancy: men	82.4 yrs
Pop. per sq km	208.3	women	86.0 yrs
Average annual rate of change		Adult literacy	...
in pop. 2020–25, %	0.6	Fertility rate (per woman)	1.6
Pop. aged 0–19, 2025, %	19.9	Urban population, %	73.8
Pop. aged 65 and over, 2025, %	20.9		per 1,000 pop.
No. of men per 100 women	98.5	Crude birth rate	10.1
Human Development Index	95.5	Crude death rate	8.2

The economy

GDP	$703bn	GDP per head	$81,994
GDP	SFr699bn	GDP per head in purchasing	
Av. ann. growth in real		power parity (USA=100)	110.8
GDP 2014–19	1.7%	Economic freedom index	81.9

Origins of GDP		**Components of GDP**	
	% of total		% of total
Agriculture	0.7	Private consumption	53.1
Industry, of which:	25.5	Public consumption	11.9
manufacturing	18.7	Investment	22.3
Services	73.8	Exports	66.0
		Imports	-53.4

Structure of employment

	% of total		% of labour force
Agriculture	2.6	Unemployed 2020	4.9
Industry	20.3	Av. ann. rate 2010–20	4.7
Services	77.1		

Energy

	m TOE		
Total output	15.5	Net energy imports as %	
Total consumption	30.1	of energy use	49
Consumption per head			
kg oil equivalent	3,504		

Inflation and finance

			% change 2019–20
Consumer price			
inflation 2020	-0.7%	Narrow money (M1)	9.0
Av. ann. inflation 2015–20	0.1%	Broad money	6.0
Deposit rate, Dec. 2020	-0.43%		

Exchange rates

	end 2020		December 2020
SFr per $	0.88	Effective rates	2010 = 100
SFr per SDR	1.27	– nominal	130.1
SFr per €	1.08	– real	108.1

Trade

Principal exports		**Principal imports**	
	$bn fob		*$bn cif*
Chemicals	115.9	Chemicals	53.2
Precision instruments, watches		Machinery, equipment &	
& jewellery	39.1	electronics	32.4
Machinery, equipment &		Precision instruments, watches	
electronics	32.4	& jewellery	12.4
Metals & metal manufactures	13.7	Motor vehicles	19.7
Total incl. others	**243.8**	Total incl. others	**206.4**

Main export destinations		**Main origins of imports**	
	% of total		*% of total*
Germany	19.7	Germany	27.8
United States	18.0	Italy	10.8
United Kingdom	11.7	France	9.2
China	8.8	United States	9.1
EU28	52.6	EU28	77.4

Balance of payments, reserves and aid, $bn

Visible exports fob	347.1	Overall balance	16.2
Visible imports fob	-271.5	Change in reserves	67.7
Trade balance	75.5	Level of reserves	
Invisibles inflows	295.1	end Dec.	854.7
Invisibles outflows	-309.6	No. months of import cover	17.6
Net transfers	-11.9	Official gold holdings, m oz	33.4
Current account balance	49.2	Aid given	3.1
– as % of GDP	7.0	– as % of GNI	0.4
Capital balance	-24.6		

Health and education

Health spending, % of GDP	11.9	Education spending, % of GDP	5.1
Doctors per 1,000 pop.	4.3	Enrolment, %: primary	105
Hospital beds per 1,000 pop.	4.6	secondary	103
At least basic drinking water,		tertiary	61
% of pop.	100		

Society

No. of households, m	4.0	Cost of living, Dec. 2020	
Av. no. per household	2.2	New York = 100	100
Marriages per 1,000 pop.	4.8	Cars per 1,000 pop.	540
Divorces per 1,000 pop.	1.9	Telephone lines per 100 pop.	36.1
Religion, % of pop.		Mobile telephone subscribers	
Christian	81.3	per 100 pop.	126.0
Non-religious	11.9	Internet access, %	93.1
Muslim	5.5	Broadband subs per 100 pop.	46.9
Other	0.6	Broadband speed, Mbps	38.9
Hindu	0.4		
Jewish	0.3		

TAIWAN

Area, sq km	36,179	Capital	Taipei
Arable as % of total land	...	Currency	Taiwan dollar (T$)

People

Population, m	23.8	Life expectancy: men	78.5 yrs
Pop. per sq km	657.8	women	83.6 yrs
Average annual rate of change		Adult literacy	...
in pop. 2020–25, %	0.1	Fertility rate (per woman)	1.2
Pop. aged 0–19, 2025, %	16.9	Urban population, %	78.6
Pop. aged 65 and over, 2025, %	19.6		per 1,000 pop.
No. of men per 100 women	98.8	Crude birth rate	8.4
Human Development Index	...	Crude death rate	8.1

The economy

GDP	$836bn	GDP per head	$35,305
GDP	T$18,933bn	GDP per head in purchasing	
Av. ann. growth in real		power parity (USA=100)	101.8
GDP 2014–19	2.5%	Economic freedom index	78.6

Origins of GDP		**Components of GDP**	
	% of total		% of total
Agriculture	1.7	Private consumption	52.2
Industry, of which:	36.7	Public consumption	14.0
manufacturing	32.0	Investment	23.6
Services	61.6	Exports	63.5
		Imports	-53.3

Structure of employment

	% of total		% of labour force
Agriculture	4.8	Unemployed 2020	3.7
Industry	35.3	Av. ann. rate 2010–20	4.1
Services	59.9		

Energy

	m TOE		
Total output	9.8	Net energy imports as %	
Total consumption	113.9	of energy use	91
Consumption per head			
kg oil equivalent	4,791		

Inflation and finance

Consumer price			% change 2019–20
inflation 2020	-0.2%	Narrow money (M1)	16.9
Av. ann. inflation 2015–20	0.8%	Broad money	9.4
Policy rate, Dec. 2020	1.13%		

Exchange rates

	end 2020		December 2020
T$ per $	28.51	Effective rates	2010 = 100
T$ per SDR	41.06	– nominal	...
T$ per €	34.98	– real	...

Trade

Principal exports		Principal imports	
	$bn fob		*$bn cif*
Machinery & electrical equip.	190.0	Machinery & electrical equip.	121.7
Basic metals & articles	27.8	Minerals	48.6
Plastic & rubber articles	22.6	Chemicals & related products	27.4
Chemicals	18.7	Basic metals & articles	20.0
Total incl. others	**304.6**	Total incl. others	**284.9**

Main export destinations		Main origins of imports	
	% of total		*% of total*
China	27.9	China	20.1
United States	14.1	Japan	15.4
Hong Kong	12.3	United States	12.2
Japan	7.1	South Korea	6.2

Balance of payments, reserves and debt, $bn

Visible exports fob	330.7	Change in reserves	19.5
Visible imports fob	-273.1	Level of reserves	
Trade balance	57.7	end Dec.	498.7
Invisibles inflows	91.0	No. months of import cover	16.9
Invisibles outflows	-80.7	Official gold holdings, m oz	13.6
Net transfers	-2.8	Foreign debt	184.7
Current account balance	65.2	– as % of GDP	30.2
– as % of GDP	10.6	– as % of total exports	43.7
Capital balance	-57.6	Debt service ratio	3.2
Overall balance	16.7		

Health and education

Health spending, % of GDP	...	Education spending, % of GDP	...
Doctors per 1,000 pop.	...	Enrolment, %: primary	...
Hospital beds per 1,000 pop.	...	secondary	...
At least basic drinking water,		tertiary	...
% of pop.	...		

Society

No. of households, m	8.0	Cost of living, Dec. 2020	
Av. no. per household	3.0	New York = 100	72
Marriages per 1,000 pop.	...	Cars per 1,000 pop.	286
Divorces per 1,000 pop.	...	Telephone lines per 100 pop.	54.6
Religion, % of pop.		Mobile telephone subscribers	
Other	60.5	per 100 pop.	123.2
Buddhist	21.3	Internet access, %	88.8
Non-religious	12.7	Broadband subs per 100 pop.	24.5
Christian	5.5	Broadband speed, Mbps	85.0
Hindu	<0.1		
Jewish	<0.1		

THAILAND

| Area, sq km | 513,120 | Capital | Bangkok |
| Arable as % of total land | 32.9 | Currency | Baht (Bt) |

People

Population, m	69.6	Life expectancy: men	74.2 yrs
Pop. per sq km	135.6	women	81.3 yrs
Average annual rate of change		Adult literacy	93.8
in pop. 2020–25, %	0.2	Fertility rate (per woman)	1.5
Pop. aged 0–19, 2025, %	21.1	Urban population, %	50.7
Pop. aged 65 and over, 2025, %	16.2		per 1,000 pop.
No. of men per 100 women	94.8	Crude birth rate	9.5
Human Development Index	77.7	Crude death rate	8.3

The economy

GDP	$544bn	GDP per head	$7,807
GDP	Bt16,876bn	GDP per head in purchasing	
Av. ann. growth in real		power parity (USA=100)	29.5
GDP 2014–19	3.4%	Economic freedom index	69.7

Origins of GDP

	% of total
Agriculture	8.1
Industry, of which:	33.6
manufacturing	25.6
Services	58.3

Components of GDP

	% of total
Private consumption	50.1
Public consumption	16.1
Investment	24.0
Exports	59.8
Imports	-50.6

Structure of employment

	% of total		% of labour force
Agriculture	31.4	Unemployed 2020	1.0
Industry	22.8	Av. ann. rate 2010–20	0.7
Services	45.7		

Energy

	m TOE		
Total output	67.7	Net energy imports as %	
Total consumption	138.8	of energy use	51
Consumption per head			
kg oil equivalent	1,994		

Inflation and finance

			% change 2019–20
Consumer price			
inflation 2020	-0.8%	Narrow money (M1)	12.9
Av. ann. inflation 2015–20	0.4%	Broad money	10.1
Deposit rate, Dec. 2020	0.44%		

Exchange rates

	end 2020		December 2020
		Effective rates	2010 = 100
Bt per $	30.04	Effective rates	2010 = 100
Bt per SDR	43.26	– nominal	...
Bt per €	36.86	– real	...

Trade

Principal exports		**Principal imports**	
	$bn fob		*$bn cif*
Machinery, equip. & supplies	105.1	Machinery, equip. & supplies	85.0
Manufactured goods	31.5	Manufactured goods	41.7
Food	31.1	Fuel & lubricants	36.6
Chemicals	24.2	Chemicals	25.7
Total incl. others	**244.8**	Total incl. others	**239.9**

Main export destinations		**Main origins of imports**	
	% of total		*% of total*
United States	12.8	China	21.2
China	11.9	Japan	14.0
Japan	10.0	United States	7.3
Vietnam	4.9	Malaysia	5.4

Balance of payments, reserves and debt, $bn

Visible exports fob	242.7	Change in reserves	18.7
Visible imports fob	-216.0	Level of reserves	
Trade balance	26.7	end Dec.	224.3
Invisibles inflows	92.4	No. months of import cover	8.9
Invisibles outflows	-88.1	Official gold holdings, m oz	5.0
Net transfers	7.2	Foreign debt	180.2
Current account balance	38.2	– as % of GDP	33.1
– as % of GDP	7.0	– as % of total exports	52.5
Capital balance	-15.7	Debt service ratio	7.8
Overall balance	13.6		

Health and education

Health spending, % of GDP	3.8	Education spending, % of GDP	...
Doctors per 1,000 pop.	0.8	Enrolment, %: primary	101
Hospital beds per 1,000 pop.	...	secondary	115
At least basic drinking water,		tertiary	49
% of pop.	99.9		

Society

No. of households, m	24.7	Cost of living, Dec. 2020	
Av. no. per household	2.8	New York = 100	74
Marriages per 1,000 pop.	...	Cars per 1,000 pop.	133
Divorces per 1,000 pop.	1.6	Telephone lines per 100 pop.	7.8
Religion, % of pop.		Mobile telephone subscribers	
Buddhist	93.2	per 100 pop.	186.2
Muslim	5.5	Internet access, %	66.7
Christian	0.9	Broadband subs per 100 pop.	14.5
Non-religious	0.3	Broadband speed, Mbps	18.2
Hindu	0.1		
Jewish	<0.1		

TURKEY

Area, sq km	785,350	Capital	Ankara
Arable as % of total land	25.6	Currency	Turkish Lira (YTL)

People

Population, m	83.4	Life expectancy: men	75.6 yrs
Pop. per sq km	106.2	women	81.2 yrs
Average annual rate of change		Adult literacy	96.2
in pop. 2020–25, %	0.6	Fertility rate (per woman)	2.0
Pop. aged 0–19, 2025, %	30.0	Urban population, %	75.6
Pop. aged 65 and over, 2025, %	10.6		per 1,000 pop.
No. of men per 100 women	97.5	Crude birth rate	14.9
Human Development Index	82.0	Crude death rate	5.6

The economy

GDP	$761bn	GDP per head	$9,127
GDP	YTL4,320bn	GDP per head in purchasing	
Av. ann. growth in real		power parity (USA=100)	43.1
GDP 2014–19	4.1%	Economic freedom index	64.0

Origins of GDP		**Components of GDP**	
	% of total		% of total
Agriculture	7.1	Private consumption	56.9
Industry, of which:	30.2	Public consumption	15.5
manufacturing	20.3	Investment	24.8
Services	62.7	Exports	32.7
		Imports	-29.9

Structure of employment

	% of total		% of labour force
Agriculture	18.1	Unemployed 2020	13.9
Industry	25.3	Av. ann. rate 2010–20	10.6
Services	56.6		

Energy

	m TOE		
Total output	44.4	Net energy imports as %	
Total consumption	161.2	of energy use	72
Consumption per head			
kg oil equivalent	1,932		

Inflation and finance

Consumer price			% change 2019–20
inflation 2020	12.3%	Narrow money (M1)	63.7
Av. ann. inflation 2015–20	12.5%	Broad money	33.9
Deposit rate, Dec. 2020	19.75%		

Exchange rates

	end 2020		December 2020
YTL per $	7.35	Effective rates	2010 = 100
YTL per SDR	10.58	– nominal	...
YTL per €	9.02	– real	...

Trade

Principal exports		**Principal imports**	
	$bn fob		*$bn cif*
Transport equipment	30.5	Mechanical equipment	43.0
Agricultural products	27.4	Transport equipment	33.4
Textiles & clothing	17.3	Chemicals	19.0
Iron & steel	13.2	Fuels	17.5
Total incl. others	**171.5**	Total incl. others	**202.7**

Main export destinations		**Main origins of imports**	
	% of total		*% of total*
Germany	9.7	Russia	11.4
United Kingdom	6.6	Germany	9.5
Iraq	6.0	China	9.4
Italy	5.7	United States	5.8
EU28	44.7	EU28	33.5

Balance of payments, reserves and debt, $bn

Visible exports fob	182.2	Change in reserves	12.5
Visible imports fob	-199.0	Level of reserves	
Trade balance	-16.8	end Dec.	105.5
Invisibles inflows	69.9	No. months of import cover	5.1
Invisibles outflows	-47.2	Official gold holdings, m oz	17.8
Net transfers	0.8	Foreign debt	440.8
Current account balance	6.8	– as % of GDP	58.0
– as % of GDP	0.9	– as % of total exports	174.2
Capital balance	5.1	Debt service ratio	34.3
Overall balance	6.3		

Health and education

Health spending, % of GDP	4.1	Education spending, % of GDP	...
Doctors per 1,000 pop.	1.8	Enrolment, %: primary	95
Hospital beds per 1,000 pop.	2.9	secondary	104
At least basic drinking water,		tertiary	113
% of pop.	98.9		

Society

No. of households, m	24.2	Cost of living, Dec. 2020	
Av. no. per household	3.4	New York = 100	47
Marriages per 1,000 pop.	6.8	Cars per 1,000 pop.	140
Divorces per 1,000 pop.	1.8	Telephone lines per 100 pop.	13.8
Religion, % of pop.		Mobile telephone subscribers	
Muslim	98.0	per 100 pop.	96.8
Non-religious	1.2	Internet access, %	77.7
Christian	0.4	Broadband subs per 100 pop.	17.1
Other	0.3	Broadband speed, Mbps	5.3
Hindu	<0.1		
Jewish	<0.1		

UKRAINE

Area, sq km	603,550	Capital	Kiev
Arable as % of total land	56.8	Currency	Hryvnia (UAH)

People

Population, m	44.0	Life expectancy: men	67.6 yrs
Pop. per sq km	72.9	women	77.3 yrs
Average annual rate of change		Adult literacy	...
in pop. 2020–25, %	-0.7	Fertility rate (per woman)	1.4
Pop. aged 0–19, 2025, %	20.9	Urban population, %	69.5
Pop. aged 65 and over, 2025, %	18.5		per 1,000 pop.
No. of men per 100 women	86.3	Crude birth rate	8.6
Human Development Index	77.9	Crude death rate	15.2

The economy

GDP	$154bn	GDP per head	$3,659
GDP	UAH3,975bn	GDP per head in purchasing	
Av. ann. growth in real		power parity (USA=100)	20.4
GDP 2014–19	0.2%	Economic freedom index	54.2

Origins of GDP		**Components of GDP**	
	% of total		% of total
Agriculture	9.0	Private consumption	75.3
Industry, of which:	22.6	Public consumption	19.9
manufacturing	10.8	Investment	12.6
Services	68.4	Exports	41.2
		Imports	-49.0

Structure of employment

	% of total		% of labour force
Agriculture	13.8	Unemployed 2020	9.5
Industry	25.0	Av. ann. rate 2010–20	8.6
Services	61.2		

Energy

	m TOE		
Total output	59.8	Net energy imports as %	
Total consumption	93.7	of energy use	36
Consumption per head			
kg oil equivalent	2,130		

Inflation and finance

			% change 2019–20
Consumer price			
inflation 2020	2.7%	Narrow money (M1)	24.8
Av. ann. inflation 2015–20	9.9%	Broad money	28.6
Deposit rate, Dec. 2020	4.37%		

Exchange rates

	end 2020		December 2020
UAH per $	28.27	Effective rates	2010 = 100
UAH per SDR	40.72	– nominal	46.2
UAH per €	34.70	– real	90.2

Trade

Principal exports		Principal imports	
	$bn fob		*$bn cif*
Food & beverages	22.1	Machinery & equipment	19.5
Non-precious metals	10.3	Fuels	13.0
Machinery & equipment	5.3	Chemicals	7.5
Fuels	4.9	Food & beverages	5.7
Total incl. others	**50.1**	Total incl. others	**60.8**

Main export destinations		Main origins of imports	
	% of total		*% of total*
China	7.2	China	15.2
Poland	6.6	Russia	11.6
Russia	6.5	Germany	9.9
Turkey	5.3	Poland	6.8
EU28	40.3	EU28	40.1

Balance of payments, reserves and debt, $bn

Visible exports fob	46.1	Change in reserves	4.5
Visible imports fob	-60.4	Level of reserves	
Trade balance	-14.3	end Dec.	25.3
Invisibles inflows	30.8	No. months of import cover	3.5
Invisibles outflows	-27.1	Official gold holdings, m oz	0.8
Net transfers	6.5	Foreign debt	123.8
Current account balance	-4.1	– as % of GDP	80.5
– as % of GDP	-2.7	– as % of total exports	133.7
Capital balance	8.9	Debt service ratio	15.1
Overall balance	6.0		

Health and education

Health spending, % of GDP	7.7	Education spending, % of GDP	5.4
Doctors per 1,000 pop.	...	Enrolment, %: primary	...
Hospital beds per 1,000 pop.	...	secondary	...
At least basic drinking water,		tertiary	...
% of pop.	93.8		

Society

No. of households, m	17.0	Cost of living, Dec. 2020	
Av. no. per household	2.6	New York = 100	53
Marriages per 1,000 pop.	5.9	Cars per 1,000 pop.	178
Divorces per 1,000 pop.	3.0	Telephone lines per 100 pop.	10.0
Religion, % of pop.		Mobile telephone subscribers	
Christian	83.8	per 100 pop.	130.6
Non-religious	14.7	Internet access, %	62.6
Muslim	1.2	Broadband subs per 100 pop.	16.2
Jewish	0.1	Broadband speed, Mbps	7.7
Other	0.1		
Hindu	<0.1		

UNITED ARAB EMIRATES

Area, sq km	83,600	Capital	Abu Dhabi
Arable as % of total land	0.6	Currency	Dirham (AED)

People

Population, m	9.8	Life expectancy: men	77.8 yrs
Pop. per sq km	117.2	women	79.8 yrs
Average annual rate of change		Adult literacy	93.2
in pop. 2020–25, %	0.9	Fertility rate (per woman)	1.4
Pop. aged 0–19, 2025, %	19.6	Urban population, %	86.8
Pop. aged 65 and over, 2025, %	2.6		per 1,000 pop.
No. of men per 100 women	223.8	Crude birth rate	9.9
Human Development Index	89.0	Crude death rate	1.8

The economy

GDP	$421bn	GDP per head	$43,103
GDP	AED1,547bn	GDP per head in purchasing	
Av. ann. growth in real		power parity (USA=100)	107.3
GDP 2014–19	2.7%	Economic freedom index	76.9

Origins of GDP

	% of total
Agriculture	0.7
Industry, of which:	46.2
manufacturing	8.7
Services	53.1

Components of GDP

	% of total
Private consumption	38.9
Public consumption	13.3
Investment	23.8
Exports	92.5
Imports	-68.5

Structure of employment

	% of total		% of labour force
Agriculture	1.4	Unemployed 2020	5.0
Industry	34.2	Av. ann. rate 2010–20	2.3
Services	64.4		

Energy

	m TOE		
Total output	253.1	Net energy imports as %	
Total consumption	116.8	of energy use	-117
Consumption per head			
kg oil equivalent	11,951		

Inflation and finance

			% change 2019–20
Consumer price			
inflation 2020	-2.1%	Narrow money (M1)	4.4
Av. ann. inflation 2015–20	0.5%	Broad money	4.6
Policy rate, Dec. 2020	1.50%		

Exchange rates

	end 2020		December 2020
			2010 = 100
AED per $	3.67	Effective rates	
AED per SDR	5.29	– nominal	143.5
AED per €	4.51	– real	...

Trade

Principal exports		**Principal imports**	
	$bn fob		*$bn cif*
Re-exports	140.7	Machinery & electrical equip.	64.9
Crude oil	29.7	Precious stones & metals	58.6
Petroleum products	22.7	Vehicles & other transport	
Gas	7.7	equipment	24.6
		Mineral products	18.0
Total incl. others	**313.8**	Total incl. others	**252.0**

Main export destinations		**Main origins of imports**	
	% of total		*% of total*
India	10.6	China	14.1
Japan	9.1	India	9.2
China	5.3	United States	6.9
Switzerland	5.2	Japan	4.4

Balance of payments, reserves and debt, $bn

Visible exports fob	315.9	Change in reserves	8.9
Visible imports fob	-241.1	Level of reserves	
Trade balance	74.8	end Dec.	108.4
Invisibles inflows	83.2	No. months of import cover	4.0
Invisibles outflows	-81.7	Official gold holdings, m oz	0.7
Net transfers	-46.6	Foreign debt	245.8
Current account balance	29.7	– as % of GDP	58.4
– as % of GDP	7.0	– as % of total exports	59.7
Capital balance	20.0	Debt service ratio	6.4
Overall balance	49.7		

Health and education

Health spending, % of GDP	4.2	Education spending, % of GDP	3.1
Doctors per 1,000 pop.	2.5	Enrolment, %: primary	114
Hospital beds per 1,000 pop.	1.4	secondary	102
At least basic drinking water,		tertiary	...
% of pop.	98.0		

Society

No. of households, m	1.7	Cost of living, Dec. 2020	
Av. no. per household	5.8	New York = 100	72
Marriages per 1,000 pop.	...	Cars per 1,000 pop.	230
Divorces per 1,000 pop.	...	Telephone lines per 100 pop.	24.2
Religion, % of pop.		Mobile telephone subscribers	
Muslim	76.9	per 100 pop.	200.6
Christian	12.6	Internet access, %	99.2
Hindu	6.6	Broadband subs per 100 pop.	31.2
Other	2.8	Broadband speed, Mbps	9.6
Non-religious	1.1		
Jewish	<0.1		

UNITED KINGDOM

Area, sq km	243,610	Capital	London
Arable as % of total land	25.0	Currency	Pound (£)

People

Population, m	67.5	Life expectancy: men	80.2 yrs
Pop. per sq km	277.1	women	83.3 yrs
Average annual rate of change		Adult literacy	...
in pop. 2020–25, %	0.4	Fertility rate (per woman)	1.8
Pop. aged 0–19, 2025, %	23.1	Urban population, %	83.7
Pop. aged 65 and over, 2025, %	19.8		per 1,000 pop.
No. of men per 100 women	97.7	Crude birth rate	11.3
Human Development Index	93.2	Crude death rate	9.5

The economy

GDP	$2,829bn	GDP per head	$42,330
GDP	£2,216bn	GDP per head in purchasing	
Av. ann. growth in real		power parity (USA=100)	76.5
GDP 2014–19	1.8%	Economic freedom index	78.4

Origins of GDP		**Components of GDP**	
	% of total		% of total
Agriculture	0.7	Private consumption	64.8
Industry, of which:	20.0	Public consumption	18.8
manufacturing	9.7	Investment	17.3
Services	79.4	Exports	31.6
		Imports	-32.7

Structure of employment

	% of total		% of labour force
Agriculture	1.1	Unemployed 2020	4.3
Industry	18.1	Av. ann. rate 2010–20	5.8
Services	80.8		

Energy

	m TOE		
Total output	138.3	Net energy imports as %	
Total consumption	208.8	of energy use	34
Consumption per head			
kg oil equivalent	3,092		

Inflation and finance

			% change 2019–20
Consumer price			
inflation 2020	0.9%	Narrow money (M1)	54.1
Av. ann. inflation 2015–20	1.7%	Broad money	9.7
Central bank policy rate, Dec. 2020	0.10%		

Exchange rates

	end 2020		December 2020
£ per $	0.75	Effective rates	2010 = 100
£ per SDR	1.07	– nominal	98.1
£ per €	0.91	– real	98.6

Trade

Principal exports		**Principal imports**	
	$bn fob		*$bn cif*
Machinery & transport equip.	173.8	Machinery & transport equip.	235.6
Chemicals & related products	69.2	Chemicals & related products	74.0
Mineral fuels & lubricants	41.3	Food, drink & tobacco	61.0
Food, drink & tobacco	30.4	Mineral fuels & lubricants	56.3
Total incl. others	**476.0**	Total incl. others	**643.0**

Main export destinations		**Main origins of imports**	
	% of total		*% of total*
United States	15.3	Germany	13.3
Germany	9.8	China	10.8
France	6.6	United States	10.1
Netherlands	6.4	Netherlands	8.5
EU28	46.3	EU28	49.7

Balance of payments, reserves and aid, $bn

Visible exports fob	476.3	Overall balance	-1.2
Visible imports fob	-643.6	Change in reserves	0.9
Trade balance	-167.3	Level of reserves	
Invisibles inflows	681.5	end Dec.	173.5
Invisibles outflows	-567.9	No. months of import cover	1.7
Net transfers	-33.8	Official gold holdings, m oz	10.0
Current account balance	-87.5	Aid given	19.4
– as % of GDP	-3.1	– as % of GNI	0.7
Capital balance	102.4		

Health and education

Health spending, % of GDP	10.0	Education spending, % of GDP	5.4
Doctors per 1,000 pop.	2.8	Enrolment, %: primary	101
Hospital beds per 1,000 pop.	2.5	secondary	121
At least basic drinking water,		tertiary	61
% of pop.	100		

Society

No. of households, m	29.5	Cost of living, Dec. 2020	
Av. no. per household	2.3	New York = 100	84
Marriages per 1,000 pop.	4.4	Cars per 1,000 pop.	505
Divorces per 1,000 pop.	1.7	Telephone lines per 100 pop.	47.8
Religion, % of pop.		Mobile telephone subscribers	
Christian	71.1	per 100 pop.	119.9
Non-religious	21.3	Internet access, %	94.8
Muslim	4.4	Broadband subs per 100 pop.	39.7
Other	1.4	Broadband speed, Mbps	22.4
Hindu	1.3		
Jewish	0.5		

UNITED STATES

Area, sq km	9,831,510	Capital	Washington DC
Arable as % of total land	17.2	Currency	US dollar ($)

People

Population, m	329.1	Life expectancy: men	76.6 yrs
Pop. per sq km	33.5	women	81.7 yrs
Average annual rate of change		Adult literacy	...
in pop. 2020–25, %	0.6	Fertility rate (per woman)	1.8
Pop. aged 0–19, 2025, %	24.0	Urban population, %	82.5
Pop. aged 65 and over, 2025, %	18.6		per 1,000 pop.
No. of men per 100 women	97.9	Crude birth rate	12.0
Human Development Index	92.6	Crude death rate	9.2

The economy

GDP	$21,433bn	GDP per head	$65,298
Av. ann. growth in real		GDP per head in purchasing	
GDP 2014–19	2.4%	power parity (USA=100)	100.0
		Economic freedom index	74.8

Origins of GDP		**Components of GDP**	
	% of total		% of total
Agriculture	0.8	Private consumption	67.9
Industry, of which:	18.0	Public consumption	14.0
manufacturing	10.9	Investment	21.0
Services	81.2	Exports	11.7
		Imports	-14.6

Structure of employment

	% of total		% of labour force
Agriculture	1.4	Unemployed 2020	8.3
Industry	19.9	Av. ann. rate 2010–20	6.4
Services	78.7		

Energy

	m TOE		
Total output	2,414.8	Net energy imports as %	
Total consumption	2,551.2	of energy use	5
Consumption per head			
kg oil equivalent	7,753		

Inflation and finance

			% change 2019–20
Consumer price			
inflation 2020	1.2%	Narrow money (M1)	52.4
Av. ann. inflation 2015–20	1.8%	Broad money	17.2
Effective fed. funds rate, Dec. 2020	0.09%		

Exchange rates

	end 2020		December 2020
$ per SDR	1.44	Effective rates	2010 = 100
$ per €	1.23	– nominal	123.6
		– real	117.8

Trade

Principal exports		**Principal imports**	
	$bn fob		*$bn fob*
Capital goods, excl. vehicles	547.9	Capital goods, excl. vehicles	677.8
Industrial supplies	529.8	Consumer goods, excl. vehicles	653.6
Consumer goods, excl. vehicles	205.7	Industrial supplies	521.5
Vehicles & products	162.5	Vehicles & products	375.9
Total incl. others	**1,643.2**	Total incl. others	**2,497.5**

Main export destinations		**Main origins of imports**	
	% of total		*% of total*
Canada	17.8	China	18.1
Mexico	15.6	Mexico	14.3
China	6.5	Canada	12.8
Japan	4.5	Japan	5.8
EU28	16.2	EU28	18.1

Balance of payments, reserves and aid, $bn

Visible exports fob	1,652.4	Overall balance	4.7
Visible imports fob	-2,516.8	Change in reserves	65.3
Trade balance	-864.3	Level of reserves	
Invisibles inflows	2,011.5	end Dec.	514.6
Invisibles outflows	-1,487.7	No. months of import cover	1.5
Net transfers	-139.7	Official gold holdings, m oz	261.5
Current account balance	-480.2	Aid given	33.5
– as % of GDP	-2.2	– as % of GNI	0.2
Capital balance	394.0		

Health and education

Health spending, % of GDP	16.9	Education spending, % of GDP	...
Doctors per 1,000 pop.	2.6	Enrolment, %: primary	101
Hospital beds per 1,000 pop.	2.9	secondary	99
At least basic drinking water,		tertiary	88
% of pop.	99.3		

Society

No. of households, m	132.7	Cost of living, Dec. 2020	
Av. no. per household	2.5	New York = 100	100
Marriages per 1,000 pop.	6.9	Cars per 1,000 pop.	360
Divorces per 1,000 pop.	2.5	Telephone lines per 100 pop.	32.7
Religion, % of pop.		Mobile telephone subscribers	
Christian	78.3	per 100 pop.	134.5
Non-religious	16.4	Internet access, %	88.5
Other	2.0	Broadband subs per 100 pop.	34.7
Jewish	1.8	Broadband speed, Mbps	32.9
Muslim	0.9		
Hindu	0.6		

VENEZUELA

Area, sq km	912,050	Capital	Caracas
Arable as % of total land	2.9	Currency	Bolivar (Bs)

People

Population, m	28.5	Life expectancy: men	68.6 yrs
Pop. per sq km	31.2	women	76.3 yrs
Average annual rate of change		Adult literacy	97.1
in pop. 2020–25, %	2.0	Fertility rate (per woman)	2.2
Pop. aged 0–19, 2025, %	33.2	Urban population, %	88.2
Pop. aged 65 and over, 2025, %	8.9		per 1,000 pop.
No. of men per 100 women	96.8	Crude birth rate	16.8
Human Development Index	71.1	Crude death rate	7.3

The economy

GDP	$64bn	GDP per head	$2,299
GDP	Bs137,482bn	GDP per head in purchasing	
Av. ann. growth in real		power parity (USA=100)	11.2
GDP 2014–19	...	Economic freedom index	24.7

Origins of GDP[a]

	% of total
Agriculture	3.1
Industry, of which:	24.5
manufacturing	7.7
Services	72.4

Components of GDP[b]

	% of total
Private consumption	100.5
Public consumption	9.0
Investment	-3.7
Exports	30.7
Imports	-36.4

Structure of employment

	% of total		% of labour force
Agriculture	7.9	Unemployed 2020	9.1
Industry	15.3	Av. ann. rate 2010–20	7.4
Services	76.8		

Energy

	m TOE		
Total output	125.1	Net energy imports as %	
Total consumption	66.9	of energy use	-87
Consumption per head			
kg oil equivalent	2,347		

Inflation and finance

			% change 2019–20
Consumer price			
inflation 2020	2,355.1%	Narrow money (M1)	1,287.1
Av. ann. inflation 2015–20	3,511.4%	Broad money	1,286.8
Deposit rate, Dec. 2020	24.00%		

Exchange rates

	end 2020		December 2020
Bs per $	...	Effective rates	2010 = 100
Bs per SDR	...	– nominal	...
Bs per €	...	– real	...

Trade

Principal exports[a]			Principal imports[a]	
	$bn fob			*$bn cif*
Oil	29.8		Intermediate goods	9.3
Non-oil	3.9		Capital goods	1.9
			Consumer goods	1.6
Total	**33.7**		**Total**	**12.8**

Main export destinations			Main origins of imports	
	% of total			*% of total*
India	30.3		China	21.6
China	19.5		United States	13.0
United Arab Emirates	11.2		Brazil	5.4
United States	10.1		Mexico	5.3

Balance of payments[a], reserves and debt, $bn

Visible exports fob	33.7	Change in reserves	-2.2
Visible imports fob	-12.8	Level of reserves	
Trade balance	20.9	end Dec.	6.6
Invisibles inflows	1.6	No. months of import cover	-26.3
Invisibles outflows	15.8	Official gold holdings, m oz	5.2
Net transfers	2.6	Foreign debt	168.1
Current account balance	8.6	– as % of GDP	281.6
– as % of GDP	8.7	– as % of total exports	901.0
Capital balance	3.8	Debt service ratio	23.1
Overall balance	8.5		

Health and education

Health spending, % of GDP	3.6	Education spending, % of GDP	...
Doctors per 1,000 pop.	...	Enrolment, %: primary	97
Hospital beds per 1,000 pop.	0.9	secondary	88
At least basic drinking water,		tertiary	...
% of pop.	95.7		

Society

No. of households, m	8.0	Cost of living, Dec. 2020	
Av. no. per household	3.6	New York = 100	30
Marriages per 1,000 pop.	2.6	Cars per 1,000 pop.	129
Divorces per 1,000 pop.	0.7	Telephone lines per 100 pop.	18.8
Religion, % of pop.		Mobile telephone subscribers	
Christian	89.3	per 100 pop.	47.3
Non-religious	10.0	Internet access, %	64.3
Muslim	0.3	Broadband subs per 100 pop.	9.0
Other	0.3	Broadband speed, Mbps	1.7
Hindu	<0.1		
Jewish	<0.1		

a 2018   b 2017

VIETNAM

Area, sq km	331,230	Capital	Hanoi
Arable as % of total land	22.5	Currency	Dong (D)

People

Population, m	96.5	Life expectancy: men	71.7 yrs
Pop. per sq km	291.3	women	79.9 yrs
Average annual rate of change		Adult literacy	95.0
in pop. 2020–25, %	0.8	Fertility rate (per woman)	2.0
Pop. aged 0–19, 2025, %	29.5	Urban population, %	36.6
Pop. aged 65 and over, 2025, %	9.8		per 1,000 pop.
No. of men per 100 women	99.7	Crude birth rate	15.1
Human Development Index	70.4	Crude death rate	6.6

The economy

GDP	$262bn	GDP per head	$2,715
GDP	D6,037trn	GDP per head in purchasing	
Av. ann. growth in real		power parity (USA=100)	12.9
GDP 2014–19	6.8%	Economic freedom index	61.7

Origins of GDP

Components of GDP

	% of total		% of total
Agriculture	15.5	Private consumption	68.2
Industry, of which:	38.3	Public consumption	6.5
manufacturing	18.3	Investment	26.8
Services	46.2	Exports	106.8
		Imports	-103.6

Structure of employment

	% of total		% of labour force
Agriculture	37.2	Unemployed 2020	2.3
Industry	27.4	Av. ann. rate 2010–20	1.5
Services	35.3		

Energy

	m TOE		
Total output	68.9	Net energy imports as %	
Total consumption	93.7	of energy use	27
Consumption per head			
kg oil equivalent	972		

Inflation and finance

			% change 2019–20
Consumer price			
inflation 2020	3.2%	Narrow money (M1)	8.4
Av. ann. inflation 2015–20	3.1%	Broad money	10.5
Deposit rate, Dec. 2020	5.00%		

Exchange rates

	end 2020		December 2020
D per $	23,131.00	Effective rates	2010 = 100
D per SDR	33,314.85	– nominal	...
D per €	28,384.05	– real	...

Trade

Principal exports		Principal imports	
	$bn fob		*$bn cif*
Telephones & mobile phones	51.4	Electronics, computers & parts	51.3
Computers & electronic products	35.9	Machinery & equipment	36.7
Textiles & garments	32.8	Telephones & mobile phones	14.6
Footwear	18.3	Textiles	13.3
Total incl. others	**264.3**	Total incl. others	**253.4**

Main export destinations		Main origins of imports	
	% of total		*% of total*
United States	23.6	China	30.3
China	16.0	South Korea	18.9
Japan	7.8	Japan	7.8
South Korea	7.6	Taiwan	6.1

Balance of payments, reserves and debt, $bn

Visible exports fob	264.2	Change in reserves	22.9
Visible imports fob	-242.7	Level of reserves	
Trade balance	21.5	end Dec.	78.3
Invisibles inflows	18.9	No. months of import cover	3.4
Invisibles outflows	-36.5	Official gold holdings, m oz	0.0
Net transfers	9.2	Foreign debt	117.3
Current account balance	13.1	– as % of GDP	35.9
– as % of GDP	5.0	– as % of total exports	39.1
Capital balance	19.4	Debt service ratio	5.5
Overall balance	23.3		

Health and education

Health spending, % of GDP	5.9	Education spending, % of GDP	4.2
Doctors per 1,000 pop.	0.8	Enrolment, %: primary	115
Hospital beds per 1,000 pop.	...	secondary	...
At least basic drinking water,		tertiary	29
% of pop.	94.7		

Society

No. of households, m	26.9	Cost of living, Dec. 2020	
Av. no. per household	3.6	New York = 100	69
Marriages per 1,000 pop.	7.2	Cars per 1,000 pop.	24
Divorces per 1,000 pop.	0.3	Telephone lines per 100 pop.	3.8
Religion, % of pop.		Mobile telephone subscribers	
Other	45.6	per 100 pop.	141.2
Non-religious	29.6	Internet access, %	68.7
Buddhist	16.4	Broadband subs per 100 pop.	15.3
Christian	8.2	Broadband speed, Mbps	7.0
Muslim	0.2		
Jewish	<0.1		

ZIMBABWE

Area, sq km	390,760	Capital	Harare
Arable as % of total land	10.3	Currency	Zim. RTGS[a] dollar (ZWL$)

People

Population, m	14.6	Life expectancy: men	60.4 yrs
Pop. per sq km	37.4	women	63.7 yrs
Average annual rate of change		Adult literacy	88.7
in pop. 2020–25, %	1.6	Fertility rate (per woman)	3.3
Pop. aged 0–19, 2025, %	50.9	Urban population, %	32.2
Pop. aged 65 and over, 2025, %	3.2		per 1,000 pop.
No. of men per 100 women	91.3	Crude birth rate	27.7
Human Development Index	57.1	Crude death rate	7.6

The economy

GDP	$21bn	GDP per head	$1,464
GDP	BS162bn	GDP per head in purchasing	
Av. ann. growth in real		power parity (USA=100)	4.5
GDP 2014–19	0.7%	Economic freedom index	39.5

Origins of GDP[b]

	% of total
Agriculture	9.2
Industry, of which:	22.9
manufacturing	11.7
Services	67.4

Components of GDP[b]

	% of total
Private consumption	77.0
Public consumption	25.6
Investment	9.3
Exports	19.0
Imports	-31.0

Structure of employment

	% of total		% of labour force
Agriculture	66.2	Unemployed 2020	5.7
Industry	6.6	Av. ann. rate 2010–20	5.3
Services	26.9		

Energy

	m TOE		
Total output	2.6	Net energy imports as %	
Total consumption	4.0	of energy use	36
Consumption per head			
kg oil equivalent	275		

Inflation and finance

			% change 2019–20
Consumer price			
inflation 2020	557.2%	Narrow money (M1)	81.7
Av. ann. inflation 2015–20	91.4%	Broad money	485.2
Deposit rate, Nov. 2020	6.24%		

Exchange rates

	end 2020		December 2020
			2010 = 100
Z$ per $	16.77	Effective rates	
Z$ per SDR	23.19	– nominal	...
Z$ per €	18.84	– real	...

Trade

Principal exports		**Principal imports**	
	$bn fob		*$bn cif*
Platinum	1.3	Fuels	1.3
Gold	1.1	Machinery & transport equip.	1.2
Tobacco	0.8	Raw materials	0.7
Ferro-alloys	0.3	Manufactures	0.4
Total incl. others	**4.7**	Total	**4.8**

Main export destinations		**Main origins of imports**	
	% of total		*% of total*
South Africa	45.1	South Africa	42.4
United Arab Emirates	17.9	Zambia	19.1
Mozambique	7.6	United States	3.1
Belgium	1.3	China	2.5

Balance of payments, reserves and debt, $bn

Visible exports fob	4.7	Change in reserves	0.1
Visible imports fob	-4.5	Level of reserves	
Trade balance	0.2	end Dec.	0.2
Invisibles inflows	0.6	No. months of import cover	0.3
Invisibles outflows	-1.3	Official gold holdings, m oz	0.0
Net transfers	1.4	Foreign debt	12.3
Current account balance	0.9	– as % of GDP	57.2
– as % of GDP	4.3	– as % of total exports	183.6
Capital balance	-0.3	Debt service ratio	26.1
Overall balance	0.0		

Health and education

Health spending, % of GDP	4.7	Education spending, % of GDP	5.9
Doctors per 1,000 pop.	0.2	Enrolment, %: primary	...
Hospital beds per 1,000 pop.	...	secondary	...
At least basic drinking water,		tertiary	...
% of pop.	64.1		

Society

No. of households, m	3.8	Cost of living, Dec. 2020	
Av. no. per household	3.8	New York = 100	...
Marriages per 1,000 pop.	...	Cars per 1,000 pop.	60
Divorces per 1,000 pop.	...	Telephone lines per 100 pop.	1.8
Religion, % of pop.		Mobile telephone subscribers	
Christian	87.0	per 100 pop.	90.1
Non-religious	7.9	Internet access, %	27.1
Other	4.2	Broadband subs per 100 pop.	1.4
Muslim	0.9	Broadband speed, Mbps	2.7
Hindu	<0.1		
Jewish	<0.1		

a Real Time Gross Settlement.   b 2018

EURO AREA[a]

Area, sq km	2,760,428	Capital	–
Arable as % of total land	23.6	Currency	Euro (€)

People

Population, m	339.8	Life expectancy: men	80.3 yrs
Pop. per sq km	123.3	women	85.2 yrs
Average annual rate of change		Adult literacy	...
in pop. 2020–25, %	0.2	Fertility rate (per woman)	1.5
Pop. aged 0–19, 2025, %	20.1	Urban population, %	76.9
Pop. aged 65 and over, 2025, %	21.2		per 1,000 pop.
No. of men per 100 women	95.9	Crude birth rate	9.4
Human Development Index	91.4	Crude death rate	10.5

The economy

GDP	$13.4trn	GDP per head	$38,976
GDP	€11.9trn	GDP per head in purchasing	
Av. ann. growth in real		power parity (USA=100)	75.6
GDP 2014–19	1.9%	Economic freedom index	69.2

Origins of GDP		**Components of GDP**	
	% of total		% of total
Agriculture	1.7	Private consumption	54.1
Industry, of which:	24.6	Public consumption	20.7
manufacturing	16.4	Investment	21.8
Services	73.7	Exports	45.8
		Imports	-42.4

Structure of employment

	% of total		% of labour force
Agriculture	3.0	Unemployed 2020	8.2
Industry	23.5	Av. ann. rate 2010–20	9.9
Services	73.6		

Energy

	m TOE		
Total output	442.7	Net energy imports as %	
Total consumption	1,284.9	of energy use	66
Consumption per head			
kg oil equivalent	3,774		

Inflation and finance

		% change 2019–20	
Consumer price			
inflation 2020	0.3%	Narrow money (M1)	13.5
Av. ann. inflation 2015–20	1.0%	Broad money	10.3
Deposit rate, Dec. 2020	-0.20%		

Exchange rates

	end 2020		December 2020
			2010 = 100
€ per $	0.81	Effective rates	
€ per SDR	1.17	– nominal	110.8
		– real	95.0

Trade[b]

Principal exports

	$bn fob
Machinery & transport equip.	927.2
Other manufactured goods	513.4
Chemicals & related products	435.2
Food, drink & tobacco	151.2
Mineral fuels & lubricants	117.0
Total incl. others	**2,280.5**

Principal imports

	$bn cif
Machinery & transport equip.	735.2
Other manufactured goods	567.2
Mineral fuels & lubricants	427.2
Chemicals & related products	243.8
Food, drink & tobacco	129.5
Total incl. others	**2,303.6**

Main export destinations

	% of total
United States	22.1
China	11.1
Switzerland	7.9
Russia	4.5
Turkey	3.6

Main origins of imports

	% of total
China	20.5
United States	14.3
Russia	7.7
Switzerland	6.4
Turkey	3.9

Balance of payments, reserves and aid, $bn

Visible exports fob	2,693.7	Overall balance	12.2
Visible imports fob	-2,332.8	Change in reserves	89.8
Trade balance	360.9	Level of reserves	
Invisibles inflows	2,078.5	end Dec.	911.4
Invisibles outflows	-1,955.6	No. months of import cover	2.6
Net transfers	-171.0	Official gold holdings, m oz	346.5
Current account balance	312.8	Aid given	56.2
– as % of GDP	2.3	– as % of GNI	0.4
Capital balance	-246.7		

Health and education

Health spending, % of GDP	10.1	Education spending, % of GDP	4.9
Doctors per 1,000 pop.	3.9	Enrolment, %: primary	103
Hospital beds per 1,000 pop.	4.3	secondary	109
At least basic drinking water,		tertiary	75
% of pop.	99.8		

Society

No. of households, m, m	151.8	Telephone lines per 100 pop.	34.8
Av. no. per household	2.2	Mobile telephone subscribers	
Marriages per 1,000 pop.	4.1	per 100 pop.	126.6
Divorces per 1,000 pop.	1.8	Internet access, %	85.7
Cost of living, Dec. 2020		Broadband subs per 100 pop.	32.3
New York = 100	...	Broadband speed, Mbps	...
Cars per 1,000 pop.	525		

a Data generally refer to the 19 EU members that had adopted the euro as at December 31 2020: Austria, Belgium, Cyprus, Estonia, Finland, France, Germany, Greece, Ireland, Italy, Latvia, Lithuania, Luxembourg, Malta, Netherlands, Portugal, Slovakia, Slovenia and Spain.

b EU28, excluding intra-trade.

WORLD

Area, sq km	134,542,704	Capital	...
Arable as % of total land	10.8	Currency	...

People

Population, m	7,713.5	Life expectancy: men	70.8 yrs
Pop. per sq km	57.3	women	75.6 yrs
Average annual rate of change		Adult literacy	86.3
in pop. 2020–25, %	1.0	Fertility rate (per woman)	2.4
Pop. aged 0–19, 2025, %	32.4	Urban population, %	55.7
Pop. aged 65 and over, 2025, %	10.4		per 1,000 pop.
No. of men per 100 women	101.7	Crude birth rate	17.5
Human Development Index	73.7	Crude death rate	7.7

The economy

GDP	$87.3trn	GDP per head	$17,811
Av. ann. growth in real		GDP per head in purchasing	
GDP 2014–19	3.4%	power parity (USA=100)	28.6
		Economic freedom index	59.1

Origins of GDP		**Components of GDP**	
	% of total		% of total
Agriculture	4.2	Private consumption	57.8
Industry, of which:	27.6	Public consumption	16.9
manufacturing	15.6	Investment	24.4
Services	68.1	Exports	30.5
		Imports	-29.8

Structure of employment

	% of total		% of labour force
Agriculture	26.8	Unemployed 2020	6.5
Industry	22.7	Av. ann. rate 2010–20	5.7
Services	50.6		

Energy

	m TOE		
Total output	15,122.0	Net energy imports as %	
Total consumption	15,116.0	of energy use	...
Consumption per head			
kg oil equivalent	1,960		

Inflation and finance

			% change 2019–20
Consumer price			
inflation 2020	3.2%	Narrow money (M1)	5.1
Av. ann. inflation 2015–20	3.2%	Broad money	4.9
LIBOR $ rate, 3-month, Dec. 2020	0.23%		

Trade

World exports

	$bn fob		$bn fob
Manufactures	12,973	Ores & minerals	747
Food	1,640	Agricultural raw materials	267
Fuels	2,466		
		Total	**18,093**

Main export destinations
Main origins of imports

	% of total		% of total
United States	12.9	China	13.4
China	9.6	United States	8.4
Germany	6.5	Germany	7.7
United Kingdom	3.7	Japan	3.9
France	3.6	Netherlands	3.2

Balance of payments, reserves and aid, $bn

Visible exports fob	18,594.2	Overall balance	0.0
Visible imports fob	-18,293.2	Change in reserves	689.0
Trade balance	301.0	Level of reserves	
Invisibles inflows	10,853.8	end Dec.	13,893.6
Invisibles outflows	-10,630.3	No. months of import cover	5.8
Net transfers	-84.5	Official gold holdings, m oz	1,118.3
Current account balance	440.0	Aid given	
– as % of GDP	0.5	– as % of GNI	...
Capital balance	-171.1		

Health and education

Health spending, % of GDP	9.8	Education spending, % of GDP	4.5
Doctors per 1,000 pop.	1.6	Enrolment, %: primary	102
Hospital beds per 1,000 pop.	2.9	secondary	76
At least basic drinking water,		tertiary	39
% of pop.	89.6		

Society

No. of households, m, m	2,190.1	Cost of living, Dec. 2020	
Av. no. per household	3.5	New York = 100	...
Marriages per 1,000 pop.	...	Cars per 1,000 pop.	131
Divorces per 1,000 pop.	...	Telephone lines per 100 pop.	18.0
Religion, % of pop.		Mobile telephone subscribers	
Christian	31.5	per 100 pop.	111.3
Muslim	23.2	Internet access, %	58.2
Non-religious	16.3	Broadband subs per 100 pop.	15.6
Hindu	15.0	Broadband speed, Mbps	...
Other	13.8		
Jewish	0.2		

WORLD RANKINGS QUIZ

Test your knowledge with our world rankings quiz. Answers can be found on the pages indicated.

Geography and demographics

1 China is larger than the United States in sq km
   a True **b** False *page 12*

2 Which country is largest?
   a Saudi Arabia **b** Argentina **c** Mexico *page 12*

3 Which country has the longest coastline?
   a Canada **b** Indonesia **c** Philippines **d** Russia *page 12*

4 What is the third tallest mountain in the world?
   a Kangchenjunga **b** Lhotse **c** K2 **d** Makalu *page 13*

5 Which of these lakes is the largest?
   a Victoria **b** Superior **c** Erie **d** Huron *page 13*

6 In which region is the largest non-polar desert?
   a Middle East **b** Northern Africa **c** South-western Asia
   d Western Australia *page 13*

7 Bangladesh has a bigger population than Japan
   a True **b** False *page 14*

8 Which country has the slowest-growing population?
   a Albania **b** Bulgaria **c** Japan **d** Lebanon *page 15*

9 Singapore has a lower birth rate than Greece
   a True **b** False *page 16*

10 Singapore has the world's lowest fertility rate
   a True **b** False *page 17*

11 Which of these has the highest median age?
   a Germany **b** Greece **c** Japan **d** Portugal *page 18*

12 New York has a larger population than Dhaka
   a True **b** False *page 19*

13 Which of these cities is the best for culture?
   a Berlin **b** London **c** Paris **d** Vienna *page 20*

Business and economics

1 Which country scores lowest in the world on the United Nations Development Programme's Human Development Index?
   a Niger b Ethiopia c Yemen d Afghanistan   *page 28*

2 Which country has the least equal distribution of household income, according to the Gini coefficient measure?
   a Brazil b Benin c South Africa d United States
   page 28

3 Which country has the highest top marginal tax rate for individuals?
   a Finland b France c Japan d South Africa   *page 29*

4 Which country achieved the highest average GDP growth over the past decade?
   a China b Ethiopia c India d Vietnam   *page 30*

5 Which country had zero average GDP growth over the past decade?
   a Barbados b Italy c North Korea d Ukraine   *page 30*

6 Which two countries, besides India, are in the top five for workers' remittances?
   a France b Germany c Mexico d Pakistan   *page 36*

7 Consumer-price inflation was more than 2,000% in Venezuela in 2020
   a True b False   *page 38*

8 Which commodity price had the biggest increase in 2020?
   a Timber b Gold c Oil d Coffee   *page 39*

9 Which of these has the highest foreign debt as a percentage of GDP?
   a Bahrain b Hong Kong c Singapore d Zambia   *page 40*

10 Which country is the least energy efficient?
   a Bahrain b Chad c Iceland d Trinidad & Tobago   *page 54*

11 Which OECD country gets the largest share of its electricity from Biomass?
   a Eswatini b France c Guatemala d Lithuania   *page 55*

12 Which country has the greatest share of women on
   company boards?
   a Belgium b France c Norway d Poland   *page 56*

13 Libya has a lower rate of youth unemployment than Jordan
   a True b False   *page 57*

14 Which country lost the most working hours due to covid-19?
   a Chile b Denmark c New Zealand d Peru   *page 58*

15 Which country has the highest foreign direct investment
   outflows?
   a China b Germany c Japan d United States   *page 59*

16 Which country has the lowest "brain-gain" (in terms of
   attracting highly skilled individuals from abroad) score?
   a Venezuela b North Macedonia c Yemen d Turkey *page 60*

17 The United States and then China spend the most on
   research and development, but which country is third?
   a France b Germany c Japan d South Korea   *page 61*

18 On an index of innovation, which of these four countries
   scores highest?
   a Israel b Germany c Switzerland d United States *page 61*

19 Amazon had a bigger net profit in 2020 than Facebook
   a True b False   *page 62*

20 Which country has the largest sovereign wealth fund?
   a China b UAE c Saudi Arabia d Norway   *page 63*

21 China has four of the five largest banks in the world by assets
   a True b False   *page 63*

22 Which is the biggest bank by market capitalisation?
   a Bank of America b Bank of China c Citigroup
   d JPMorgan Chase   *page 63*

23 Which of these is the largest by market capitalisation?
   a Japan Exchange b Nasdaq c Shanghai SE   *page 64*

24 Which is larger by market capitalisation?
   a London Stock Exchange Group b Hong Kong exchanges
                                                      page 64

Politics and society

1 Which country is most democratic?
 a Sweden b Denmark c Norway d Finland *page 67*

2 Which country has the highest percentage of female members of parliament?
 a Cuba b Rwanda c New Zealand d Norway *page 67*

3 Which country has the highest secondary school enrolment?
 a Belgium b Estonia c Hong Kong d Sweden *page 68*

4 Niger has the lowest adult literacy rate
 a True b False *page 69*

5 Which of these countries has the highest marriage rate?
 a Cyprus b Egypt c Turkey d Uzbekistan *page 70*

6 Which country has the lowest divorce rate?
 a Brunei b Ireland c Uzbekistan d Vietnam *page 71*

7 The mean age of a woman at her first marriage is higher in Ireland than in Hungary
 a True b False *page 71*

8 Which country has the smallest average household size?
 a Austria b France c Germany d Sweden *page 72*

9 The United Kingdom is not one of the ten most expensive places to live
 a True b False *page 73*

10 Which country has the lowest cost of living?
 a Algeria b Colombia c Syria d Venezuela *page 73*

11 Which country has the most speed cameras per km of road?
 a Iran b Italy c United Arab Emirates d United Kingdom *page 75*

12 Which country has the fewest cars per person?
 a Ethiopia b Haiti c Madagascar d Sudan *page 76*

13 Which airport is the busiest?
 a Atlanta b Beijing c Frankfurt d Heathrow *page 78*

Health and welfare

1 Which country has the highest life expectancy?
a Singapore b South Korea b Spain d Sweden *page 90*

2 Women in Nigeria can expect to live longer than men in Zimbabwe
a True b False *page 91*

3 Which country has the highest death rate?
a Cuba b Japan c Russia d South Sudan *page 92*

4 Pakistan has a higher infant mortality rate than Afghanistan
a True b False *page 93*

5 Which country has the lowest death rate?
a Algeria b Kuwait c Oman d Qatar *page 93*

6 Which country has the highest prevalence of diabetes?
a Egypt b Pakistan c Saudi Arabia d Sudan *page 94*

7 More people are likely to die of pollution-related causes in Ivory Coast than North Korea
a True b False *page 94*

8 In which of these countries is HIV/AIDS most prevalent?
a Eswatini b Malawi c South Africa d Zimbabwe *page 95*

9 Cuba spends more as a percentage of GDP on health than Switzerland
a True b False *page 96*

10 Which country has the highest out-of-pocket health spending per person?
a Austria b Italy c Liberia d Switzerland *page 96*

11 Which country will lose the most years because of overweight people?
a Chile b Greece c Mexico d United States *page 97*

12 Which country will suffer the highest rate of deaths because of overweight people?
a Argentina b Bulgaria c Peru d Russia *page 97*

Culture and entertainment

1   Which country has the most landline telephones per person?
    a France b Japan c Taiwan d United Kingdom   *page 98*

2   Which country has the most broadband subscribers
    per 100 population?
    a Andorra b Monaco c Taiwan d Singapore   *page 99*

3   On a survey of population trust in news media, which two
    countries tied top in 2020?
    a Germany and Sweden b Finland and Portugal c Australia
    and New Zealand d United Kingdom and United States
    page 100

4   Which country tops the index of abuse against journalists?
    a China b Saudi Arabia c Syria d Turkey   *page 101*

5   There are more visits to the cinema per person in Iceland
    than the United States
    a True b False   *page 102*

6   Which country has won the most Oscars for best foreign
    film?
    a Denmark b France c Italy d Spain   *page 102*

7   Which country has produced the most Nobel prize winners
    in Peace?
    a Germany b Italy c France d United States   *page 103*

8   Which country consumes the most beer per person?
    a Austria b Czech Republic c Germany d Poland *page 104*

9   Which country is the biggest tourist spender?
    a United States b China c France d Italy   *page 105*

10 Spain earns more from tourism than any other country
    a True b False   *page 105*

11 Which country had the most covid deaths per million
    population by April 2021?
    a Belgium b Czech Republic c France d Italy   *page 107*

12 Which country had the highest rate of covid vaccination by
    June 2021?
    a Bermuda b Israel c Malta d United Kingdom   *page 107*

Glossary

Balance of payments The record of a country's transactions with the rest of the world. The **current account** of the balance of payments consists of: visible trade (goods); "invisible" trade (services and income); private transfer payments (eg, remittances from those working abroad); official transfers (eg, payments to international organisations, famine relief). Visible imports and exports are normally compiled on rather different definitions to those used in the trade statistics (shown in principal imports and exports) and therefore the statistics do not match. The **capital account** consists of long- and short-term transactions relating to a country's assets and liabilities (eg, loans and borrowings). The **current and capital accounts**, plus an errors and omissions item, make up the **overall balance**. **Changes in reserves** include gold at market prices and are shown without the practice often followed in balance of payments presentations of reversing the sign.

Big Mac index A light-hearted way of looking at exchange rates. If the dollar price of a burger at McDonald's in any country is higher than the price in the United States, converting at market exchange rates, then that country's currency could be thought to be over-valued against the dollar and vice versa.

CFA Communauté Financière Africaine. Its members, most of the francophone African nations, share a common currency, the CFA franc, pegged to the euro.

Cif/fob Measures of the value of merchandise trade. Imports include the cost of "carriage, insurance and freight" (cif) from the exporting country to the importing. The value of exports does not include these elements and is recorded "free on board" (fob). Balance of payments statistics are generally adjusted so that both exports and imports are shown fob; the cif elements are included in invisibles.

CIS is the Commonwealth of Independent States, including Georgia, Turkmenistan and Ukraine.

Crude birth rate The number of live births in a year per 1,000 population. The crude rate will automatically be relatively high if a large proportion of the population is of childbearing age.

Crude death rate The number of deaths in a year per 1,000 population. Also affected by the population's age structure.

Debt, foreign Financial obligations owed by a country to the rest of the world and repayable in foreign currency. The **debt service ratio** is debt service (principal repayments plus interest payments) expressed as a percentage of the country's earnings from exports of goods and services.

Debt, household All liabilities that require payment of interest or principal in the future.

Economic Freedom Index The ranking includes data on labour and business freedom as well as trade policy, taxation, monetary policy, the banking system, foreign-investment rules, property rights, government spending, regulation policy, the level of corruption and the extent of wage and price controls.

Effective exchange rate The nominal index measures a currency's depreciation (figures below 100) or appreciation (figures over 100) from a base date against a trade-weighted basket of the currencies of the country's main trading partners. The real effective exchange rate reflects adjustments for relative movements in prices or costs.

EU European Union. Members as at mid 2020 are: Austria, Belgium, Bulgaria, Croatia, Cyprus, Czech Republic, Denmark, Estonia, Finland, France, Germany, Greece, Hungary, Ireland, Italy, Latvia, Lithuania, Luxembourg, Malta, Netherlands, Poland, Portugal, Romania, Slovakia, Slovenia, Spain and Sweden. The United Kingdom officially left the EU on January 31st 2020.

Euro area The 19 euro area members of the EU are Austria, Belgium, Cyprus, Estonia, Finland, France, Germany,

Greece, Ireland, Italy, Latvia, Lithuania, Luxembourg, Malta, Netherlands, Portugal, Slovakia, Slovenia and Spain. Their common currency is the euro.

Fertility rate The average number of children born to a woman who completes her childbearing years.

G7 Group of seven countries: United States, Japan, Germany, United Kingdom, France, Italy and Canada.

GDP Gross domestic product. The sum of all output produced by economic activity within a country. GNP (gross national product) and GNI (gross national income) include net income from abroad, eg, rent, profits.

Import cover The number of months of imports covered by reserves, ie, reserves ÷ $\frac{1}{12}$ annual imports (visibles and invisibles).

Inflation The annual rate at which prices are increasing. The most common measure and the one shown here is the increase in the consumer price index.

Life expectancy The average length of time a baby born today can expect to live.

Literacy is defined by UNESCO as the ability to read and write a simple sentence, but definitions can vary from country to country.

Median age Divides the age distribution into two halves. Half of the population is above and half below the median age.

Money supply A measure of the "money" available to buy goods and services. Various definitions exist. The measures shown here are based on definitions used by the IMF and may differ from measures used nationally. Narrow money (M1) consists of cash in circulation and demand deposits (bank deposits that can be withdrawn on demand). "Quasi-money" (time, savings and foreign currency deposits) is added to this to create broad money.

OECD Organisation for Economic Co-operation and Development. The "rich countries" club was established in 1961 to promote economic growth and the expansion of world trade. It is based in Paris and now has 37 members from April 2020 when Colombia joined.

Official reserves The stock of gold and foreign currency held by a country to finance any calls that may be made for the settlement of foreign debt.

Opec Set up in 1960 and based in Vienna, Opec is mainly concerned with oil pricing and production issues. The current members (2021) are: Algeria, Angola, Congo-Brazzaville, Equatorial Guinea, Gabon, Iran, Iraq, Kuwait, Libya, Nigeria, Saudi Arabia, United Arab Emirates and Venezuela.

PPP Purchasing power parity. PPP statistics adjust for cost of living differences by replacing normal exchange rates with rates designed to equalise the prices of a standard "basket" of goods and services. These are used to obtain PPP estimates of GDP per head. PPP estimates are shown on an index, taking the United States as 100.

Real terms Figures adjusted to exclude the effect of inflation.

SDR Special drawing right. The reserve currency, introduced by the IMF in 1970, was intended to replace gold and national currencies in settling international transactions. The IMF uses SDRs for book-keeping purposes and issues them to member countries. Their value is based on a basket of the US dollar (with a weight of 41.73%), the euro (30.93%), the Chinese renminbi (10.92%), the Japanese yen (8.33%), and the pound sterling (8.09%).

List of countries

	Population	GDP	GDP per head	Area	Median age
	m, 2019	$bn, 2019	$PPP, 2019	'000 sq km	yrs, 2019
Afghanistan	38.0	19.3	2,156	653	18.2
Albania	2.9	15.3	14,648	29	36.1
Algeria	43.1	171.1	12,020	2,382	28.3
Andorra	0.08	3.2	...	0.5	45.8
Angola	31.8	88.8	6,966	1,247	16.6
Argentina	44.8	445.4	23,040	2,780	31.3
Armenia	3.0	13.7	14,258	30	35.1
Australia	25.2	1,396.6	53,381	7,741	37.8
Austria	9.0	445.1	60,418	84	43.4
Azerbaijan	10.0	48.0	15,041	87	31.9
Bahamas	0.4	13.6	38,743	14	31.9
Bahrain	1.6	38.6	47,003	0.8	32.2
Bangladesh	163.0	302.6	4,964	148	27.2
Barbados	0.3	5.2	16,331	0.4	40.2
Belarus	9.5	63.1	19,997	208	40.1
Belgium	11.5	533.1	56,349	31	41.8
Benin	11.8	14.4	3,433	115	18.7
Bermuda	0.06	7.5	85,418	4	42.2
Bolivia	11.5	40.9	9,111	1,099	25.3
Bosnia & Herz.	3.3	20.2	16,289	51	42.6
Botswana	2.3	18.3	18,553	582	23.8
Brazil	211.1	1,839.8	15,300	8,516	33.1
Brunei	0.4	13.5	64,848	6	31.8
Bulgaria	7.0	68.6	25,312	111	44.4
Burkina Faso	20.3	16.0	2,275	274	17.5
Burundi	11.5	3.0	785	28	17.3
Cambodia	16.5	27.1	4,583	181	25.3
Cameroon	25.9	39.0	3,803	475	18.6
Canada	37.4	1,736.4	51,669	9,985	41.0
Cayman Islands	0.07	5.5	73,292	0.3	39.0
Central African Rep.	4.7	2.2	987	623	17.5
Chad	15.9	11.3	1,650	1,284	16.5
Channel Islands	0.17	10.4	...	0.2	42.4
Chile	19.0	282.3	27,002	757	35.0
China	1,433.8	14,342.9	16,830	9,563	38.1
Colombia	50.3	323.6	16,012	1,142	30.9
Congo-Brazzaville	5.4	12.3	3,836	342	19.1
Congo-Kinshasa	86.8	50.4	1,147	2,345	17.0
Costa Rica	5.0	61.8	21,738	51	33.0
Croatia	4.1	60.8	31,131	57	44.1
Cuba	11.3	100.0	...	110	41.9
Curaçao	0.16	3.1	25,563	0.4	41.5
Cyprus	1.2	24.9	41,254	9	36.7
Czech Republic	10.7	250.7	44,296	79	42.8
Denmark	5.8	350.1	62,090	43	42.2
Dominican Rep.	10.7	88.9	19,228	49	27.7
Ecuador	17.4	107.4	11,879	256	27.6
Egypt	100.4	303.1	12,284	1,001	24.5

	Population	GDP	GDP per head	Area '000 sq	Median age
	m, 2019	$bn, 2019	$PPP, 2019	km	yrs, 2019
El Salvador	6.5	27.0	9,164	21	27.2
Equatorial Guinea	1.4	11.0	19,379	28	22.3
Eritrea	3.5	2.0	1,836	118	19.2
Estonia	1.3	31.5	39,986	45	42.2
Eswatini	1.1	4.5	9,003	17	20.5
Ethiopia	112.1	95.9	2,320	1,104	19.3
Fiji	0.9	5.5	14,290	18	27.7
Finland	5.5	269.3	53,172	338	43.0
France	65.1	2,715.5	50,993	549	42.1
French Guiana	0.3	...	...	84	25.0
French Polynesia	0.3	5.9	...	4	33.2
Gabon	2.2	16.9	15,612	268	22.5
Gambia, The	2.3	1.8	2,321	11	17.7
Georgia	4.0	17.5	15,656	70	38.2
Germany	83.5	3,861.1	57,530	358	45.7
Ghana	30.4	67.0	5,652	239	21.3
Greece	10.5	209.9	32,506	132	45.2
Guadeloupe	0.4	...	...	2	43.3
Guam	0.17	5.9	35,600	0.5	31.1
Guatemala	17.6	76.7	9,020	109	22.6
Guinea	12.8	12.3	2,675	246	17.8
Guinea-Bissau	1.9	1.3	2,077	36	18.7
Guyana	0.8	5.2	13,661	215	26.4
Haiti	11.3	14.3	3,034	28	23.7
Honduras	9.7	25.1	5,981	112	23.9
Hong Kong	7.4	365.7	62,496	1	44.5
Hungary	9.7	163.5	34,966	93	43.0
Iceland	0.3	24.2	60,132	103	37.2
India	1,366.4	2,868.9	6,997	3,287	28.1
Indonesia	270.6	1,119.2	12,335	1,914	29.5
Iran	82.9	581.2	12,858	1,745	31.5
Iraq	39.3	234.1	11,363	435	20.8
Ireland	4.9	388.7	89,684	70	37.9
Isle of Man	0.1	7.5	...	0.6	44.0
Israel	8.5	394.7	42,898	22	30.4
Italy	60.6	2,003.6	45,723	301	46.9
Ivory Coast	25.7	58.5	5,443	322	18.8
Jamaica	2.9	16.5	10,193	11	30.4
Japan	126.9	5,081.8	43,594	378	48.0
Jordan	10.1	44.5	10,517	89	23.5
Kazakhstan	18.6	181.7	27,518	2,725	30.4
Kenya	52.6	95.5	4,521	580	19.9
Kosovo	1.8	7.9	11,871	11	29.0
Kuwait	4.2	134.6	52,060	18	36.1
Kyrgyzstan	6.4	8.5	5,486	200	25.8
Laos	7.2	18.2	8,173	237	24.1
Latvia	1.9	34.1	33,021	64	43.6
Lebanon	6.9	52.0	15,196	10	29.2

	Population	GDP	GDP per head	Area	Median age
	m, 2019	$bn, 2019	$PPP, 2019	'000 sq km	yrs, 2019
Lesotho	2.1	2.4	2,824	30	23.8
Liberia	4.9	3.1	1,491	111	19.3
Libya	6.8	52.1	15,846	1,760	28.5
Liechtenstein	0.04	6.9	139,100	0.2	42.8
Lithuania	2.8	54.6	40,016	65	44.6
Luxembourg	0.6	71.1	124,591	3	39.6
Macau	0.6	53.9	129,451	0.03	38.9
Madagascar	27.0	14.1	1,720	587	19.4
Malawi	18.6	7.7	1,107	118	17.9
Malaysia	32.0	364.7	29,620	330	29.9
Maldives	0.5	5.6	20,395	0.3	29.6
Mali	19.7	17.3	2,424	1,240	16.2
Malta	0.4	15.0	47,578	0.3	42.3
Martinique	0.4	...	42,581	1	46.6
Mauritania	4.5	7.6	5,427	1,031	20.0
Mauritius	1.3	14.0	23,882	2	37.1
Mexico	127.6	1,268.9	20,944	1,964	28.9
Moldova	4.0	12.0	13,627	34	37.2
Monaco	0.04	7.2	7,272	0	53.1
Mongolia	3.2	14.0	12,862	1,564	28.0
Montenegro	0.6	5.5	24,036	14	38.6
Morocco	36.5	119.7	7,826	447	29.2
Mozambique	30.4	15.3	1,338	786	17.5
Myanmar	54.0	76.1	5,370	677	28.7
Namibia	2.5	12.4	10,064	824	21.7
Nepal	28.6	30.6	3,568	147	24.1
Netherlands	17.1	907.1	61,285	42	43.1
New Caledonia	0.3	9.8	56,329	19	33.3
New Zealand	4.8	206.9	45,382	268	37.9
Nicaragua	6.5	12.5	5,646	130	26.1
Niger	23.3	12.9	1,279	1,267	15.1
Nigeria	201.0	448.1	5,363	924	18.1
North Korea	25.7	30.3	5,991	121	35.1
North Macedonia	2.1	12.5	18,108	26	38.8
Norway	5.4	403.3	70,006	625	39.7
Oman	5.0	76.3	28,507	310	30.3
Pakistan	216.6	278.2	4,898	796	22.6
Panama	4.2	66.8	32,851	75	29.4
Papua New Guinea	8.8	24.8	4,548	463	22.2
Paraguay	7.0	38.1	13,246	407	26.0
Peru	32.5	226.8	13,416	1,285	30.3
Philippines	108.1	376.8	9,302	300	25.4
Poland	37.9	595.9	35,165	313	41.3
Portugal	10.2	238.8	37,918	92	45.7
Puerto Rico	2.9	105.0	36,045	9	43.2
Qatar	2.8	175.8	94,029	12	32.1
Réunion	0.9	...	...	3	35.6
Romania	19.4	250.1	33,340	238	42.8

	Population	GDP	GDP per head	Area '000 sq	Median age
	m, 2019	$bn, 2019	$PPP, 2019	km	yrs, 2019
Russia	145.9	1,699.9	29,181	17,098	39.4
Rwanda	12.6	10.4	2,325	26	19.9
Saudi Arabia	34.3	793.0	49,040	2,150	31.4
Senegal	16.3	23.6	3,545	197	18.4
Serbia	8.8	51.5	19,495	88	41.4
Sierra Leone	7.8	4.1	1,794	72	19.3
Singapore	5.8	372.1	101,649	1	41.7
Slovakia	5.5	105.1	33,516	49	40.8
Slovenia	2.1	54.2	42,431	21	44.2
Somalia	15.4	4.9	954	638	16.6
South Africa	58.6	351.4	13,034	1,219	27.4
South Korea	51.2	1,646.7	44,011	100	43.1
South Sudan	11.1	4.1	862	659	18.9
Spain	46.7	1,393.5	43,496	506	44.4
Sri Lanka	21.3	84.0	13,657	66	33.7
Sudan	42.8	30.5	4,123	1,879	19.5
Suriname	0.6	3.7	17,256	164	29.8
Sweden	10.0	530.9	56,632	447	41.1
Switzerland	8.6	703.1	72,376	41	42.9
Syria	17.1	60.0	6,375	185	25.2
Taiwan	23.8	612.2	53,429	36	41.9
Tajikistan	9.3	8.1	3,529	141	22.3
Tanzania	58.0	63.2	2,771	947	17.9
Thailand	69.6	543.5	19,277	513	39.7
Timor-Leste	1.3	2.0	3,710	15	20.6
Togo	8.1	5.5	1,667	57	19.3
Trinidad & Tobago	1.4	24.3	27,334	5	35.7
Tunisia	11.7	38.8	11,232	164	32.5
Turkey	83.4	761.4	28,133	785	31.2
Turkmenistan	5.9	40.8	15,207	488	26.6
Uganda	44.3	35.2	2,284	242	16.5
Ukraine	44.0	153.8	13,341	604	41.0
United Arab Emirates	9.8	421.1	70,089	84	32.6
United Kingdom	67.5	2,829.1	49,932	244	40.4
United States	329.1	21,433.2	65,298	9,832	38.2
Uruguay	3.5	56.0	22,515	176	35.6
Uzbekistan	33.0	57.9	7,308	447	27.5
Venezuela	28.5	64.0	7,344	912	29.1
Vietnam	96.5	261.9	8,397	331	32.1
Virgin Islands (US)	0.1	3.9	...	0.3	42.3
West Bank & Gaza	5.0	16.3	6,495	6	20.5
Yemen	29.2	22.6	2,575	528	20.0
Zambia	17.9	23.0	3,624	753	17.4
Zimbabwe	14.6	21.0	2,961	391	18.6
Euro (19)	340.4	13,365.0	49,336	2,760	44.4
World	7,713.5	87,345.0	17,811	135,543	30.6

Sources

Academy of Motion Picture Arts and Sciences
AFM Research
Airports Council International, *Worldwide Airport Traffic Report*

Bank of East Asia
Bloomberg
BP, *Statistical Review of World Energy*

Cable
CAF, *The World Giving Index*
CBRE, *Global Prime Office Occupancy Costs*
Central banks
Central Intelligence Agency, *The World Factbook*
Committee to Protect Journalists
Company reports
Cornell University
Council of Tall Buildings and Urban Habitat
Credit Suisse

The Economist, www.economist.com
Economist Intelligence Unit, *Cost of Living Survey; Country Forecasts; Country Reports; Liveability Index*
Encyclopaedia Britannica
Eurostat, *Statistics in Focus*

Finance ministries
Food and Agriculture Organisation

Global Democracy Ranking
Global Entrepreneurship Monitor
Global Internal Displacement Database
Government statistics

H2 Gambling Capital
The Heritage Foundation, *Index of Economic Freedom*

Holman Fenwick Willan

IMD, *World Competitiveness Yearbook*
IMF, *International Financial Statistics; World Economic Outlook*
INSEAD
Institute for Criminal Policy Research
Internal Displacement Monitoring Centre
International Civil Aviation Organisation
International Cocoa Organisation, *Quarterly Bulletin of Cocoa Statistics*
International Coffee Organisation
International Cotton Advisory Committee, *March Bulletin*
International Diabetes Federation, *Diabetes Atlas*
International Grains Council
International Institute for Strategic Studies, *Military Balance*
International Labour Organisation
International Organisation of Motor Vehicle Manufacturers
International Publishers Association
International Rubber Study Group, *Rubber Statistical Bulletin*
International Sugar Organisation, *Statistical Bulletin*
International Telecommunication Union, *ITU Indicators*
International Union of Railways
Inter-Parliamentary Union

Johnson Matthey

McDonald's

National Institute of Statistics and Economic Studies
National statistics offices

Nobel Foundation

OECD, *Development Assistance Committee Report; Economic Outlook; Government at a Glance; OECD.Stat; Revenue Statistics*
OMDIA
Our World In Data
Oxford Internet Institute

Pew Research Centre, *The Global Religious Landscape*
Progressive Media

Reporters Without Borders, *Press Freedom Index*
Reuters Institute

Sovereign Wealth Fund Institute
Space Launch Report
Stockholm International Peace Research Institute

Taiwan Statistical Data Book
The Times, *Atlas of the World*
Thomson Reuters

Union of Concerned Scientists
UN, *Demographic Yearbook; National Accounts; State of World Population Report; World Fertility Report*
UNAIDS
UNCTAD, *Review of Maritime Transport; World Investment Report*
UNCTAD/WTO International Trade Centre
UN Development Programme, *Human Development Report*

UNESCO Institute for Statistics
UN High Commissioner for Refugees
UN Office on Drugs and Crime
UN, Population Division
US Department of Agriculture
US Energy Information Administration
US Federal Aviation Administration
US Geological Survey

Visionofhumanity.org

Walk Free Foundation
WHO, *Global Health Observatory; Global Immunisation Data; World Health Statistics*
World Bank, *Doing Business; Global Development Finance; Migration and Remittances Data; World Development Indicators; World Development Report*
World Bureau of Metal Statistics, *World Metal Statistics*
World Economic Forum, *Global Competitiveness Report*
World Federation of Exchanges
World Health Organisation
World Intellectual Property Organization
World Tourism Organisation, *Yearbook of Tourism Statistics*
World Trade Organisation, *Annual Report*

Yale University

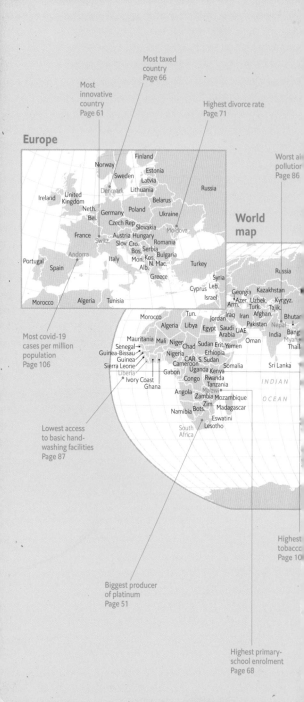

Most innovative country
Page 61

Most taxed country
Page 66

Highest divorce rate
Page 71

Worst air pollution
Page 86

Europe

World map

Most covid-19 cases per million population
Page 106

Lowest access to basic hand-washing facilities
Page 87

Biggest producer of platinum
Page 51

Highest tobacco
Page 10

Highest primary-school enrolment
Page 68